LUDMILA PETRUSHEVSKAYA

Ludmila Petrushevskaya was born in Moscow in 1938. After a war-time childhood of great deprivation, she entered Moscow University to study journalism, graduating in 1961 into a job in Moscow Television. She also attended Alexei Arbuzov's playwrights' workshop. In 1969 when she submitted some short stories to the journal *Novyi Mir*, the then editor, Tvardovsky, noted: 'Withhold publication, but don't lose track of the author.' (A year later Tvardovsky himself was removed.) Her first publication was in fact two stories in *Avrora.Teatr* magazine published some of her plays in 1979, ranking her with other up-and-coming writers like Galin, Chervinsky and Arro. Also in 1979 Yuri Norstein's full-length animated film of her scenario, *The Tale of Tales*, received six international awards and in 1984 was nominated by an international jury of film critics as the best animated feature ever made. Meanwhile her plays, though still largely unpublished, were being widely performed in factory and amateur drama groups. With the coming of *glasnost* in the mid-eighties, her work has been staged in various Moscow theatres and increasingly, abroad, while from 1988 onwards several collections of her stories and plays have been published in the Soviet Union. Her story 'A Modern Family Robinson' appeared in the Harvill anthology *Dissonant Voices* in 1991. She still lives in Moscow and has three children.

STEPHEN MULRINE is a senior lecturer at Glasgow School of Art, and has been writing since the late 1960s, mostly plays for radio and television. In recent years he has turned an interest in Russian themes to translation, and in addition to the work of Ludmila Petrushevskaya, his versions of plays by Alexander Gelman have been performed on stage and radio to critical acclaim.

Cover picture c

D1323711

A Nick Hern Book

Cinzano: Eleven Plays first published in 1991 as an original
paperback by Nick Hern Books, a Random Century Company,
20 Vauxhall Bridge Road, London SW1V 2SA

Set in Baskerville by BookEns Ltd, Baldock, Herts.
Printed in Great Britain by
T.J. Press (Padstow) Ltd, Padstow, Cornwall.

A CIP Catalogue record for this book is available from the British
Library

ISBN 1 85459 106 1

LUDMILA PETRUSHEVSKAYA

CINZANO
Eleven plays

Translated and introduced by
Stephen Mulrine

CINZANO
SMIRNOVA'S BIRTHDAY
MUSIC LESSONS
THREE GIRLS IN BLUE
THE STAIRWELL
LOVE
NETS AND SNARES
THE DARK ROOM
The Execution
The Meeting
A Glass of Water
Isolation Box

NICK HERN BOOKS, LONDON

Contents

Ludmila Petrushevskaya: Introduction

While the prospects for *perestroika*, in the sense of a rebuilt Soviet economy, remain distinctly gloomy, its symbiotic partner, *glasnost*, has produced more tangible results, and the impact of the new freedoms has been felt perhaps nowhere more strongly than in the theatre, traditionally a forum for ideological debate in a society which has always taken its art seriously.

This has been reflected in the emergence, since 1985, of literally hundreds of new theatres, some little more than cleared basements and attics, and also in the rise to international note of an important group of playwrights – not a generation, since they are united less by age and background than by their willingness to break silence on the conditions of Soviet life. The latter, in the post-Gorbachev thaw, has come under intense scrutiny in all media, and the Soviet Union's unenviable dual status of Third World country and developed nation is as cruelly exposed in the theatre as anywhere, with the removal of taboos on a wide range of subjects: sex, crime, drunkenness, corruption, unemployment, homelessness, pollution, etc.

Such themes are central to the work of Ludmila Petrushevskaya, although it has no obvious programmatic character – not a conscious exposé, but a truthful record of the daily lives of Soviet citizens. Running counter to the tradition of Socialist Realism, its often painful honesty guaranteed that Petrushevskaya would remain unpublished, though not unperformed, until very recently. She had been writing, initially short stories, since the late sixties, but not until 1979 did the prestige monthly *Teatr* publish her early play, the relatively innocuous *Love*. And in his foreword to the play, the distinguished playwright Alexei Arbuzov then wrote: 'When I think of Petrushevskaya, all I wish is that her talent be spared misunderstanding.'

Paradoxically, Soviet officialdom understood Petrushevskaya rather too well, and it is for that reason that *Cinzano*, for example, with its thoroughly negative picture of three young men drinking themselves into a stupor, to escape their drab lives and family responsibilities, lay unpublished for fifteen years, during which it was nevertheless widely staged.

And while the Brezhnev 'period of stagnation' in which it is set, now seems to Westerners remote, it is a measure of the deep-rooted ills of Soviet society, and how little life has changed for the ordinary citizen, that the play is still fresh and relevant today.

Prostye lyudi, simple folk, have been Petrushevskaya's concern from the outset. A graduate of the Faculty of Journalism at Moscow State University, and later of Alexei Arbuzov's playwrights' workshop, her true exemplar in drama was Alexander Vampilov, the voice of critical realism throughout the sixties, until his tragically early death in 1972. Her own first experiments were in prose, and in 1969 she submitted several short stories to the radical editor of *Novyi Mir*, Alexander Tvardovsky, the brave spirit who had published Solzhenitsyn's *One Day in the Life of Ivan Denisovich*.

By 1969, the climate had already changed, however, and while her self-evident talent and uncompromising honesty impressed Tvardovsky, he did not publish the stories, but noted on the manuscript: 'Withhold publication, don't lose track of the author.' A year later, Tvardovsky was removed from his post.

Not until 1988, in fact, was any substantial body of Petrushevskaya's work published, and the volume of plays entitled *Songs of the 20th Century*, from which this selection (*Cinzano* and *Smirnova's Birthday* excepted) is taken, is the result of an independent venture, the first title in a projected series by the RSFSR Union of Theatre Workers.

Such organisations are now empowered to act on their own initiative, without the Party's *imprimatur*, and the Union's declared policy is to publish controversial, and hitherto neglected authors. In that respect the choice of Petrushevskaya is significant, as A. Smelyansky notes in his introduction:

> 'The right to inaugurate this playwrights' series has been won by Ludmila Petrushevskaya, above all through her unique gifts. In the course of the past decade there has been no more complex and clearly expressed talent in our theatre. Her piercing vision, and interpretation of the commonplace as an unexplored area of Soviet reality, her understanding of so-called "simple people" as they truly are, formed by their history, her precise writer's ear, tuned to contemporary speech, the ways in which people actually speak and communicate – all these things have made Ludmila Petrushevskaya's plays immensely attractive to the theatre . . . '

Smelyansky goes on to observe that the author herself determined the content of *Songs of the 20th Century*, and it is an indication how hard old habits die that the editorial board debated whether or not to print a group of short plays, known collectively as *The Dark Room*, and here translated as *The Execution*, *The Meeting*, *A Glass of Water*, and *Isolation Box*. Speaking like a true *perestroishchik*, however, Smelyansky concludes:

' . . . A talented author ought to be able to show herself to the reader in whatever guise she thinks fit. For too many years now the "levelling out" of dramatists by editorial taste has removed from writers the capacity and courage, even, to stand one to one with their public. We have extinguished the dramatists' feeling of responsibility for their own words, and that has led to serious consequences . . . '

In fact, Petrushevskaya's work is rootedly apolitical, as the term is commonly understood. Even the wretched prisoner, whose fate is the subject of both the short trilogy *The Execution*, and *The Meeting*, is significantly no dissident, but a multiple murderer, and there is scarcely a line in her plays that could be construed as direct criticism of the system, the Party, the *nomenklatura*, or a named official. Where reference is made to the labour camps, for example, in *Smirnova's Birthday*, it is in the form of an oblique comment about food parcels. On a rare occasion, her characters do express political opinions, as in the short story *Circle of Friends*, but they speak with their own voices, not Petrushevskaya's. Her concern, as always, is with their personal relationships.

Petrushevskaya's work is often described as 'Chekhovian', and in the sense that her plays deal with the everyday, yet complex processes of living, the description is apt enough. Like Chekhov, she insists her work is fundamentally comic, and though it is anything but consoling, there is admittedly a degree of wry amusement to be got from both, in contemplating the gulf between human aspiration and achievement.

It is perhaps that same insight which accounts for the apparently unresolved character of much of Petrushevskaya's work. We look in vain for the strong curtain line, or the tidy conclusion, and her characters' lives are mostly as chaotic and confused when we leave them, as when they first step out onto the stage. Her dramatic manner is that of the natural storyteller, and indeed there is very little discernible difference between a monologue like *Nets and Snares*, and her short stories, with their sharply characterised narrator voices. Certain of her dialogues, *A Glass of Water* and *Isolation Box*, for example, are effectively monologues for long stretches, and Petrushevskaya in a sense writes through a spectrum of narrative, the actual genre being determined by the varying amounts of time she permits her characters to tell their stories. This is so typical of her work, even her large-cast plays, that these rambling meditations and reminiscences should not be thought of as digressions, but rather the very essence of the drama.

Petrushevskaya is an unashamed realist; her work is almost wholly devoid of non-naturalistic devices, and the symbols of the threatening swing, in the final scene of *Music Lessons*, and the log-cum-prison guard, in *The Meeting*, are the only examples of their kind in this collection. Likewise her handling of dramatic time and place is relatively straightforward, and the complexities of *Three Girls in Blue*, say, derive more from its relationships than its structure.

Such difficulties should not be minimised, however, and on a personal note, I have more than once had to draw up a diagram to keep track, in translating *Cinzano*, for example, of just who is married to, or divorced from whom, who's staying in whose flat, and who owes whom, and how much money! It is the small change of existence, indeed, that gives Petrushevskaya's work its dense texture, and articulates so compelling a picture of Soviet life. While Petrushevskaya can be seen as belonging to the tradition of Socialist Realism in aesthetic terms, this is emphatically not life 'depicted in its revolutionary development', with its positive heroes, and optimistic messages for posterity. Petrushevskaya draws very few conclusions herself, but it is possible to identify recurrent themes in her work – the desperate shortage of living space, for example, and its destructive effect on family relationships. Square metres, in a sense mercifully unfamiliar to most Western audiences, are the stuff of dreams and nightmares both, in play after play.

And although Petrushevskaya maintains she is no feminist, the backwoodsman attitudes of the average Soviet male, and his convenient double standards, are wickedly exposed on almost every page of her work. Her women characters are frequently self-sacrificing to the point of absurdity – the pathetic Nina, and her mother, in *Music Lessons*, the three young women of *Smirnova's Birthday*, the monologue speaker of *Nets and Snares*; the list could easily be extended, and while they clearly conspire in their own subjugation, Petrushevskaya's attitude to them is much harder to determine. About her male characters, however, couch potatoes, hooligans, and opportunists almost to a man, we are left in little doubt.

To say that Petrushevskaya's view of family life was jaundiced would be an understatement; mothers and daughters bicker tirelessly, accusations of neglect on the one hand, and manipulation on the other, resound within the cramped, plaster-boarded private hells of her Moscow high-rise apartment blocks; siblings cheat one another out of their rights; children are hostages to fortune, or spheres of influence to battle for. Yet her description of her plays as comedies is not ill-founded. Many of her characters exhibit a form of emotional dislocation, and the most appalling personal tragedies are referred to almost casually, accorded the same status as trivial reminiscence. Petrushevskaya's people lack a sense of scale, or decorum, and our compassion for their plight is often tinged with superior amusement. In truth, they are incapable of fully comprehending their fate, or of perceiving what is important amid the clamour of their short-term needs and anxieties. In that respect, they resemble us all, and our ambiguous attitude to them is an acknowledgement of both their, and our human condition.

In the event, Petrushevskaya's precisely detailed recording of life, 'un-retouched', as Smelyansky observes, makes her work also very specifically Soviet. Nevertheless, from their beginnings in unsanctioned productions in experimental studio-theatres, all over the Soviet Union, her plays have now been performed in most Western European countries, the United States and Australia. They may permit few concessions to non-Russian readers, or translators for that matter, but in a real sense they bear out the contention of the American poet William Carlos Williams, that the only true universal is the local.

Stephen Mulrine
Glasgow
April 1991

I owe a debt of gratitude to Laura McFarlane, and Kathy Clugston, and most especially to Galina Androchnikova, without whose help a difficult task would have been impossible.

CINZANO

Characters

PASHA (male)
VALYA (male)
KOSTYA (male)

Cinzano was first performed in English in Stephen Mulrine's translation at the Tron Theatre, Glasgow on 9 November 1989. The cast was as follows:

PASHA	Forbes Masson
KOSTYA	Peter Mullan
VALYA	Paul Samson

Directed by Roman Kozak
Designed by Valery Firsov
Lighting by Nick McCall

Evening. An empty room. Two chairs, picked up from a rubbish tip, a garden seat, a large empty confectionery box. Enter PASHA, VALYA *and* KOSTYA.

PASHA. So, you found it okay?

KOSTYA. We've brought you some furniture, Pasha. Took a seat on the tram.

PASHA. Muchas gracias.

VALYA. Yeh, Kostya humped it out. (*Laughs.*)

PASHA. Come on in, sit yourself down.

VALYA. Listen, me and Kostya met up coming from work, and I don't understand why we've had to truck away out here. It could all've been fixed up back there.

KOSTYA. Yeh, it's miles away. Sit down, have a seat.

PASHA. Hey, first things first. (*To* KOSTYA.) Have you got the money?

KOSTYA. Yeh, I've got it.

VALYA. Look, you guys, I've got to go. Let's wrap this up quickly, and I'll clear off.

PASHA. Wait a minute, I'm busy.

VALYA. What d'you mean busy? Give us the money.

PASHA. I'll give you the money, but not right now.

VALYA. Kostya, give us the money, same as we agreed. You should've given us it earlier, I knew this would happen.

KOSTYA. Look, don't get ratty.

PASHA. Listen, guys, they're flogging off Cinzano down there. Top quality – full litre bottles. And I'm taking three bottles home, no messing. So I'll make up the ten roubles to you later, Valya – one way or another. I've got to lay in a supply.

VALYA. That's a different story. So where's home then?

PASHA. Home's yon place, anywhere I hang my hat.

VALYA. What – you don't live here?

PASHA. It's temporary.

VALYA. What d'you mean, you live here temporary, or you don't live here temporary?

KOSTYA. He's here today, and that's it, right?

VALYA. But where do you usually stay?

PASHA. Nowhere, till the next time, again already.

VALYA. Eh?

PASHA. Listen, guys, time's short.

KOSTYA. Me and Valya took ages getting out here. (*Takes out the money, peels off two ten-rouble notes.*)

PASHA. There's enough there for six. So I'll take five home, if that meets with your approval. Five'll do me, that'll cover it. The Cinzano'll make up for everything! And I'll owe you – what, twenty roubles, Valya, okay?

VALYA. No, I'm sorry, but why did I come all the way out here, Pasha, eh? I mean, I'm asking myself.

PASHA. Okay, I'm sorry, but I didn't invite you.

VALYA. Well, *I'm* sorry, but that's no good, pal.

PASHA. Hey, *I'm* sorry, right? But is that not enough, I'm giving you back thirty? I mean, we're talking Cinzano here.

VALYA. Well, okay – but one of them's mine.

KOSTYA. It's a deal. Wonderful.

VALYA. Hurry up, I need to go. Where's the bog around here?

PASHA. Going to powder your nose, dear? Second door on the right.

VALYA *exits.* KOSTYA *takes out the money.*

PASHA. Right, come on – hand it over. (*He stuffs the money without counting it into his pocket, and exits. VALYA re-enters.*)

VALYA. Okay, give us the money. The thirty.

KOSTYA. I've just given it to Pasha, the whole lot.

VALYA. Christ, that's brilliant. Look, pal, you were supposed to hand that over to me.

KOSTYA. I was supposed to give you it before the holidays. But you were diving about all over the shop. See me after the holidays, I'm going away, you said. Well, it's after the holidays now, and here you are.

VALYA. Christ, pal, you're something else. I don't get this. Who did you give it to? Eh? Pasha? What for?

KOSTYA. Look, he gave it to me – I just gave him it back.

VALYA. That money's mine!

KOSTYA. Well, it'll *be* yours. In a while. I told you already on the way out from work, I says, just don't count on me today, Valya, I'm going out to give Pasha back this money. And what did you say? I'll be bombed out on a Friday for Chrissakes, flat stony, that's what you said. So then you got onto the tram.

VALYA. Listen, man, I'm not pleased with you. Not pleased at all. You know what's happening to you, I don't need to tell you, 'cause you've said it often enough yourself, but you're going down the drain, you're sinking lower and lower. (KOSTYA *flings his arms around* VALYA.) Well, Christ, I didn't expect this, no way. (KOSTYA *kisses* VALYA.) Piss off!

KOSTYA. We'll get a drink in a minute. He's bringing it back. He's coming back with five bottles.

VALYA. And I'm taking one of them home. No, two. I mean, at the end of the day –

KOSTYA. So who's arguing? Take the two.

VALYA. It's my money.

KOSTYA. No, no, you're definitely wrong there. It's not yours yet. I mean, we were all set to return it before the holidays, and you didn't take it.

VALYA. No, it's *you* that's wrong. I came out here specially, so's Pasha could hand over what he owes me. And you've brought the money? So what's the hold-up?

KOSTYA. You're dead right. But that doesn't mean he's got to give you exactly the same money as I brought him. He'll give it back when he's able. I mean, how's he going to hand over something he doesn't actually possess – (*Looks at* VALYA's *watch.*) – at this moment in time? You can't give back what you don't have. See, I didn't give him the fifty roubles, because I didn't have it. I gave him forty.

VALYA. What d'you mean you didn't have it?

KOSTYA. Well, it *was* the holidays.

VALYA. I don't understand this attitude to other people's money.

KOSTYA. I mean Pasha literally dumped these fifty roubles on me, just before the holidays. Pass them on to Valya, he says. I didn't want to take them, kept on refusing, but Pasha, conscious of his . . . well, bearing in mind his . . . um . . . not unmindful of his little weakness, right? And not a hope in hell of getting that kind of money together again – well, he just turns up at the flat – Polina wouldn't let him in, slammed the door on him, but he keeps on ringing the bell regardless, must've been a dozen times, and eventually Polina and old Ivan poke their noses out, and Pasha hands them an envelope – this is for Kostya, he says, there's fifty roubles in there. Ivan does his nut, as usual, keeps shouting there's nobody lives here by that name. But he's no mug, he wasn't going to refuse fifty roubles, and he even stood counting it in front of him. I mean, he thought, if Pasha's getting shot of fifty roubles, then it's got to be dodgy money, surely. He wouldn't be *giving* it away, would he, unless it was hot. Anyway, I get in in the small hours, Polina's asleep, they're all out for the count, and on the table there's the envelope with a note inside, compliments of Koltsov, it says. I didn't bother getting up in the morning for breakfast, I'll just let them all clear out, I think. And at the table they didn't mention my name, except that Ivan kept laying it off about needing to buy Vladik a little fur coat at fifty roubles, exactly fifty roubles, but there was no money, or to be more accurate, there *was* money but it belonged to the kind of person that wouldn't scruple to steal a fur coat for the winter off his own kid's back. *And* that doesn't give anything towards its keep. Vladik wasn't going to ask whose coat it was, but Svetka asked. Svetka's always winding Ivan up. The little childish voice, you know? Grandad, who's stolen a fur coat off our Vladik? There was a really strained atmosphere at the table. Silence reigned. Meanwhile I'm asleep behind the partition, with a pillow over my ears. Vladik told Svetka it was her dad that stole it, but Svetka wasn't ready for that, she wanted the full-length performance, same as always. Only it didn't pan out like that, Vladik, he's a good kid, he killed it stone dead. Otherwise old Ivan would've started his usual guessing game with them, oh no, poor little Svetka, you've got no cream today and no nice garlic sausage for Vladik, because a certain person has squandered all your money, your black caviar, and your red caviar, *and* your white – spent it all on wine. Svetka's delighted. Who is it? Who is this person? The same person, says grandfather Vanya, that stole the fur coat off Vladik's back. At which point everybody clams up. Vladik's saying nothing and the triumphant mother-in-law, she's saying nothing either. Polina's silent as well, but she's got a face like thunder. And old Vanya doesn't answer the kid. You can imagine what it's like.

VALYA. Yeh, yeh, I get the picture. But I'll tell you a better one . . .

Enter PASHA with two briefcases.

PASHA. You know the funny thing, there was no queue or nothing. I think they're all into tonic wine and anti-freeze down there. Anyway I says, 'Give us Cinzano'. And a guy at my back says, 'What's that, then?'

KOSTYA. How much did you get?

PASHA. What we agreed, you guys.

KOSTYA. You didn't forget about Valya?

PASHA. Two bottles.

KOSTYA. I don't suppose you thought to get me one?

PASHA. More.

KOSTYA. Thank Christ.

PASHA. The shop was on the point of closing, that's the thing.

VALYA. Well, meanwhile . . .

PASHA. Uno momento . . . (*Exits to the kitchen.*)

KOSTYA. He's a good guy. 'Cause, I mean, you can come to in the middle of the night, looking for a drink, and there's bugger all. Remember that time at Kondakov's, we had to drink tea at two o'clock in the morning.

VALYA. That's right!

KOSTYA. Tea's nasty stuff. It does in your kidneys, and your heart as well. You know, I got home in the morning, went for a shave before work, and had a look at myself in the mirror – Jesus, my face would hardly fit in the mirror! That's tea does that.

VALYA. Really?

PASHA *enters with a tea-plate.*

KOSTYA. Is that something to eat?

PASHA *takes a paper bag out of the briefcase and empties some sweets onto the plate.*

VALYA. Such extravagance – that's too much.

PASHA. Nothing's too good for you, kid.

VALYA. Is that so?

KOSTYA. Are we going to drink out the bottle?

PASHA. Hey, guys – here's a joke: these two vampires tear the head off this guy, and one says to the other, 'Shall we just drink out the bottle?'

PASHA *partly raises the cardboard box, and takes out a half-loaf of bread.*

KOSTYA. Food!

VALYA. Cut us a slice of that. I've just come from work.

KOSTYA *takes out a penknife and carefully cuts off a slice.*

PASHA (*opening a bottle*). Kostya, hand us up the other two packets – there's cheese, and sliced salami.

VALYA. Have you gone nuts?

PASHA. I bought them for you, Valya.

KOSTYA. Hey, one of these parcels has got some sort of rags in it.

PASHA. That's not it, that's the wrong one – (*Snatches it away.*) That's them there, the packets.

KOSTYA. I'm just looking. There's clothes or something in one, and shoes in the other.

VALYA. What, are you taking them to sell?

PASHA. Right, mate, eat.

VALYA. You can't drink and eat at the same time.

PASHA. So, eat up. Right, you guys, here's to us! And here's to my old ma! (*They drink.*)

VALYA. Yeh, Kostya, you didn't finish about the ten roubles.

KOSTYA (*mysteriously*). Ah.

PASHA. What ten roubles?

KOSTYA (*deliberately*). Yeh, what ten roubles?

VALYA. Well, it seems he's spent one of the five tenners.

PASHA. Eh? Well, Jesus – (*Laughs delightedly.*) I couldn't figure it out – I kept on counting the change.

KOSTYA. What ten roubles, I said.

VALYA. You told me yourself, you'd blown a tenner.

KOSTYA. What tenner?

PASHA. Hey, drink up, you guys! (*They drink.*) Christ, Valya, you're still eating. You should get false teeth, man, you'll be able to eat quicker.

VALYA. Yeh, I know, I just don't have the time. If it's not one thing it's another. I'm making a cupboard at the wife's flat.

PASHA. What wife's?

VALYA. Olga's, whose d'you think?

PASHA. Since when?

VALYA. Since when what?

PASHA. Since when did she have a flat?

VALYA. Well, they allocated her one. Her and her mother. Only her mother's got married again and moved in with him. Olga says for once in her life she's going to live like a human being, and not with your so-and-so relatives. So off she goes with the kid. She's got little Alyosha into a new nursery already. And that's me there now every night.

KOSTYA. What d'you mean every night? What about yesterday?

PASHA. And Monday?

VALYA. Yeh, well, Olga hasn't got a phone.

KOSTYA. Oh, I get it. Your old dear thinks you're at the wife's.

PASHA. But won't Olga phone up your parents?

VALYA. Not Olga, man. She's had it right up to here, she says, all that family life crap. But I'm still making furniture for her!

PASHA. And then she just says, right, that's it, on your bike?

VALYA. No way, pal. She wants me to move in with them, and I'm not actually against that. But what about the old folks? They'll be left on their own in that big place, fifty square metres, in their old age? They've knocked their pan in for me their whole life, and I just give them the elbow? I mean, who's going to drive the old man's car?

PASHA. Is he buying a car?

VALYA. He's practically bought it.

PASHA. Hey, great, we'll go for a drive!

VALYA. It's the old guy's, it's not mine.

KOSTYA. Yeh, but on the other hand, you can't get a divorce, can you?

PASHA. Why not?

KOSTYA. Valya's applying to go abroad.

PASHA. Abroad where?

VALYA. Never-never land, where d'you think?

PASHA. The free world, you mean.

VALYA. So? I've been to Czechoslovakia, and Bulgaria – Bulgaria's Golden Sands.

PASHA. I applied to go to Mongolia.

VALYA. So what happened?

PASHA. They were supposed to be expanding at work, and then they didn't. Changed their minds.

VALYA. So they turned you down. Anyway, you can't buy much with Mongolian money. One of our guys brought back an East German fur coat for his wife. He got it there, artificial fur, only, no padding. She'd to take it to a dressmaker's to get a padded lining put in. Daren't step outside the door if it's below minus fifteen. Listens to the weather forecast every day, cursing. He'd have been better bringing back plain leather.

PASHA. By the way, talking about women – phone up, Konstantin, on you go –

VALYA. Phone up who?

KOSTYA. Druzhinina, he means. But she won't be in just now.

VALYA. Who's Druzhinina?

PASHA. A little blonde bird.

KOSTYA. It's her girlfriend's birthday, she'll be at her place.

VALYA. Who's that?

KOSTYA. Smirnova, she works in our department.

VALYA. Hey, guys, we should go there!

KOSTYA. Nah, Pasha's barred.

VALYA. Well, we'll go without Pasha.

KOSTYA. I'm barred there as well.

VALYA. You're kidding. I don't believe you guys! It's terrific at Smirnova's place – they dish up roast lamb.

KOSTYA. Yeh, and gin. But me and Pasha had to spend the night there last time. (*They drink.*) Yeh. We were sitting in the kitchen, and eventually we drank her old man's blood-pressure medicine out the fridge. A quarter bottle. I mean, from the outside it looks exactly like pepper vodka. You can't tell the difference. And in the morning we got onto the metro, and the blood-pressure went right down. Either that or it was the row they kicked up starting to affect us – auto-suggestion, you know?

PASHA. That's the likeliest. Rows make my blood pressure drop, definitely.

KOSTYA. Anyway, we fell asleep on the Circle line, couldn't help it. And we finished up inside the depot, worse luck. Signalling for ages, to get out.

VALYA. How d'you mean?

PASHA. Battering at the doors.

KOSTYA. Smirnova's old man kept shouting at us, we were killing him – Christ, we were killing ourselves – 'cause we'd drunk all his medicine. He was on two drops, man, three times a day. It's sent from the Far East, you've got to pay gold for it. Lowers your body metabolism, instantly.

PASHA. That's crap, all that stuff. A pure con. My old man used to send for it as well.

KOSTYA. Anyway, it put us right out the game. We had to stay off work, took ages to recover.

VALYA. So. I'll nip out and phone, then. (*Eats.*)

PASHA. Eat up, it's your money that's bought it.

VALYA. You haven't given us anything back yet.

PASHA. Who are you going to phone?

VALYA. Whoever answers. Meantime I'm having a bite to eat. (*Eats.*) By the way, the wool's fantastic in Mongolia. You'd have been able to bring Tamara back a nice woollen jacket if you'd gone there. But what can you do, if they won't let you go? I suppose Tamara would've been pleased?

PASHA. Tamara? Ah, she's giving me a hard time. I've got to get home before twelve. If I'm not in by twelve Tamara withdraws my conjugal rights, you know? That means I've got to get the bus at 23.02. And on top of that, from here to the bus is what . . . a half-hour, minimum.

KOSTYA. Thirty-five minutes.

PASHA. So, if it's the 23.02 bus . . . (*Looks at* VALYA's *watch.*) Jesus, that leaves me practically no time at all. Hey, Valya, go and phone.

VALYA. I don't get it, I thought you were already divorced?

PASHA. That's right. It's so's I could establish residence at my old dear's, get registered there.

VALYA. Oh, I see – you mean otherwise you could lose the flat? Is your mother old?

PASHA. What's that got to do with it?

VALYA. Well, they're all old more or less. Happens to us all.

KOSTYA. Hey – his mother's in the hospital right now, okay?

PASHA. I'm getting her home soon, tomorrow.

VALYA. Tomorrow's Saturday, they don't discharge them on Saturdays.

PASHA. I'm picking her up, right?

KOSTYA. Is it anaemia she's got?

PASHA. Let's drink to the repose of her soul.

VALYA. Idiot. You run off at the mouth. (*Drinks.*)

PASHA. That's the good thing about drink. Everything else fades into the background.

VALYA. What's the point of that? What's the point of escaping from reality, if the reality's just that we like a drink? We just like the stuff and that's it. None of this high-minded crap about drinking in order to forget. I mean, why have we always got to hide behind some sort of fancy language. We're sitting here drinking 'cause it's terrific. For its own sake, right? The drink is. And here we're even having to justify this little party. We don't need to justify ourselves to anybody, I mean, what business is it of theirs? (KOSTYA *kisses* VALYA.)

VALYA. Hey, come on . . . So, how did your Tamara react to the divorce? I mean, when you filed for it?

PASHA. She filed the papers herself. Even before I brought it up.

VALYA. So it was actually her . . . that's better.

PASHA. Mutual. The parties arrived at a mutual understanding.

VALYA. So you're living here?

PASHA (*shrugs*). When I'm here.

VALYA. So in fact you don't need to go anywhere – what are you counting the seconds for? I don't need to go, either. You and all, Kostya – you'll get in behind your partition, before the gates close. (*Imitates Metro announcement.*) 'Mind the doors, please!' Come on you guys, let's drink. Hand us up another bottle. How many's that, by the way? Two of them's yours, right, and that's three, no, four to me, and we'll drink what's left.

PASHA. Look, go and phone, will you, I've got no time to waste.

VALYA. What d'you mean no time? Christ, you – I mean, how come? You don't live anywhere, there's nobody waiting up for you.

PASHA. If I'm late, the conjugal rights get withdrawn, okay?

VALYA. Conjugal what?

PASHA. Rights. She locks the door on us.

VALYA. What's all this about your conjugals? I've got conjugals as well, and so has Kostya, behind his little partition. By the way, are you still crashing out at your old dear's?

KOSTYA. Nah, we've had a bit of a row.

VALYA. Hey, that's bad. One of these days you'll end up on the street.

KOSTYA. We've had a row. Polina keeps going on about it – 'What do we want with their chickens?', she says. I mean they come to visit the grandchildren, and they bring a chicken. For eight people. So there they are, they walk in, and the dinner's been ready for ages without this chicken, and we would've sat down hours ago, but oh no, they want it cooked. We're having cold meat and stuff, and they're that stupid they don't realise their benevolence is just a prize pain in the arse as far as Polina and old Vanya are concerned. Polly says to me, tell them we don't need it. So I tells them, and of course the old dear gets all upset, and the old man has to take his drops. We brought this for your kids, they say, 'cause you spend everything on drink. So it all comes down to me, naturally. And the old dear says right, if you and Polina are that cosy, don't bother coming to spend the night with us. That's you finished! You can go and shoot yourselves!

PASHA. You know, there isn't a single car goes up our way after twelve. You could take a bird, and spread her out on the main road and do whatever you want with her, as many times as you liked. So I'll need to get moving, you know? Need to shift. (*Drinks.*)

VALYA. And you're still not officially separated from Tamara, right?

PASHA. No, it's official. I've just got to get registered at my old dear's – some sort of bullshit red tape. I've been putting it off, but that's all there is now.

VALYA. Yeh, you'd better register. I mean, if you don't watch, you could be left with no flat.

PASHA. Christ, I'll need to hurry. Really shift, I'm not going to make that bus!

KOSTYA. Listen, you could catch twenty buses, you've stacks of time. You'll be on it, don't worry. Wait another five minutes, Valya's just nipping out to phone.

VALYA *makes a sandwich, exits.*

KOSTYA. So, how are things with your mum?

PASHA. She's got to have an operation, for a bone-marrow transplant. Urgent. Actually tomorrow. She's going to need bone marrow, and I'm giving it to her. I'm donating it tomorrow in fact, they've already tested it. It matches up. A wife can't accept it from a husband. You can take it from your offspring, and it'll match up, but no way a wife. She's not a blood relative, and it's got to be a blood relative. Anyway, that's it. It's going to be okay. Let's drink to it, right?

KOSTYA. You went out to see her today?

PASHA. Yeh, I did. Jesus, man, don't ask. Some things you don't ask about. She was white as a sheet. (*They drink.*)

KOSTYA. My old guy's sick the whole time. I'll need to ask Smirnova what it was we were drinking that time. It's great for lowering the blood pressure.

PASHA. Yeh, took us forever to claw our way out of that carriage! (KOSTYA *laughs.*) So, what about them, will they not allocate you some space?

KOSTYA. Nah, the old dear's saying, you'll just divorce Polina and come and sponge off us.

PASHA. That's garbage! If you got part of their flat you could divorce her and live on your own, be independent.

KOSTYA. Yeh, well, in the first place they've said they want to die on their own patch, same as they've got used to. And I'll tell you, old Vanya's been giving them a lot of support, apparently, which I didn't know about. I mean they've been going on and on, no contact between them, and suddenly the old man phones up Vanya, and they're as thick as thieves. Yeh, believe you me, says Vanya, old people shouldn't change their way of life – they can't stand the shock to their system. They shouldn't give up their territory, or they'll die very quickly. So what's at the bottom of it? Polly's asked her parents as well, to do an exchange and get her a flat, supposing it's only one room. He's my husband, I've got to live with him and all that. No, no, says Vanya – we can't do that, it'll cause a shock to the system. So he's discussed the whole business with my old guy and sorted it all out. Yeh, who does this, who gets that, who gets the kids, they're that attached to the grandchildren. I mean, do you understand me, they're attached to my kids! (*Mimics them.*) No, no, Polina, you can't manage on your own, Konstantin'll just sell you out at the first pub that stocks beer!

PASHA. Yeh, so you've said.

KOSTYA. I mean, I'm all for live and let live. I wouldn't lift a finger for myself. And I wouldn't interfere in anybody else's life. I don't want to go to court, and make a fuss, just to see them clear out in a removal van. But basically I don't give a shit. I'll survive. There's nothing they can do about it, they're just standing with their mouths shut, waiting for me to go down the drain. But I'm not, right? I'm getting by. The kids are fed, shod, clothed, and the telly's working, as old Vanya says. Yeh, we get paid on Monday, and I've got to buy Vladik a little pair of winter boots. Druzhinina's bringing us a pair of her daughter's boots for four roubles.

PASHA. She might give you them for nothing. You know, just hand them over.

KOSTYA. Well, if she was giving them, I'd take them.

PASHA. Of course.

KOSTYA. So I'll make four roubles out of that deal. I'll tell Polina I'm bringing in boots. I've bought them, I'll say, so you can deduct four roubles off the housekeeping.

PASHA. It's the same with me. Tamara's used to me getting a rouble five, right? Only now they've given me a raise. And she's asking me, Pasha, she says, are you not on a rouble twenty these days? And I'm saying, what, you must be joking! Yeh, and she's still not found out.

VALYA (entering). Her gran says she'll be in in twenty minutes. She phoned to say she was on the way.

KOSTYA. Who did?

PASHA. The blonde bird?

VALYA. Yeh, right, Irka Stroganova.

A pause.

KOSTYA and PASHA look reproachfully at VALYA.

KOSTYA. Christ, she's a dawg, a pedigree hound, man. She'll come and drink everything in sight.

VALYA. I saw her at a class reunion this year. Give us a call, she said, whenever you fancy a drink.

KOSTYA. She just arrived out the blue at our place with her

daughter. Jesus, she drank as much elderberry wine as old Vanya could put on the table. It was Svetka's birthday party. Relatives going at it for two days, the two lots. God, her daughter's the spitting image of Semyon, I tell you. (*Makes a wry face.*)

VALYA. Well, at least she won't get kidnapped.

KOSTYA. Irka sat there at the table, telling us that no matter where she crawled home from, or however much she'd been drinking, she would always fold and iron her daughter's clothes at night, leave a little pile of things ready for the nursery. Of course all the relatives were ecstatic.

VALYA. She's got a Ph.D, you know.

KOSTYA. But it was funny how it turned out, 'cause Semyon arrived as well, with his new wife – you know, for Sveta's birthday party. Only Irka got it wrong and turned up a day late. Or maybe she didn't get it wrong, just did it deliberately. Yeh, that's more likely. Anyway, she came on the Sunday, when there was a second sitting of the relatives. Otherwise the two wives would have met up.

PASHA. Did Semyon give you back the watch?

VALYA. What watch?

KOSTYA. Oh, yeh, about the watch. Semyon took us into this bar on payday. He says, 'I've got to give the new wife an account of everything I spend, so you and me'll have a little drink, and you can give me a loan of your watch. I'll tell her I bought it off some guy for five roubles.' So I took the watch off.

PASHA. Yeh, you've told us.

KOSTYA. Anyway, a week goes by, I give Semyon back his money, and ask him where's the watch? He says the strap broke, and he's lost it. Okay, fair enough. Next time we meet up, he says, come on back with me to the house, there's nobody in, the wife's in hospital having the kid. So we walk in, and I'm looking around, and there's the watch, lying on the windowsill. And in fact, the strap *is* broken.

VALYA. I don't know what it is you see in that guy.

KOSTYA. Hey, come on, I think he's a great bloke, I really admire him. We went to this restaurant for foreigners, the two of us – it's open till 3 a.m. The headwaiter's a mate of

Semyon's, and we'd been drinking before that at some geezer's wedding reception. Semyon was chatting up the musicians and we sat in with the band, all pals together. Then they took us out, up to the hard currency bar, and we got absolutely pig-drunk. They all baled out then, and Semyon and me stripped off and went for a swim in a goldfish pond. And Vitalik, that's the headwaiter, he kept running round the edge shouting, 'Hey, come on, lads, you'll get me into trouble, hold it in, hold your water, you'll poison the fish! Come on, give over'.

VALYA. That Irka used to be a good-looking bird.

KOSTYA. She drinks too much. Says it's her circumstances drives her to drink. Semyon left her in a right mess, her mother had just died, her little girl was sick, and he just up and walked out on her.

VALYA. What d'you mean, it's her circumstances makes her drink? She drinks because she wants to. It's the same as us, we drink because we like it, nothing to do with circumstances. I just like the stuff, and I love you guys, my good mates.

KOSTYA. I went on a real bender a while back, out the game completely. So I rolls home a week later, straight into bed, and the quack gives us a sick-line, with a diagnosis: disfunction.

VALYA. What's that, your intestines?

KOSTYA. No, the whole bit. The whole system – disfunction. He gave us a line off work, and me and Pasha went out, wound up standing in this queue. They were doing fur hats at thirty roubles. We stood for a while, then left. No money. I phones two or three people to try and get a loan. Pasha gave it a shot as well, no use, so we just gave up the idea.

VALYA. So how did this disfunction show up then?

KOSTYA. Blood pressure. A hundred and eighty over a hundred and ten. That's the first time it's been measured, by the way. But that's okay, I mean, people can get up to two-fifty, and still live. Like my old man . . .

VALYA. Hey, I've just remembered! There's somebody else I've to phone.

PASHA. The blonde bird?

KOSTYA. Hey, Pasha – d'you remember that blonde chick we met on the metro? We were sitting alongside her, and I says to her, allow me to introduce my friend, Pasha Koltsov, same as the great poet. And she bursts out laughing. You're never going to believe this, she says, but my name's Koltsov as well. And I says, I don't believe you, let's see your passport. So she produces it, and there it is, straight up – Koltsov. We all checked it out – I mean, the whole train was clocking her passport – address, place of work, age – she was forty.

VALYA. Give her a phone.

KOSTYA. The passport doesn't have to show the phone number. Yet.

VALYA. I'll go and phone a few names out the little black book.

He picks up the bottles and makes to exit. KOSTYA *detains him, and after a struggle* VALYA *leaves without the bottles.*

PASHA (*after a pause*). We were having a serious talk about something.

KOSTYA. Yeh, I know, and then you can't remember. It was something really important, but what about? Hey, remember last summer, sitting drinking in our kitchen for three whole days – Vanya and the mother-in-law were away in the country, best time of the year, the blessed season. And we were talking all the time, non-stop, but about what – I was trying to remember afterwards, and I couldn't.

PASHA. I'm going to be late.

KOSTYA. That was really great. We had everything we needed. The whole of Saturday and Sunday, as well as part of Friday and part of Monday. But I'm on the wagon these days, strict regime, Saturdays and Sundays. Got to take the kids out walkies.

PASHA. I'll be late for my bus. Then I'm not going to get back. And I've got to . . .

KOSTYA. Yeh, we had everything we needed in that kitchen: a couple of old coats on the floor, and a bottle on the table. And you don't need anybody else.

PASHA. I've got to go. (*Stands up.*)

KOSTYA (*reaching out*). Hey, pass us over the bottle, since you're up.

PASHA. It's time I wasn't here, I'm going. (*Sits back down.*)

KOSTYA *pours out two glasses.*

KOSTYA. I'm packing in that job, you know. I've already told them.

PASHA. I'm off. That's it. Finished. I mean, what have I got here? Nothing. Absolutely fuck all. I can get drunk. Christ, I should be getting drunk. Today of all days.

KOSTYA. I'll go and get a job as a lorry-driver, same as Sobolyev. He's pulling down five notes a trip, and that's times 'n' trips, you know?

PASHA. How much money have I got?

KOSTYA *(emphatically)*. En.

PASHA *(begins rummaging in his pockets)*. How much money have I got? *(Takes out a note.)* Three roubles . . . One rouble . . . Three roubles . . . Much is this? *(Peers at a note.)*

KOSTYA. Let's see.

PASHA. How much is this?

KOSTYA. Let's see it. That's a postcard you've got there.

PASHA *(continues rummaging in his pockets)*. Death certificate. I'm supposed to give this to Tamara. What business is it of Tamara's? My mother's not related to her. Certificate No. MU 280574. *(Kisses the certificate.)*

KOSTYA. How much did you say?

PASHA. MU 280574.

KOSTYA *(suddenly interested)*. Hey, I wonder how much I've got? I need four roubles for boots. I'll get that off Polina. And I'll get the boots off Druzhinina. So how much is that I'll have left? I'll take four roubles off Polina, I'll say, you can deduct them off the housekeeping, I won't put them in, so that means those four roubles I'm taking off you for the boots, you just deduct them from the housekeeping money, right? And I'll bring the boots next time I'm up. And I've got more here. *(Brings out a ten-rouble note.)* So that's ten roubles, right, plus I'll take four off Polina, plus I can flog the boots at the market . . . for fifteen. They're good winter boots.

PASHA. I definitely had five tenners, right?

KOSTYA. Ten plus four . . . plus sixteen.

PASHA (*pounds his forehead with his fist*). Where's the money gone? Where's my money?

KOSTYA. Hey, relax, take it easy. Come on, I'll give you a kiss. How's this for a kiss, eh? (*Kisses* PASHA *on the ear.*)

PASHA. Let's have a drink.

Enter VALYA.

VALYA. Hey, what's this? What's all this, eh? How much have you got there?

PASHA. Where's my money?

KOSTYA. Hey, Valya – did you get through on the phone?

VALYA. What d'you mean your money? It's mine!

PASHA. That's garbage, man.

KOSTYA (*displaying his postcard*). This is four roubles for boots, right? That's what the boots cost, four roubles. And the rest can go towards the housekeeping.

PASHA (*dejectedly*). I've got the certificate . . . it's all ready. Just give us the money and I'll go.

VALYA. So he took the ten off you?

KOSTYA (*firmly*). For boots . . . and for the housekeeping.

VALYA. Come on, give us it.

KOSTYA. Here, have a drink. (*Drinks.*) I'm not handing over the housekeeping this time, no way. (*Mimicking.*) He does that every time with the housekeeping, never hands it in.

PASHA. I've got to buy everything. Nobody else'll do it. Only I've not to get paper flowers for the grave. That's what she said. Doesn't matter what kind, but they've got to be fresh. So I've just got to find the money and that's that.

KOSTYA. And I've got this as well (*Shows a ten-rouble note.*)

VALYA (*angrily*). Fucking give us that, you! (*Snatches the note from* KOSTYA, *who slumps forward and falls asleep.*)

PASHA. And you're going to give that to me, right? (*Reaches to take it.*)

VALYA. That's where you're wrong, pal. (*Takes* PASHA's *money from him, begins to count.*) You're giving it to *me*. That's five . . .

three . . . two notes . . . and a tenner. That's twenty roubles, just. So when are you giving us the other thirty?

PASHA. Hey, give us that back. It's not mine.

VALYA. You're dead right it's not. It's you owes me money, for starters.

PASHA. Fling us that back, before I make you.

VALYA. I need it, it's mine. It's not yours. Fucking moral freak!

PASHA *gets up to threaten* VALYA, *and falls back down.*

VALYA. Christ, it's totally legless.

PASHA. I need flowers.

VALYA. What, to make it up with the wife? (*Pockets the money.*)

PASHA. They're for my mother.

VALYA. What's your mother want flowers for? They don't need much, you know, just so's their little son turns up for a bite to eat, and sits still a minute, so they can get a look at him. Your mother doesn't need flowers. I don't take flowers to my old dear. No way. I just turn up in the flesh, and that's better than flowers, far as she's concerned. I mean, while they're still living, I'm duty bound to visit them, so they can get a good look at me. Flowers for the old dear's just ridiculous. I could buy them, if I wanted, I don't need you to tell me. But I'm not. (*Exits.*)

PASHA. I've got to go. (*Makes an effort to rise.*) Kostya! Hey, Kostya? (*Shakes him.*) I'm going. What's the time?

KOSTYA. I've lost my watch . . . the strap broke.

PASHA (*panicking*). I'm not going to make it! I'll never make it! What's the time?

KOSTYA (*holds out his arm, no watch*). Have a look.

PASHA. I can't see a thing. My eyesight's been getting worse and worse. I'm going blind.

KOSTYA (*his eyes closed*). I've gone blind as well. Disfunction.

PASHA. It's time I was out of here.

KOSTYA. You don't need to go anywhere, have you forgotten? You and Tamara are divorced, right? You don't owe anybody anything. That time's past. And I don't owe anybody anything, except a hundred roubles. Give us over a bottle. Feel around for one.

PASHA. I've gone blind. I can't see any, not one.

KOSTYA. You're looking in the wrong place. Give us it here. (*Rummages in the briefcase, takes out packages.*) That's grub, that's not it. (*Unwraps packages: a woman's headscarf and a pair of shoes. He puts on the headscarf.*)

PASHA. Not that way. (*Covers his own face with the headscarf.*)

KOSTYA. Here's a bottle. Here, Pasha, you have a drink as well.

PASHA. I can't see a thing.

KOSTYA. I can't make you out either. Where's your mouth? I'll give you a drink. (*Pours the wine onto the headscarf.*) Hey, your face has turned black.

PASHA. My face? (*Feels the scarf.*) That's grief. My mother's died, and her funeral's tomorrow. I'd just better not be late, that's all.

KOSTYA. Just don't think about it, that's the main thing. I mean, there's no such thing as being totally late. You imagine you're late, but the way it works out, in the long run, there's never any harm done. Just keep an eye on the time. (*Holds his wrist up to* PASHA's *face.*)

PASHA. I can't see a thing.

KOSTYA. Me neither. It doesn't matter. What's the odds? You can go tomorrow.

PASHA. That's right. I mean, so what? Everything's shut today anyway. So what's the hurry? What am I going for? What, like I've got to see Tamara urgently?

KOSTYA. That's it, you're dead right. You've got to train them up gradually, educate them, so's they don't get agitated and start throwing their weight about. So's whenever you *do* arrive they're pleased to see you. You just keep on not turning up, and then suddenly you're there, right?

PASHA (*rummaging in the briefcase*). I've got these apples from somewhere. I was taking them in to the hospital, for my mother. That's a couple of days I've had them.

KOSTYA. So, you were taking them in, and now they're back here. A gift from the gods.

PASHA. So eat them, then.

KOSTYA. We've knocked it off, eh – something to drink, and something for eating. Hey, listen! I mean, Jesus, tomorrow's Saturday. What's the rush? What are you in a hurry for? We've got all day tomorrow as well. I mean, it *is* Saturday – we're not beholden to anybody tomorrow.

PASHA. You reckon?

KOSTYA. Yeh, but on Sunday I've got to be at Polina's without fail. I've got this strict routine with the kids on a Sunday. Like, I wake up on a Sunday morning, and there's my two little monsters sitting on top of me. And they're saying, right, we're going to torture you, Daddy, until you beg for mercy. So on you go, I say. And they've got needles. Until you start screaming. And I don't say a word. And they stick them in deeper. Daddy, why are you not screaming? And I tell them: Partisans don't talk.

PASHA. But you're staying here with me till Sunday. You gave your word.

Curtain

SMIRNOVA'S BIRTHDAY

Characters

ELYA SMIRNOVA (female)
POLINA SHESTAKOVA (female)
RITA DRUZHININA (female)
VALENTIN (male)

POLINA *and* ELYA *are sitting at table.*

ELYA. No, it's me that should be thanking you for remembering my birthday. Nobody remembered, and here you've come, a total stranger. Actually, I'm not having anybody this year, I've told them all to stay away. My father's been taken to hospital, and my mother's in bed, she's recovering from a heart attack.

POLINA. I wouldn't have remembered your birthday myself, I've been rushing around so much, but some woman rang up, she said Kostya'd be at your place today, and she asked me to come. This woman badly needs to see Kostya. It was her that told me it was your birthday.

ELYA. Well, she's mistaken. My birthday was the day before yesterday.

POLINA. So what's with today?

ELYA. Today's Friday, that's what. I have my birthdays once a year on Fridays, it's well known. I mean, you know what people are like, you've got to fill their faces at least once a year, or they turn nasty on you.

POLINA. But this woman said Kostya would definitely be here.

ELYA. She must be pretty stupid, then. Pigheaded. Who is she?

POLINA. Her name's Tamara.

ELYA. Tamara who?

POLINA. She's one of Kostya's pals' ex-wife. I don't know her surname.

ELYA. What's the pal's name?

POLINA. He's called Pasha.

ELYA. That figures. Pasha's wife's already chucked him out. So – is she coming here too?

POLINA. I shouldn't think so. She was phoning from out of town.

ELYA. Huh, you never know with these ex-wives.

POLINA. By the way, Elya, his mother's just died. Pasha's mother.

ELYA. God, what a life!

POLINA. Yes, wonderful, isn't it? Pasha went to the morgue a couple of days ago, to get the death certificate, and he hasn't been seen since.

ELYA. So what was up with his mother?

POLINA. Something to do with her blood. The white corpuscles.

ELYA. Most likely Pasha's gone on a bender.

POLINA. Most likely. That's what Tamara thinks as well. And that's why Kostya's the only one in contact with Pasha.

ELYA. Okay. We'll wait. (*Pause.*) But won't Kostya phone home?

POLINA. Whenever he phones, my father says there's nobody there by that name.

ELYA. Kostya used to tell stories about that. He's forever spinning yarns. He says, there I am getting dressed for work, and I come out, and the mother-in-law's standing by the bookshelf, dusting, and she has this grim face on her for some reason. Maybe that's their hiding place, in the books, I mean. They keep the housekeeping money inside the books. The kids can't read yet, and I never read books, needless to say. Anyway, they try not to leave me alone, but there's this phone call for the mother-in-law, and she has to go out into the hall. It's obvious from the conversation that it's one of her cronies, her first husband's wife, and she's going to be on there for an hour. So I picked up one of their books – *Fifty Years in the Ranks* – but there's nothing inside it.

POLINA. We haven't much money, just Father's pension, and nothing at all from my mother – I'm only a junior research assistant, and there's two kids . . . and of course Kostya doesn't bring anything in.

ELYA. Well anyway, he said he found it. In a novel called *The Fireraisers*, by Nikolai Shpanov. And his mother-in-law's out in the corridor, on pins and needles, shouting, 'I'm sorry, I can't talk right now, I just can't . . .', and so on. Seems this first husband's wife's hard of hearing. Anyway, Kostya says, this is what I'm thinking I'll do. The mother-in-law'll ask where's the money? And I'll tell her just to take it off the grand piano – or at least the first hundred roubles of it anyway!

POLINA. We don't have a grand piano, where did he dream that one up? And he would never take money.

ELYA. Yes, they're what you'd call decent people, he says, so I didn't actually touch their money.

POLINA. We've only got an upright piano.

ELYA. Polina, I've been meaning to ask – how are things between you and Kostya?

POLINA. How d'you mean?

ELYA. You know, how are things going?

POLINA. About the same as usual – about average.

ELYA. I mean, Kostya's a friend of mine. I sign in for him, whenever he's late – you see, he'll nip out, hang up his coat, he has a session with Pasha every morning at eleven, in some boozer. And when the boss emerges, I jump in pretty damn quick, Shestakov's down at the isotope block, I tell him. And of course they're not on the phone.

POLINA. Well, he just worships you, you fixed up his industrial accident claim, you remember, that time he broke his rib?

ELYA. Of course I remember, I'm supposed to have brought him in off the stairs. What did actually happen?

POLINA. Him and one of his pals, a removal man, they were shoving a piano against a wall.

ELYA. It's a good job our working day wasn't over, and Kostya wasn't late. What he calls 'late for work' is arriving at knocking-off time.

POLINA. Anyway, you were asking how things were between us? Kostya's insisting we clear out of my parents' house. But I can't just dump them, they're too old. And I mean who'll look after the kids? Besides, you can't get an apartment if you've got bugger-all money. So everything's ground to a halt.

ELYA. Polina, there's only one solution – you've got to get a divorce.

POLINA. And deprive the children of a home?

ELYA. You can settle down again. You're still young.

POLINA. What are you talking about?

ELYA. You're throwing yourself away on Kostya. You want to love him a bit less. Don't run after him so much. Find yourself somebody else.

POLINA. I can't think of somebody else without a shudder.

ELYA. What, have you found somebody already?

POLINA. Eh?

ELYA. That you can't think about without a shudder. I mean really, I *am* Kostya's friend, but this is news to me. I'll have to mention it to him!

POLINA. I haven't found anybody! Nobody!

ELYA. Well, you should. You need to fight fire with fire.

POLINA. Oh yes, of course, and then more fire to fight *that* fire.

ELYA. Well, what do you expect? Personally, I've been on fire my whole life.

POLINA. You know, when I was just a young girl, I had lovely long braids, right down to here . . . and a certain lieutenant was chasing after me. And I was still at school. Well, anyway, he got a posting and had to go away. So when I married Kostya after that, I had to ask his forgiveness, mentally. That's how I thought of Kostya – fire to fight fire. Only as it turned out, it was my whole life.

ELYA. That's nonsense, you've got your whole life ahead of you.

POLINA. You know, Kostya was only the second time in my life.

ELYA. That goes for bugger-all, frankly. There was a man at our work started propositioning me – my parents were away for the summer, at the dacha, and he kept coming to the house. Anyway, this time he overstayed, and the metro was off, and you couldn't get a train or nothing out the place. Of course he'd no money for a taxi. And I don't give money on occasions like that, on principle, I refuse. I mean, why should I dole out money to them? You'll have to hoof it, I told him, really spelt it out, you know? So then he says, 'Okay, I'll just crash out here with you'. But I mean I've had washing soaking in the bath for God knows how many days, so what the hell, I just started washing at the dead of night. Anyway, I take it out to hang up on the balcony, and when I get back in he's already stretched out on the sofa in his underpants, and he's saying, 'And please don't tell me, Smirnova, that I'm only the second man you've had'. Talking about the second time in your life, as you say. Well, anyway, I nip smartly into my parents' room and bolt the door. And he's standing outside the door a full half-hour, begging me to open it, saying we're both adults, what difference does it make to you, and all of that. What they all say on these occasions. Then he just flakes out as if nothing's happened and starts snoring. He's snoring so loud, that when I go out past him to the bathroom, he doesn't even hear me. I can't get to sleep, and he's snoring. I tell you, I was turning the air blue. Then I had to travel with him into work, the next morning, like we were an item. Anyway you were saying, the second time in your life . . .

POLINA. There's your fire to fight fire.

ELYA. Yes, well, as a general rule, a woman should get married not when she's in *love*, but when she's *loved*. Right? So next time, get married *without* love.

POLINA. They'll have to drug me first. (*A ring at the doorbell.*) If that's Konstantin, don't tell him I'm here.

ELYA *opens the door, and* RITA DRUZHININA *enters.*

ELYA. Druzhinina, what a coincidence! I was just this minute thinking about you, thinking I hope she won't come!

RITA. Many happy returns, Smirnova, I've brought you a present – *Vermutto Italiano*. It's called 'Cinzano'.

ELYA. And there's another one there on the table – somebody's already dumped one on me.

RITA. Must be a big delivery, then?

ELYA. Yes, most likely. Let me introduce you, this is Rita, my girlfriend, and this is Polina Shestakova, she's married to Kostya Shestakov, that you've heard so much about.

RITA. Pleased to meet you. Yes, this Cinzano was delivered to our canteen.

POLINA. And I bought this at our local wine shop.

RITA. Seems there's been a big consignment, right enough. I still had to pay old Masha over the odds for it, though.

ELYA. There's a special canteen at Rita's place, would you believe. And d'you know where she works? At the Novodevichy cemetery.

RITA. It's just an ordinary snackbar, with old Masha.

POLINA. At the Novodevichy? Hey, I'll bet you get plenty of fresh air in that place.

RITA. Fresh air? You must be joking. It's like a crypt we're sitting in – walls this thick. We have to keep our overcoats on.

POLINA. Do you want to know a coincidence? My father dreams about getting into the Novodevichy, day and night.

RITA. You should bring your father up some time.

POLINA. He gets a special pension, you know, from the Republic. Every so often they all get together at some old woman's, and this old dear raises her glass and says, 'When we started out, we had so many dreams, and now all our dreams have come true. We're all on special pensions'. So there you are. And it turns out you actually work there – in that famous place, eh? Now *there's* a coincidence for you.

RITA. Well, I'm not personally in the cemetery, I'm in the museum. There's a museum of statistics close by. It's not connected.

POLINA. And my father just dreams about the Novodevichy!

RITA. If he's interested, get him to look in. We have a set text for excursions, but I'll expand on it for you.

POLINA. The big thing is, we have a grandmother buried there, on my mother's side. But they don't allow you more than four burials in one tomb. And there's three stacked in there already. And my mother's sister's still alive, and she's determined – he's not in direct line, she says, he's a son-in-law, the distaff side, you know? But Papa wants to lie alongside Mama.

RITA. Have you been a long time without your mother? Mine's been dead a year.

POLINA. No, God forbid! They're alive, thank God. They're both alive. They have a strict daily routine. They're made of iron.

They'll outlive me. I sometimes wish I would die first. Then I wouldn't have to bury anybody.

RITA. That's sneaky.

ELYA. Hey, what kind of talk's this, then? Let's drink up, girls, I mean, it is my birthday.

RITA. That's right, absolutely. So – who'll be coming?

ELYA. Yes, you might've given me a call. My birthday's been cancelled.

RITA. My offspring's sick, I've got to stay in with her, and we've no telephone in the block, you know yourself. I mean, just in order to come here, I've had to pay a childminder, sixty kopecks an hour, to sit with my little girl. I managed to get her down to sleep, and it was only then I could get out. So, your birthday's been cancelled?

ELYA. My father said he couldn't take any more mess in the house, he's not long for this earth, all of that – you know what it's like. Anyway, a month before this he'd started trying to get himself into a clinic. I mean, there's not a lot you can do, with a sick father, when they're supposed to be taking him into hospital, but nobody'll sign the admission papers. However, they signed the chit today at last, he's away now, and my mother's worn out, and I stayed off work . . .

POLINA. What's wrong with your father?

ELYA. The usual. Diabetes, high blood pressure, hardening of the arteries.

POLINA. My father has swelling of the prostate, incontinence, *and* hardening of the arteries.

RITA. We'll be the same ourselves one day.

POLINA. That's the whole point.

ELYA. What do you mean? He's having a rest-cure in hospital, away from us. And he says I've not to have any more birthdays in the house.

POLINA. Well, for ages now we've always celebrated birthdays and suchlike just within the immediate family circle. Papa has trouble walking, and visitors make such a mess, plates everywhere, and the expense, and all that.

ELYA. That's absolutely true. Two years in a row I've done roast leg of lamb, and salads, and even managed to get hold of tomatoes. Forty or fifty roubles out the window, and they bring nothing but bottles – and drink them all up themselves, thank you very much. Last year they gave me a glass cigarette holder, and one of those books, *Ancient Buryat Monuments*, and some other junk . . .

POLINA. Well, my mother gave me earrings, with emeralds.

ELYA. Anyway – let's just pretend today's my birthday all the same. Let's clink glasses. The first toast is to the mistress of the house, the second toast is to the lovely ladies, the third . . .

RITA. The third to the children. At sixty kopecks per hour.

ELYA. Did I hear you have a big family?

POLINA. Two kids, what about you?

ELYA. No, I've none.

RITA. I have a little girl. A lovely little thing, five years old, her name's Tanya.

POLINA. Well, my Vladik's seven, and Svetochka is four and a half. I've got to live somehow for their sake. I was on a field-trip in the summer, at Karakumi one time. And I went out onto the sand, lay down on a sand-dune, and thought, wouldn't it be nice just to get sunstroke and die? But you can't leave the kids, you've got to bring them up. The old folks are too old now.

ELYA. Well, okay, they'll grow up, everybody in this wonderful country of ours has to grow up. Look at me, I'd no father, no mother, and I lived God knows how long with my grandmother at Chulkovo. And grew up to be a free agent. My father and mother were abroad – in one of the planet's hot spots, you know? You can't fly off to these places with a child.

POLINA. My mother's father was a governor-general under the Tsar. And my mother's mother was a governess.

RITA. So how old is your mother, then?

POLINA. Well, her parents had her late on in life. And I was a late birth as well.

ELYA. I don't like late pregnancies – 30 per cent of late pregnancies turn out imbeciles, the Americans've got statistics.

RITA. Well, okay, but I'm writing a thesis myself just now, I'm on my second chapter, third year, and I've been working stuff out too, fiddling the statistics, so I know how it's done. But the main thing, Polina, is how are you managing to get along with two old people and two kids! I mean, when my mother was ill I stuck my little girl into a five-day crèche. She got covered in scabies in there, and my mother was dying, and then my boss told me to apply for leave of absence, she was short of tour-guides. 'I've got a really bright young comrade,' she says, 'for your post, he'll soon get on top of it.' Some fresh graduate or other . . .

ELYA. Yes, somebody's pet, most likely.

RITA. I suppose your husband helps out, otherwise how can you manage, really, with two kids and two old folks on your hands!

POLINA. He's no help whatsoever.

RITA. Well, that must be tough. You have my sympathy.

ELYA. It's tough for you and me both, but it's a bed of roses for her.

POLINA. Oh sure, I've got it made. I do the washing twice a week. We don't put anything into the laundry, I don't want it boiled up with everybody else's muck. I bath the kids twice a week, go to the shops every day. Mama does the cooking, and I'm still writing my thesis.

RITA. You're doing a thesis too?

POLINA. Of course, why not? You're not the only one. And I'm typing it myself. Our typists want thirty kopecks per page, with diagrams.

ELYA. Ours take twenty-five, do you want me to fix you up?

POLINA. Five kopecks isn't a saving. Anyway my mother has quite a good Underwood, which her own mother left her. She worked as a typist. What used to be called an amanuensis. Just after the Revolution. I mean, what's five kopecks, you can't make a meal off it. In fact, I don't have a lunch, I take sandwiches, and brew up tea on the stove. Summertime's the worst, when they're all away at the cottage, and there's nobody at home to cook. So I eat packet soup. One packet does two days. One time I went hungry for two whole days. Kostya brought his pal Pasha, and they ate all my soup for two days, just like that. I came home from work and just burst into tears. The fridge was empty. I'd been counting on some hot soup, and there wasn't any. I sat down to type, start typing and crying. Kostya shouts at me, what's the matter, he says, there's plenty of people around, why don't you just borrow a rouble, and nip out to a snackbar? But I just sat there crying. Anyway, I had to go hungry two days and two nights. I had bread and cheese for lunch with me in my bag – also for two days, otherwise I wouldn't have lasted out. That's all I had to eat.

ELYA. Well, I'm forever in debt. Living on tick, loans out the social fund. I've no money, and never will have, but I do all right clothes-wise. My parents feed me now and again. Everything else is pin-money.

RITA. Yes, we went to this girl's formal dinner once. You know, to celebrate her defence of her thesis. In a restaurant. And in the morning the girls at work ask me what everyone was wearing. And what were *you* wearing, they ask. And I tell them I was dressed same as always, in rags.

POLINA. I'm always well turned out, because I make over old things. We have a Singer sewing machine, and I run up things out of my old schoolgirl dresses – you know how we used to wear them very long and wide.

RITA. Oh, I really love that, when you can make something out of nothing, out of old rags.

ELYA. Yes, well, once an old rag, always an old rag.

POLINA. I recently found my grandmother's old quilt cover in a trunk and stripped the lace edging off it, and ran myself up a lovely little blouse.

ELYA. Oh sure, a filthy old rag.

POLINA. What do you mean? It's Alençon lace, real French lace, I had to darn it. Some people actually thought it was gauze scrim, the sort of stuff they'd buy for a rouble a kilometre.

RITA. Yes, well, I go around in old stuff, too. So what?

ELYA. All the same I envy you two. You've got three kids, and I've got nobody, that's my chances gone. I didn't dare get pregnant without a husband. You know, if you have a kid, eventually they'll start asking questions, they'll want to know how babies are made, and all that. But I wasn't for marrying this man either, I mean, he was a lot younger than me.

POLINA. So what? There's plenty of examples, nowadays a lot of women marry younger men. It's a kind of fashion, to take a toy-boy.

ELYA. Well anyway, I couldn't do it.

POLINA. What was the age difference?

ELYA. Twelve years.

POLINA. Well, at our work, I know of an instance with eighteen years' difference. He was just out of the army, and she worked in the accounts department, a bright, lively sort of person. She was thirty-eight, he was twenty. And at first they just lived together. At least, they'd keep each other's place, in the canteen queue. All kinds of rumours started up, and there was some sort of anonymous letter. Women are in the overwhelming majority at our place, 80 per cent, and she was hauled up to explain herself. She was really annoyed, and he got upset too. That in itself forced them together. People were trying to split them up, and they only made things worse. Because in the end she lays her passport on the table, and there's the stamp saying she's got married. They made plenty of noise about it, but she's a smart woman. She did what she had to, worked her way into the system.

ELYA. Did she go through the trade union?

POLINA. No, no way – she joined the mutual aid fund. Nobody was that keen to work there, so she became the treasurer. She was a real live wire, went at it hammer and tongs, squeezing money out of everybody, even struck up a deal with the cashier, so she could collect the debts on payday. Anyway, they all tried to keep on the right side of her, supposing it was for a hundred roubles or whatever.

ELYA. Quite right too. That would shut them up. So how are they getting on these days?

POLINA. They're getting on fine now. She's on invalidity. His kidneys have just about packed in. They support each other, go for walks every Saturday in the woods. They eat according to some kind of Yoga organic system, a bit of turnip for lunch, raisins and walnuts.

RITA. I tried a Yoga diet, when I was absolutely blown out, all puffed up. But a Yoga diet's even more expensive. For a start, Yogis eat from the market. It's all good quality, certainly, but that same turnip costs as much as a turkey. Besides which, you can't stick a turnip down in front of a kid. They need chicken.

ELYA. Chicken and fruit for the kids, as our neighbour says. Come on, girls, let's drink up this wine which costs as much as two chickens for the kids, plus tax at sixty kopecks an hour.

RITA. Don't remind me.

ELYA. It's for my birthday. So anyway, Polina, what happened after that?

POLINA. Well, she became an invalid, and it was actually his fault, two years ago. Motorbike accident. She was a passenger in the sidecar, and they picked her up just about in pieces, afterwards. She stood up to it well, it took guts, lay in hospital a whole year, then crutches, and she can still just about put one foot in front of another. But he says he can't even think of a life without her, and that's our girls got it wrong again, so shit on them.

ELYA. Polina!

POLINA. Well, serves them right. Certainly, he seemed to have got off lightly at first, from the accident, but now he's got a pain in his kidneys, you see, so it seems he's done in his own kidneys.

ELYA. No, that'll be caused by nerves.

RITA. We've got 90 per cent women in the museum as well. Nine women and one vacant place up for grabs at eighty-five roubles. Our lady director's desperate to bring in some young boy. She'll keep on hoping and praying till eventually they'll just cut the position. She can't get a man to work there. And she won't take on a woman.

ELYA. I can't stand women either.

POLINA. Present company excepted.

ELYA. You shut your face, French lace! No, I couldn't marry somebody younger than myself. I'd be too conscious of what people were saying. Polina, is Kostya much older than you?

POLINA. We're the same age.

ELYA. But he *is* older?

POLINA. No, he's actually younger than me by nine months and three days.

ELYA. Well, I couldn't be doing with it, if I'm older and he's younger. I'd think they were all laughing at me, saying that's the old bag baby-snatching.

RITA. Our boss told us a joke recently. This little kid comes home from the nursery, he's eating his yoghurt, and he takes a mouthful, rests his chin on his hands, and says, 'Phoney weed a man'. And he takes another sip, and says it again, 'Phoney weed a man'.

POLINA. Oh, I know this one, they were telling it at our place.

RITA. Well anyway, the mother asks him, what's all this 'Phoney weed a man' stuff? And the kid says, 'That's what our teacher and the nurse say when they're drinking out of their little glass – 'Oh, phoney weed a man, right now.'

ELYA. I don't get it?

RITA. Oh, if only we had a man right now!

ELYA (to POLINA). I've been meaning to ask for ages. What kind of ring is that?

POLINA. It's emerald, with brilliants and platinum. It's part of a set with earrings.

ELYA. Really? And it's so like paste, the kind of thing the Czechs make. You'd never guess it was real. Good for you, Polina! And good for the Czechs!

RITA. Well, we lost everything in our family. During the evacuation everything went in exchange for bread, or potatoes. We were stupid.

ELYA. God knows where it all went, but we've nothing like that in Chulkovo. Although there were refugees. And there was a big estate nearby.

POLINA. We'd lost everything to begin with as well. Everything was left to my mother's older brother, and the girls only got their dowry. But that brother had a skivvy, Nora, her name was. She worked in a factory throughout the war, and kept him fed, so nothing was sold. And when the war ended, he married Nora out of gratitude. And all our family turned their backs on them. But after he died, my mother started to invite Nora home, and we eventually teamed up with her, and got a bigger flat in an exchange. Mama's sister still hasn't forgiven us for that to this day. Anyway, that's how we've got the family heirlooms.

ELYA. And now everything'll be passed on to the children.

POLINA. Yes, and it's a good thing it's a daughter, too, so the jewellery'll be passed on to her, and not to some daughter-in-law.

RITA. It must've been hard work, looking after a stranger, the old woman.

POLINA. Yes, it was hard. On holidays, she'd be stretching out her paw with a glass in it, to clink just like one of the family. But she died on the very same day as Svetochka was born. It was as if she felt it was time to give up her room. The quack said trying to treat her was a form of torture.

ELYA. Anyway, you did well, getting shot of her. Lucky you didn't poison her, maybe.

RITA. Yes, on our side they've all snuffed it, just died out. Ours was a good family, too – establishment people. Grandfather had been a brilliant student before the Revolution, tearing around in his motorcar, all the young ladies, playing the violin – I wish I knew where that violin was, it was a good one, probably made by a master.

ELYA. Nobody managed to keep anything at Chulkovo, either, although we weren't under the Germans. We had refugees staying with us, that was all. Later on, I subscribed to the Dostoevsky and World Literature series in one of the bookshops. You could do that then, but now everything gets snapped up, the locals know a good thing when they see it. All we've got left these dark days, is if anybody's getting put in jail, they'll go straight to my father. To this day he's quoted among them like an authority. He helped somebody once in his life, and now he's paying for it.

RITA. A good deed never goes unpunished, that's a fact, Smirnova.

ELYA. What do you mean a good deed? It was an old uncle of ours he helped, Yuri Smirnov, and as it turned out, he'd chopped up somebody with an axe, at a wedding. They released Uncle Yuri, which didn't please the other side, I can tell you. There was absolute mayhem in the village.

POLINA. My father's village is called Salvation-on-the-Sands, and there's a whole street of Sharapovs. My father's name's Sharapov, and the street's called Sharapov Street. Kostya and I went there once after we got married. The forest, the Volga, and all that stuff. We went from house to house, spent a whole week doing nothing else. They were stewing up beets, making moonshine, Kostya recalls it to this day. Yes. And right after that they started visiting us, as a regular event, but father's on a strict diet, he absolutely doesn't drink. He doesn't use vodka either, especially home-brew.

ELYA. Of course, they're all bag-men, you know what I mean. But my mother got rid of them once and for all. I was still young, but I remember it well. Uncle Yuri Smirnov arrived with Uncle Pyotr, and they're sitting with my father, the room's full of smoke and spittle, my father's laying it off, pig-drunk, and he shouts to my mother – we've just come in from a walk – 'Come on, Mama,' he shouts, 'Bring us out the Cuban rum!' And all that business with Batista was still going on then, so my mother grabbed a five-litre jar of mushrooms off the table and flung it on the floor.

RITA. Did they get cut?

ELYA. Just missed.

RITA. I couldn't stand our relatives either, but now there's hardly anybody left, and I've got to run around after them. They were forever telling tales on each other, going on about how many housing points they had, applications for this and that, anonymous letters, ration coupons, who didn't send Grandma a parcel in the labour camp, who made off with all Grandpa's things, whatever happened to his big box with the manuscripts, where's the silverware, where are all the books? And I don't need all that. I've got a co-operative flat, and I'm up to my neck in stuff. One minute they're painting the concrete toadstools in the yard, collecting two roubles each off us, next they're wanting books for a library. And I don't have any heirlooms.

POLINA. Yes, we've been through a few battles.

ELYA. It's the coming thing these days, heirlooms. There's already a fashion for collecting diamonds, and gold. Even me, I've stood in a queue for some.

POLINA. Yes, well, you soon run through your inherited wealth, if you've got to live off it day to day.

RITA. I know somebody that got an unexpected windfall from

Switzerland. He bought a car, a Zhiguli, and other stuff. A co-operative flat for himself and his mother, a fridge, an upright piano, carpets, various other things. His Zhiguli's always full of junk – he used to go around like a tramp, still does, and he hauls all kinds of tree-stumps and roots out of the woods, sort of sculpture, in his Zhiguli. He takes the dog to the vet in it, too. His dog has a mild form of schizophrenia. It's pure bedlam in the flat.

POLINA. That's because he's got no culture.

RITA. No, he's got culture all right – he's one of the Ryurikoviches, in fact the last of the line. And he's only produced daughters, they're expecting his third soon, and everybody's waiting. He's in a panic, he says there'll be nobody to carry on the family name. His wife's the daughter of some general, quite a common person. But he's one of the Ryurikoviches. His fridge is leaking already, three times he's had to call out the repairman. And his daughters have refused to learn music, all of them, unanimous. And he says, I've made a bad mistake buying all these things. Carpets need a vacuum cleaner and so forth. I've made a real blunder.

POLINA. Well, he should have bought gold, of course.

ELYA. And lived on what? Sandwiches?

RITA. He says he should have blown the lot on art books. That would have been an investment. Something for posterity. And I mean you can read them, so that doubles their value.

POLINA. Yes, but you can wear gold.

RITA. Then you'll look like some floor-walker, going around dripping in the stuff.

ELYA. What do you know about floor-walkers? A person's worth whatever she's worth.

RITA. That's true enough, I suppose. My hairdresser, Zinka, goes around wearing gold the whole time, like a shop-window dummy, but she's a kind soul. This'll show you – her little boy was taking out the garbage, and when he comes back in he says, 'There's somebody sleeping beside our bin, and he's saying "Don't chuck it here, son!", in this hoarse voice.' So she hurries out with him, and true enough there's this old man, sitting up against the wall, settling himself down for the night. He'd come into town to the Social Services to see about his pension, her neighbours had told him to clear off out the entry, and he'd fetched up at the dustbins. So anyway they took that old man in, and I mean, what can you do with somebody straight out of a bin? They put him in a bath, then cleaned the bath out and that was that.

ELYA. Why are you telling us this?

RITA. Well, she goes around dripping with gold. Certainly, she's a lousy hairdresser.

ELYA. Yes, that's obvious, you always look a fright, your hair's like rats' tails.

RITA. Yes, well, my hair gets dirty so quickly. I've got to wash it every two days. And there's all that rushing around – work, nursery, nursery, work. So why bother?

ELYA. And your Zinka's gold'll be nine carat, same as her hairdressing. The one thing matches the other, the gold and the workmanship. The gold's found its own level.

RITA. Well, anyway, as a friend of mine used to say, she married the son of a good family, and got a drunken slob.

POLINA. Who told you that?

RITA. You don't know him, just somebody I knew.

ELYA. Relax, it was him that told her, Ryurikovich.

RITA. No, Ryurikovich isn't from a wealthy family, his old woman was an art historian. I used to go to them, and they'd pour out tea, and apologise because they'd no sugar. And the general's daughter married him for love, it was a really intense personal thing with her – he could've had his pick from about ten fiancées.

ELYA. And you were the tenth.

RITA. The eleventh.

Pause.

ELYA. Anyway, Druzhinina, you're wearing gold as well, a wedding ring, did you forget? But if I were you I wouldn't wear it on your left hand – only widows wear it there, definitely not unmarried mothers.

POLINA. On the subject of gold, my mother's always frightened of a war. She says, if anything happens, do the same as Nora. Sell nothing, keep it for the children.

ELYA. Yes, and the children'll pass it on to their children. So when do we get to live?

POLINA. We live for the children's sake.

ELYA. Well, for the sake of the children, just the same, I once committed a crime. To cut a long story short, I'd wound up with a five-month old foetus, and I couldn't get a legal abortion. So I started taking pills, to get rid of it, I mean, what could I do? Anyway, I damn near snuffed it, next thing there I am in hospital having the abortion, that very same D & C, absolutely ghastly, black sunken eyes, you know? I just lay there dying. And there was this really young doctor there, I'll never forget him, he scrapes the whole mess into a basin, and says, 'Oh dear, what a fine little lad you've killed!' I just passed out.

POLINA. Five-month-old foetuses sometimes cry.

RITA. Well, I say to myself, no matter how many I have, they're all mine.

POLINA. So you'll keep them all.

RITA. All of them.

POLINA. Yes, you can count yourself lucky, you've only copped for one.

ELYA. She's never had the opportunity.

RITA. That's true enough.

ELYA. That's because you frighten men off. But they cling on to me, I use my head. A person's first got to come to terms with themselves, their situation in life. I mean, should you have a child by somebody younger than yourself? But that's what happens, you bring them into the world, they do the same, and nobody ever so much as stops to think, have they got the right? Setting up house with somebody younger than yourself, ruining a young lad's life, so he's going around with his kidneys done in, chomping turnips.

POLINA. What are you getting all upset about? You're a woman, you'll still find happiness out there, believe me.

ELYA. Well, you haven't, and you're not going to.

POLINA. You've never even had it.

ELYA. And your second-time-around fire hasn't put out the first one, has it!

POLINA. And she kills babies, too!

ELYA. Fire! Fire!

RITA. We're really pissed. My head's spinning. How am I going to get home? The babysitter'll be on her way out now, most likely. I mean, what's sixty kopecks to her? And why am I sitting here, what am I waiting for? Tanya'll wake up alone, she'll start crying in the darkness.

ELYA. I had to take my father to the hospital. I got home frozen, totally whacked, I'd just got my head down, and then she appears. Just look at her, chasing after her husband, but he can't get far enough away from her.

POLINA. Me? It's not me that wants him. It's some woman called Tamara, she's looking for him because Pasha's mother's died.

ELYA. So let bloody Tamara find him herself. Tamara's looking for Pasha, but you're using it as a pretext to hunt for Kostya.

RITA. Pasha's mother's dead!

POLINA. Besides which, Tamara told me Kostya's woman would be here, at this birthday do – this is his current attraction, she says, her name's Rita Druzhinina.

ELYA. That's right, now that Tamara's divorced from Pasha, she's started to expose all his hidey-holes. So you shut up, Rita. Pasha's got to be found.

RITA. Polina, he dumped me a long time ago.

POLINA. Well, for God's sake, I know that. Tamara's news is old hat. Kostya's going with some woman called Ira now.

RITA. Who told you that?

POLINA. Rita, you can't just dismiss the children. Nobody else'll have his kids. He's an alcoholic. And he's paying too much alimony.

ELYA. This idiot would have his child.

POLINA. What's your ex-husband paying in alimony?

RITA. Sometimes it's eight, sometimes ten roubles.

POLINA. Multiply that by four . . . let's see . . . eh? What sort of wage is that? I don't get it?

RITA. I don't know. Seems he's deliberately gone onto some kind of part-time rate, so as not to pay. And he's making money on the side, in the book black-market. He's also collecting pictures.

ELYA. Well, that'll be a nice heirloom for Tanya.

RITA. He went on half-time because he was against having the child. He was dead set on an abortion. He didn't want Tanya, he hasn't once seen her. We got divorced before she was born.

ELYA. What have I just been saying? Mine was against it as well, and he dumped me. Of course, I was really disgusting, throwing up at every street corner. I used to howl for days on end. Ate everything in sight. One time I ate a whole herring. So that's why he baled out on me. I mean, what sort of life is it, a single parent, with the father twelve years younger than the mother, and that doesn't even want to know the child, and absolutely no hope? Is that a nice life for a child? . . . Oh, my poor little darling . . . what have I done, what have I done?

RITA. Anyway, Polina, just give over. I mean, who's this Ira person? What Ira are you talking about? There's no Ira, he's destroying himself, and you're going on about Ira.

POLINA. Ira and some other woman, Koltsova, appear in his little black book. And there's another child somewhere, that suffers from weeping eczema. He asked me to get hold of a quartz lamp to treat it, this one that's got the weeping eczema.

RITA. That's for my little Tanya, it's for her. For my Tanya. Did he ask a while ago?

POLINA. Oh yes, he asked long before you turned up.

RITA. When?

POLINA. Before we were married.

ELYA. There's so many kids around these days, you can hardly bloody move for them.

POLINA. A father ought to be with his children. You can have as many girlfriends as you like, but he's got two legitimate offspring, it's them he should be looking out for.

ELYA. And what have I just been saying? I've missed my chance (*A ring of the doorbell.*) Who the hell's ringing that bell!

She opens the door and admits VALENTIN *who is carrying a briefcase.*

VALENTIN. Hey, many happy returns! Look what I've brought you. (*Opens the briefcase, shows* ELYA.) It's a rare find, expensive stuff. I got it through the old man, he gets special vouchers. Have you ever heard of it? Cinzano?

ELYA. Yes, well – hello, goodbye, here's your hat and what's your hurry!

VALENTIN. Hey, hold on, it's Italian vermouth.

ELYA. What are you doing here?

VALENTIN. I'm going to Japan. I've just dropped in to say goodbye.

ELYA. Japan, eh? That's pretty good.

VALENTIN. By the way, you'll soon be paying your subs to me. I've wangled my way onto the young graduates' council – president, not bad, eh? (*Takes off his coat.*) My old man's bought a car. (*He enters the room, sees* POLINA *and* RITA.) Oh, you've got company, *Velly nice.* We'd better introduce ourselves. Hi, I'm Valentin, en route to Japan, urgent business . . . (*Pause.*) What's the matter with them?

ELYA. Pasha's mother's dead, you know.

VALENTIN. So is this a wake?

ELYA. No, she hasn't been buried yet. Pasha's buggered off somewhere and they won't bury her without him. You don't know where he is?

VALENTIN. Me? How would I know? Why are you asking me?

ELYA. We're all waiting for Kostya, he's supposed to be coming.

VALENTIN. Yeh, yeh, he'll probably come. So, let's sit down and wait a while. It's a cold night, I've been diving around all over the place, I'm frozen stiff, and I was just thinking, where can I go to kill the evening? It's nice and warm here, though. And it's cold out there. So, d'you mind if I heat myself up from your bottle, until we get to mine . . . (*He pours out a glass, drinks.*)

ELYA. Listen, I still haven't any money for a taxi, absolutely not.

VALENTIN. So you're not any richer yet, since that time?

ELYA. And my mother's sick, so just keep the noise down.

VALENTIN. I still haven't got a divorce. I'm getting all these trips abroad now, and you can kiss that goodbye if you're divorced.

ELYA. That's your business.

VALENTIN. Of course. So – Pasha's mother's dead. That's a shame.

ELYA. And there's nobody to bury her. And we're sitting here like idiots – what'll we do, where'll we go?

VALENTIN. Never mind, there's some decent people around, they won't leave her lying out. I'll get onto it tomorrow first thing. You can depend on me. Man of action, I've got my finger on the button. Hey, girls, don't cry, your golden boy's here.

RITA. Well, anyway, me and Tanya are watching the TV and she says to me, 'Oh look, Mama, look who's just galloped past!' and I said, 'Yes, that was two horses'. And she says, 'No, it wasn't, Mummy, it was a horse and a she-horse'.

POLINA. I was down at the cottage once – Vladik was still young, and Svetochka wasn't born yet, and I see Kostya coming with two kids: holding Vladik's hand, and carrying a little girl on one arm. And I had this idea, these are our future children. The two kids really suited Kostya. But it turned out it was a neighbour's little girl, from an adjoining plot. I tell you, if I'd had a second boy, I'd have hanged myself, but I had a little girl. Anyway, this one, the neighbour's little girl, runs through our plot all the time onto the road. Vladik runs after her, and then he comes back and says, 'Mama, she's eating our raspberries!' And Kostya says to him, 'Hey, son, you're surely not growing up to be a greedy boy? You're not a greedy boy, eh?'

VALENTIN. You're really great, Smirnova, you know that?

The End

MUSIC LESSONS

Characters

The GAVRILOVS:

> GRANYA, thirty-eight years old.
> NINA, her daughter, eighteen years old.
> VITYA, her son, a schoolboy.
> IVANOV, GRANYA's husband, thirty-five years old.

The KOZLOVS:

> FYODOR IVANOVICH (FEDYA)
> TAISA PETROVNA (TAYA)
> NIKOLAI, their son. (KOLYA)
> VASILIEVNA, the grandmother.
> KLAVA, TAISA's sister. (KLAVDIA)
> UNCLE MITYA, KLAVA's husband.
> NADYA, NIKOLAI's girlfriend.

> Girls in the student hostel.

> ANNA STEPANOVNA, the GAVRILOVS' and KOZLOVS'
> neighbour.
> SERGEI ILYICH, her husband.

ACT ONE

Scene One

The scene is a large room in the GAVRILOVS' *apartment. It is clean and tidy, although the signs of hardship are everywhere. In the corner, a television set is switched on, and the* GAVRILOV *family,* GRANYA, NINA, *and* VITYA *are watching a programme.* GRANYA *and* VITYA *are lying on the bed.* NINA *is sitting at the table, weeping. The doorbell rings, and* VITYA *springs up to open the door.* NINA, *her eyes red with weeping, rushes to the door at the same time and stops him, calling out* 'Who is it?'

WOMAN'S VOICE. Open the door, love, it's me.

NINA hooks up the security chain and part-opens the door. She stands looking at her a few moments before admitting their neighbour, ANNA STEPANOVNA. ANNA STEPANOVNA *is a little old dried-up woman who works as a night concierge and is thus free during the day. She is wearing a pinafore, with her sleeves rolled up, and a profoundly sad expression.*

ANNA STEPANOVNA *(to no-one in particular)*. So what's happening, eh? Flat on his back, is he, the dirty pig? We should call the police right now. Use the phone-box. *(To* GRANYA.) Is she asleep?

GRANYA. I think so.

There is a faint smile on GRANYA's *face. She is a tall, thin, subdued woman, with metal false teeth, wearing earrings. She speaks softly, even at moments of intense emotion.*

ANNA STEPANOVNA. She's a little sweetheart, as good as gold, eh? My first was like that, Gena – just ate and slept, a right little dumpling. That's what everybody said, a little dumpling. But your little Galya – well, who'd have thought it? Her father – *(a cautious nod in the direction of the hall door.)* – her father's thin as a rake, skin and bone. And your people, the Gavrilovs, they're just the same. (*Then, out of the blue.*) Has he arrived yet? Is he home?

GRANYA. Yes, he's home.

ANNA STEPANOVNA. What a carry-on! (*Wringing her hands.*) And what are you going to do now? (GRANYA *shrugs.*) Well, I suppose one way of looking at it, he is the baby's father. He is her father. But then again – he won't forgive you. He's not going to forgive you, no way. Maybe he's come back to get you, eh? You think about that.

NINA *is sobbing now.* GRANYA *absently watches television.*

I mean he's going to remember it was you got him put in jail. D'you think he won't remember? He will. What was it he said when they were taking him away? Granya? 'I'll be back.'

GRANYA *nods in agreement, sends* NINA *into the adjoining room.* ANNA STEPANOVNA *looks around her.*

Well, you've got a really nice place here, you keep it nice, everything clean and tidy. Still, Nina'll soon be bringing home a good wage, Vitya's a boarder, you'll be able to buy some clothes, a few things for the house. Not all at once, of course. Three kids, it's nothing but expense. Just one thing – don't you let that man of yours hang round your neck, let him go to hell! I mean, you weren't exactly happy when he was living here, were you? Eh? Just thank your lucky stars they put him in jail for a year, and not thirty days. You should get down on your knees and thank the court – I mean, just look, a whole year he's been away and you've had your little Galya in peace, nobody's been beating the kids, or swearing at them. And you yourself –

GRANYA. He didn't swear at them.

ANNA STEPANOVNA (*regardless*). And you're on your own – a great life. Come home in the evening, pamper yourself, have a nice warm bath, get into bed all nice and fresh, your own boss. And if you need a man, well, just whistle, there's plenty of them all ready and waiting. They'll give it to you in a gift!

NINA (*entering*). Mama, Galya's woken up, and she's hungry. (GRANYA *exits.*)

ANNA STEPANOVNA. And she's not crying? Just lying there? Just smacking her little lips? Well, she's a darling. My first was the same. Gena would wake up and turn his head round and give a sort of little cough. But he wouldn't cry. Just this little coughing sound . . . ahah-ahah . . . like that. (*Laughs.*) And the minute he started, I'd wake up instantly. Nothing else'd waken me, shouting or whatever. And we were two families living in that room, me and little Gena, and my Sergei, my husband. And there was another woman, Marta, with her little boy – he was born same day as Gena. Me and Marta were in the same maternity hospital, in adjoining beds. Marta had no place to go – she'd been brought up in an orphanage, and she'd no husband. I took her home with me. And her little boy used to howl the place down, and I'd just sleep on. But the second my little Gena started to cough, I'd be out of bed like a shot. He just used to whimper, never cried. So that's why – it's because of that me and Sergei used to be so quiet. Sergei's still quiet, maybe even too quiet. It's all boiling up inside, but it doesn't show on the surface. Me, I can't sit still, I've got a bee in my bonnet the whole time. I've got clothes soaking and I was going to wash them. Then our Yuri went down for a newspaper and when he comes back he says Ivanov's asleep beside the radiator in the entry.

NINA *exits*. ANNA STEPANOVNA *is shouting into the next room, but watching television at the same time.* VITYA *is also entranced, watching TV.*

Anyway I took Marta home, although we'd hardly room to turn round. Twelve square metres, and a stove, the three of us, plus the two of them. The neighbours started complaining, kicking up a fuss. I used to hang my nappies up in the kitchen, and nobody said a word. But when Marta started to hang hers up, they complained and took them down. So we had to dry Marta's nappies in our room. And what with the condensation and damp, the window steamed up – it was winter, of course. So anyway, we messed about like that for two months, and I took Gena out for a walk one time, and when I came back, Marta was gone. She understood, and she just left of her own accord. Certainly the neighbours had called out the police twice, because Marta hadn't a resident's permit. But I never said a single word to her, nor did Sergei. She wasn't like some people, you could spit in their eye and they'd just wipe it off and carry on regardless.

There is a patriotic war film on TV. ANNA STEPANOVNA *waits for the occasional lull in the fighting, then hurriedly speaks her piece.*

Well, anyway, I thought he'd come back to you. Not because

he'd said he would, or thinks anything about you at all. No, it's because he's got no place else to go. You mark my words – he's no good. Don't take him in – we need drunks in this block like a hole in the head. And your Nina's a young woman now, what's she going to do with somebody else's old husband? She's not going to wash and clean for him.

GRANYA (*appearing in the doorway*). He's not that bad. Nina's been like a daughter to him.

ANNA STEPANOVNA. Oh, God forgive you, Granya!

GRANYA. What do you mean?

The baby suddenly begins to cry.

ANNA STEPANOVNA. I'm going, I'm going. I'd better go, love.

NINA *enters carrying a bundle of nappies.*

And your fiancé's back home from the army, did you know? The Kozlovs' boy Nikolai, you remember. He always used to laugh at you – that's my girlfriend just run past, he'd say. (NINA *nods*.) That's my fiancée in the fifth grade. Yes, he's come home a big grown-up fellow. Drove up in a taxi just this evening. And he had a girl with him. Maybe he picked her up at the station, or else he's brought her home with him from the army, who knows? Anyway I had to run and get the washing on. Nikolai says to me, he says, 'Why don't you pop in, Stepanovna?' But I haven't got the time.

Scene Two

A large room in the KOZLOVS' apartment. The layout is similar to that of the GAVRILOVS', but the furnishings, etc., are very different. True, the television set stands in the same corner, the screen turned from the audience, but there are carpets, crystal, highly-polished furniture. The table is extended, and the KOZLOVS are seated round it. NIKOLAI's mother, TAISA PETROVNA, his father FYODOR IVANOVICH, NIKOLAI himself in civilian clothes, with a moustache, and his girlfriend NADYA TIMOFEYEVNA. In appearance, she is the perfect image, in our modern situation, of the well-paid department store salesgirl, hairdresser, factory worker, or, as in this case, house-painter. NADYA is smoking, opposite her sits NIKOLAI's grandmother, VASILIEVNA, as if mesmerised, following

with her eyes each puff of smoke as it rises to the ceiling, ANNA
STEPANOVNA *is also there, wearing the same house-coat, and with her
sleeves still rolled up. She is sitting on the edge of her chair, with her glass
raised high. She appears rather ingratiating, her face is flushed, and she is
silent. Indeed, everyone at the table looks a little flushed.*

FYODOR IVANOVICH. So you'd a good time in the army, had a
bit of luck, too, as you've been telling us. And we'll fix you up
with a good job. Not what you were doing before. Now on you
go, son, over to the piano, it's time we had a few songs. I've
missed the singing while you've been away, the vocals. On you
go, you can do your courting later, now it's your father calling
you to your duty. What did you study six years for, eh? And if
you hadn't given up you'd have finished music school, you'd
have a certificate by now. Anyway, I've wasted my money, six
years out of my life. All you can do is accompany your old
man, and I've got to persuade you to do that, even.

NIKOLAI. Give over, Papa!

FYODOR IVANOVICH. Well, come on – ye gods, the coaxing it
took when you were a child! Go on, sit down at the instrument,
for God's sake!

NIKOLAI. I even tried to keep quiet about it in the army, that I
could read music. Then this lieutenant comes up and says,
'You've got an intellectual face, you can sing in the choir.' So, I
wound up in the choir. Still, it often got us out of duties,
travelling away to competitions and reviews.

ANNA STEPANOVNA. Come on, Nikolai, play for us, please!

FYODOR IVANOVICH (*about to fly into a rage*). Well?

NIKOLAI *shrugs and sits down at the piano, his father stands
alongside. The influence of television is obvious, his father sings a gypsy
romance, 'As Soon As Azure Night Falls . . .' He sings tensed up and
straining – not in the manner of someone singing at the dinner table,
wholeheartedly – but like someone whose whole life's ambition has been to
sing. Singing of this kind doesn't produce a pleasant or joyful impression –
on the contrary, everyone at the table averts their eyes. Only* ANNA
STEPANOVNA, *who is extravagantly pleased with everything, joins in,
in a quavering treble.* TAISA PETROVNA *pays no attention to her
husband and busies herself looking after her guests – she picks up their
plates, takes them out to the kitchen.* TAISA PETROVNA *pushes a
pastry slice at* ANNA STEPANOVNA. *The latter, jolted out of her
reverie, briefly protests, then immediately launches into song again with*

her mouth full, rocking on her chair. NADYA *pours herself some wine.*
VASILIEVNA's *fierce staring eyes follow her every move, but* NADYA
*is not in the least embarrassed, she pays no heed to anybody. The song
comes to an end, and only* ANNA STEPANOVNA *applauds.*
NIKOLAI, *his face flushed, stands behind* NADYA's *chair leaning over
her. His face practically buried in her back-combed, silvery-pink rinsed
hair.* ANNA STEPANOVNA's *eyes are burning.*

NADYA. Listen, to hell with this crap, I want to dance.

FYODOR IVANOVICH *is standing by the piano, ready to sing on
and on, but* NIKOLAI *takes* NADYA's *arms and leads her to the
radio,* NIKOLAI *turns the volume up full – it is playing the
'Adagio' from* Swan Lake. NIKOLAI *and* NADYA, *pressed tightly
against each other, mark time on the spot to the music.*

ANNA STEPANOVNA *(suddenly clutching at her pocket).* Oh, what's
the o'clock! Oh, I've got the washing on to soak! Oh!

FYODOR IVANOVICH. You've let the whole world slip away,
that's what you've done. Your Sergei'll think you've disappeared
off the face of the earth, most likely he'll be killing himself
laughing.

ANNA STEPANOVNA *(coming to her senses, coldly).* Sergei? My
Sergei'll come for me and take me home and never say a word.

FYODOR IVANOVICH *(nodding sarcastically).* No doubt, no doubt
– you'll say enough words on his behalf, so he won't get a look
in. (ANNA STEPANOVNA *hurries out.*) She's running out . . .
there goes people power in action, the granny police!

The dancing at the KOZLOVS' *continues.* NADYA *and* NIKOLAI
are now dancing to Khachaturyan's 'Sabre Dance'. *The* FATHER
leaves the piano and sits down at the table. MOTHER *carries in
the tea-pot,* GRANDMOTHER *stares fixedly at* NADYA, *at her
boots, her dress, etc.* NADYA *has a bandage on one of her
fingers.*

TAISA PETROVNA *(projecting over* 'The Sabre Dance'). We'll have
a drink of tea at least, before you go home. It's getting late, and
Fyodor Ivanovich has to get up at six for work tomorrow.

NIKOLAI *(he is already in a wild state of excitement from jumping
around, and he is shouting).* What work, Mother! Tomorrow's
Sunday!

TAISA PETROVNA. Oh, I'm getting the days all mixed up. Anyway, sit down and have some tea just the same.

NIKOLAI. And you're chasing our guests out too early. Anybody else's house they'd have invited forty people, and they'd be partying till morning.

FYODOR IVANOVICH. Other people's houses are one thing, ours is another.

NIKOLAI. I mean, you only come home from the army once in your life. Isn't that right, Nadya?

NADYA. Of course.

NIKOLAI. That's it, sweetheart, you stick up for me!

A news broadcast on the radio. NIKOLAI *and* NADYA *dance to the news for a little while, but eventually the jollification peters out, of its own accord, and the two young people sit down at the table.*

NADYA. Oh, it's cake. I don't eat cake.

GRANNY (*putting in her oar*). Oh yes, and what *do* you eat?

NIKOLAI (*pedantically*). Grandma, you've got to respect other people's tastes.

GRANNY (*sotto voce*). Respect my arse. Her taste's all in her mouth, that one.

TAISA PETROVNA (*kindly*). Have some jam, Nadya. I made it myself in the summer, our own strawberries. We have a little garden plot, and the strawberries were just unbelievable!

NADYA. You have a plot? And a house? How many rooms?

TAISA PETROVNA (*gently*). How many do you need?

NIKOLAI. Mama, I've just got out of the army!

TAISA PETROVNA. No, really, how many rooms do you young people need? And how many will you leave us for our old age?

NADYA. How many do we need? You've got two rooms, haven't you? Well, we'll take whichever is the smaller.

FYODOR IVANOVICH. Thanks very much, you're too kind.

NADYA. Because when the children arrive, they'll be sleeping with their grandparents, not their mother and father.

GRANNY (*loudly*). Over my dead body. What damnable cheek!

NADYA (*in a loud, distinct voice, without a trace of embarrassment*). The furniture in here takes up too much room.

GRANNY. And the furniture's wrong as well!

Nobody takes any notice of her. As if spellbound, everyone turns to look at the objects NADYA directs her attention to.

NADYA. You shouldn't have so much furniture. What do you want that dresser for, that crockery exhibition? And what do you want with that coffee table? You've no books to put on it. And carpets should be deep pile, so your feet sink into them.

NIKOLAI is nodding mechanically, his arm round NADYA's shoulders.

FYODOR IVANOVICH. Oh, of course, we're the ignorant masses. Working class origins.

NIKOLAI. Nadya's working class too. (*Lays his head on NADYA's shoulder.*)

GRANNY (*suddenly*). So, you get that room, where do I go? Into the kitchen?

NADYA. Of course your flat is a bit cramped for three generations.

TAISA PETROVNA (*placating*). Well, it doesn't matter. We'll get by somehow. Nadya love, come and give me a hand, and we'll wash the dishes.

NADYA. No fear. You're on your own.

FYODOR IVANOVICH slams his fist down on the table, gets up decisively and follows his wife through to the kitchen. GRANNY takes herself off to her own room, carefully jamming the door shut behind her with a piece of paper. NADYA and NIKOLAI converse in whispers about something, then he rushes, dishevelled, into the kitchen. NADYA goes up to the piano, and plays 'Chopsticks' with her thick, clumsy fingers. In the kitchen they all stand rooted to the spot, listening.

FYODOR IVANOVICH. Now she's wrecking the instrument. Go right ahead! Give it hell!

NIKOLAI. You see, Mama? I'm just back, just home from the army and he's started already!

TAISA PETROVNA. Fedya, Nadya wants to stay the night here with us.

NIKOLAI. I want her to!!!

FYODOR IVANOVICH. Oh yes, and is there anything else she wants?

TAISA PETROVNA. Wait, Fedya. I mean, if you think of it, we can put Mama on the couch, and the two of us can sleep on the divan.

NIKOLAI. Yes, you can crash down there for one night, surely.

FYODOR IVANOVICH. Yes, if it is just one night, but supposing she doesn't leave.

NIKOLAI (cheerfully). So maybe I'll have to go?

FYODOR IVANOVICH. You keep quiet, Kolya, while you've still got a tongue in your head. You've said too damn much today already.

NIKOLAI. See? There he goes again.

FYODOR IVANOVICH. How can you speak like that to your father?

In the lounge, NADYA is playing 'Chopsticks', NIKOLAI brings a pillow, etc., out of his grandmother's room, trailing the sheets along the floor. GRANNY rushes after him, picking up the sheets. TAISA PETROVNA takes fresh linen into GRANNY's room. All of this takes place at high speed, to the music of 'Chopsticks'. Suddenly GRANNY is already sitting on the couch in her nightgown, staring dumbly at her bedroom door, which NADYA and NIKOLAI are jamming closed with the paper wad, from the other side.

Scene Three

Morning in the GAVRILOVS' flat. GRANYA is carrying the baby through into the kitchen, and pauses en route beside NINA.

GRANYA. Honestly, I'm surprised at you. For a start he's got no place else, that's why he's come here. Anyway, he'll be going soon, I couldn't just leave him sprawled out in the entry. People would talk. So he's spent the night in the bathroom, big deal. I threw some old rags down for him on the floor. (*Exits.*)

VITYA *enters.*

VITYA. Ivanov's sitting in the kitchen with Galka.

NINA. It's all right, he'll be leaving soon.

VITYA. He says he's staying with his daughter from now on.

NINA. Yes, well Mama won't let him stay here.

VITYA. She's telling him, 'Go away, for God's sake, or it'll all just start over again.' And he's saying, 'No, it won't, definitely not, no way.' That's what he's saying, I knew he would. She's given him a mirror to have a shave.

NINA. Well, it certainly won't make life easier for him, if he goes away looking like that.

VITYA. And she's told him to hang on, we're going to have breakfast.

NINA. And where's Galka? Bring her in here.

VITYA. He's holding onto her. She's told him to get shaved now, and give Galka back. But he keeps saying wait, wait.

NINA. Yes, he's only like that when he's sober.

VITYA. Too true.

NINA. Go and get Galka. If he's going to shave, and Mama's making breakfast, they won't know where to shove Galka anyway.

VITYA *exits.* NINA *gazes absently out of the window.* VITYA *re-enters.*

VITYA. Mama's taken the pram through there. They've put Galka in the pram. He's shaving and watching Galka at the same time.

NINA. And what about Mama?

VITYA. Mama's making the kasha.

NINA. He'll be going soon.

VITYA. Mama says he should go to the country, to our folks. She'll give him a letter. And in the summer she'll take Galka down there, to Granny's.

NINA. Of course. He'll get work there – as something, maybe a nightwatchman.

VITYA. Yes, and he'll get blind drunk, and that'll be the end of the nightwatchman's job. They'll kick him out. Uncle Vanya at Auntie Marusya's just the same. She told Mama, your Ivanov's incorrigible, a drunken slob, same as my Ivan.

NINA. Well, it doesn't matter, he'll be leaving anyway.

Scene Four

Morning in the KOZLOVS' *apartment. The beds have been tidied away, and the table laid.* MOTHER *is wearing her Sunday best,* FATHER *an open-necked shirt,* GRANNY *in a flower-patterned dress, all seated at the table, waiting to see what transpires. The door opens and the wad of paper falls to the floor.* NADYA *emerges, without make-up, in her silver dress, and mules on her bare feet.* NIKOLAI *enters behind her, screwing up his eyes.*

NIKOLAI. Mama, give Nadya a towel, to get washed.

TAISA PETROVNA *(cheerfully)*. Of course, dear.

She takes a large towel from the cupboard. NIKOLAI *accepts it, and the young couple go out. There is the sound of running water, then the bathroom door is closed.* MOTHER *goes back to the table, shrugs.* FATHER *settles down to his breakfast. They all watch television, a childrens' programme of some kind. A little boy is singing.*

GRANNY. She's put us all in our place, that one. She's taken over. That's what's in store for us. We'll all be jammed in together, then we'll die off, give way to the kids, die the death of the righteous. You here, us there, the grandchildren in with the grandparents, and me off to the boneyard. And the carpet's not deep enough for her.

TAISA PETROVNA Yes, well she likes everything *too* much, just as long as she can have her own way. This'll do her nicely. I mean, she's from a hostel. She's got her beady eyes on this apartment, and that's a fact. But she doesn't want our Nikolai for love nor money. It's him that's trailing after her. She's only got to snap her fingers.

GRANNY *(an afterthought)*. She's a gold-digger.

FYODOR IVANOVICH. Isn't she just! They're not even like that in our place. Personally I wouldn't have her kind on the payroll.

TAISA PETROVNA. She's a painter on a building site.

FYODOR IVANOVICH. Well, you get all sorts of painters. But this one gave herself away immediately.

TAISA PETROVNA. I didn't like her any better the last time, when Nikolai wasn't here, and she came to introduce herself.

FYODOR IVANOVICH. What I can't fathom is why she behaves like that? Eh? Why is she so obvious, coming straight out with it? Anybody else would have washed the dishes, and helped clear the table – they'd have held their tongue and not made an exhibition of themselves right off! For God's sakes, she was in her fiancé's *house!*

GRANNY (*splutters*). Fiancé?

FYODOR IVANOVICH. No, but why is it – I mean, does she really not understand that she can't behave like that? Rubbishing us all because of the furniture!

GRANNY. And she couldn't even dream of buying a suite like that.

FYODOR IVANOVICH. And she's spent the night with a strange man, eh?

TAISA PETROVNA. That's true, we could've put up a folding bed for Kolya in the kitchen.

GRANNY. Yes, and they'll get married, then it'll be *me* on a folding bed in the kitchen!

FYODOR IVANOVICH. God, you're like a stuck record.

GRANNY. Of course I am. Kolya'll get married, and I'll have to live in the kitchen, but you and our Kolya'll have a room to yourselves, that's *very* nice. And eventually I'll go further than the kitchen, into my grave!

TAISA PETROVNA. Oh, you and your grave – you keep on about it the whole time. On the slightest pretext, you're going to your grave!

GRANNY. So where else would I go? There's no room for me here, I've outstayed my welcome. There's no room at Klavdia's either. It'll have to be the old folks' home.

TAISA PETROVNA. Klavdia has the same kind of apartment as ours, except it's in a bigger mess.

GRANNY. Don't shout at your mother.

TAISA PETROVNA. Who said a word to you?

A silence. The sound of running water.

FYODOR IVANOVICH. That Stepanovna turned up yesterday, we hadn't seen her for ages. She came to sniff out what kind of fiancée Nikolai's got himself. What did you invite her for?

TAISA PETROVNA. Me? (*Highly indignant.*) It was Nikolai invited her – if he had his way he'd invite the whole block, the whole crowd of them.

GRANNY. Well, you've done it now. They'll all want to know, all the old wives down on the benches.

FYODOR IVANOVICH. They can all just bugger off!

A procession passes through the room, NADYA *at its head,* NIKOLAI *following, jamming the door shut behind them with the paper wad.*

GRANNY. Not so much as a by your leave.

TAISA PETROVNA (*exaggeratedly loud*). Who wants tea? Kolya? Kolya? Will you have tea, or instant coffee?

NIKOLAI (*from his room*). Mama, give it a rest!

FYODOR IVANOVICH. Don't bother them. You see? They're not pleased.

NIKOLAI *emerges, jams the door with the paper wad as before.*

NIKOLAI. Well, good morning.

FYODOR IVANOVICH. Good morning! We didn't get round to saying it last time.

NIKOLAI. That doesn't count. You should have closed your eyes while we slipped past. It's these damn connecting rooms. It'll be like that all the time now – 'Excuse me, I hope I'm not disturbing you?' and all that.

FYODOR IVANOVICH. Why's that? Why is it going to be like that?

TAISA PETROVNA. Fedya.

FYODOR IVANOVICH. Yes, well nobody's asked *me* yet, by the way, how it's going to be in my own house. I mean, I am still actually here in my own home!

NIKOLAI. Oh yes, so what does that make me? Am I not?

FYODOR IVANOVICH. No, you're in your parents' home, all right?

NIKOLAI. God almighty – does that mean I'm just here on sufferance?

TAISA PETROVNA. Father, go into the kitchen. I've got a pie in there, check it's not burning.

FYODOR IVANOVICH (*furious*). A pie! (*Exits.*)

TAISA PETROVNA. Kolya, Kolya, you really shouldn't! I mean, after all . . .

NIKOLAI. Nadya came to see me at Syzran twice. She's my wife.

TAISA PETROVNA. She came to see you twice, but your father's devoted his whole life to you. He's brought you up, fed and clothed you.

NIKOLAI. I won't speak like that to my children.

TAISA PETROVNA. You haven't got any yet. You've got to live a bit, before you raise your own.

NIKOLAI. Here we go again!

TAISA PETROVNA. Nobody's said anything to you, have they? We need to sit down and discuss all this calmly.

NIKOLAI. Yes, and meanwhile you're rubbishing her.

TAISA PETROVNA. Listen, if you want my opinion, it's like water off a duck's back with her.

NADYA *enters.*

NADYA (*in her impertinent voice, expressionless*). What's all the noise? I'll hold your coats, if you like?

NIKOLAI. It's okay, there's no problem. Sit down and have some tea.

TAISA PETROVNA. Sit down, sit down, Nadya dear, take the weight off your feet. (NADYA *sits.*) And good morning.

NADYA. Good morning.

GRANNY. Huh – that's them got the formalities over!

FYODOR IVANOVICH (*enters*). Taya, you'd better take out that pie.

TAISA PETROVNA *exits*, FYODOR IVANOVICH *sits down*.

Well, look who's here. Cheers!

NADYA. Cheers.

FYODOR IVANOVICH. What are we thinking of, a day like this and no wine. Kolya, get your skates on, nip down to the corner shop. We'll drink to the bride and groom.

NIKOLAI. Now you're talking, Papa. That's a great idea! Absolutely, I'll be back in a second. Nadya, don't be getting up to mischief now. (*Hurries out.*)

FYODOR IVANOVICH. There's money in my coat, in my purse! (*Pause.*) Meantime, let's have a drink of tea, okay?

NADYA. I won't have any tea. I'll wait for the wine.

FYODOR IVANOVICH. So you don't like mixing your drinks? Well, that's something at least.

GRANNY. Bloody hell!

FYODOR IVANOVICH. My wife's mother's a great woman. She'll call a spade a spade. You're still swithering, wondering whether or not to speak, and she's already jumped in, with both feet.

NADYA. That's a sign of ill-breeding.

GRANNY. Oh-ho-ho-ho! Oh, that's priceless! (*Laughs, starts to cough.*)

FYODOR IVANOVICH. Oh yes, and what kind of upbringing d'you think our grandmother had, eh? She worked in a mill, she was a weaver. Three years at school, and bye-bye, that's your lot! That's all the education she's had. And what sort of culture do you pick up on the shop floor, eh? All swearing like troopers. But of course, your building site, that's a different story. They say 'How do you do' when they clock in, 'Thank you' when you pass them the mortar, 'Excuse me' when they stand on your foot. And in the hostel, no doubt you get lectures all the time on the cultured life. Like how to behave in somebody else's house!

NADYA. We had a lecture recently on love and friendship.

GRANNY. Yes, love and friendship behind the bush!

NADYA. No, just love and friendship. What love is, ideologically, and how to disprove it. You wouldn't happen to have a match?

FYODOR IVANOVICH. Granny and I don't smoke.

NADYA. I need to pick my teeth. I'm going into the kitchen.

TAISA PETROVNA *enters with the pie.*

TAISA PETROVNA. Nadya, dear, where are you going?

FYODOR IVANOVICH. She's looking for matches.

TAISA PETROVNA (*calls after her*). They're by the cooker, on the little shelf.

They sit in silence at the table, watching television. The outside door slams.

FYODOR IVANOVICH. That'll be Kolya back, Kolya! (*A silence.*) Nikolai?!

TAISA PETROVNA. He's probably gone into the kitchen, to see Nadya.

FYODOR IVANOVICH. She's a real bitch, that one. She'd bite you as soon as look at you.

TAISA PETROVNA. Kolya chose her, Kolya knew what she was like.

FYODOR IVANOVICH. Kolya chose *her*? He was hand-picked, I'm telling you, and they've just strung him along.

TAISA PETROVNA. Well, so? I mean, I picked you, didn't I.

FYODOR IVANOVICH. I was the only one after you, there was nobody else to pick. I was the only one tempted.

GRANNY. Is that how you remember it? You don't remember how I wouldn't let you into the house? You'd come in and sit down, your eyes never away from the door. When's Taya coming, when's Taya coming? I had to ask you to leave with a brush in my hand! And you'd go out and stand in the entry. I sent Klavdia out to have a look, and she comes back: 'He's still there, Mama, what'll we do with him?'

FYODOR IVANOVICH. Yes, you were ill-bred then, and you've remained ill-bred. Nadya was telling the truth.

GRANNY. Oh, of course, and you were so *well*-bred. The minute you moved in you showed yourself in your true colours, your foul temper. I didn't know how the hell to get rid of you!

TAISA PETROVNA. Mama! . . .

GRANNY. He raised his hand to me.

FYODOR IVANOVICH. Oh God, here she goes again!

The outside door slams.

TAISA PETROVNA. What's that?

NIKOLAI *enters, flushed and out of breath.*

NIKOLAI. There was a queue. At this hour in the morning, would you believe. I got a bottle of white. So where's Nadyezhda then?

TAISA PETROVNA. She's in the kitchen.

NIKOLAI. Have you chased her out? (*Exits, re-enters.*) She's gone. She's just left. (*Sits down, still in his overcoat.*)

GRANNY. And a good thing too.

FYODOR IVANOVICH. Young girls are headstrong. Don't worry about it.

TAISA PETROVNA. I wasn't here. What happened?

GRANNY. She told me I was ill-bred. I'm too ill-bred for her.

NIKOLAI. Granny, really – for Heaven's sake, Gran.

TAISA PETROVNA. Anyway, take off your coat.

NIKOLAI. I'm going out after her.

TAISA PETROVNA. You're not serious? Where will you go? Maybe she's not even in the hostel now. She could be anywhere.

NIKOLAI. Where else can she go? She doesn't have anybody here, she's practically an orphan.

TAISA PETROVNA. All right, all right. But you'll drink some tea first, and have a piece of pie, and this bottle of yours . . . do you want anything else? I'll make some sandwiches. And there's some sweets there, a few biscuits. Take your coat off, have some breakfast, and then you can go.

Scene Five

Breakfast at the GAVRILOVS'. VITYA, IVANOV *and* GRANYA *are sitting at the table. The pram is also in the room.*

GRANYA. We should have had something to celebrate your return, but there's no money. Nina gets paid on a Thursday, she gets a junior's wage, twenty-three roubles. And I don't get paid until Monday.

IVANOV. That's enough, I said! I'm off the drink.

GRANYA. You could've had a glass of something, but there's no money for it.

IVANOV. I've already told you.

GRANYA. Anyway, about your residence permit. That's only if you keep off the drink. Or else I'm not registering it. I can't register you staying here otherwise, I just can't.

IVANOV. You can't?

A pause.

GRANYA. I mean, what are you to me? They'll say: what's your relationship to the person you wish to register? Just passing?

A pause.

IVANOV. Possibly.

GRANYA. Well, you think about it.

A pause.

IVANOV. What's to think about?

GRANYA. What?

IVANOV. I'll go and enlist.

GRANYA. I'm not throwing you out.

IVANOV. Yes, well they won't register me anyway.

GRANYA. They won't register you just like that.

IVANOV. So how?

GRANYA. How, how – they'll register a husband with a wife, that's how.

IVANOV. But you and I . . .

GRANYA. You and I what?

IVANOV (*finally understands*). Well, carry on . . .

GRANYA. Your neighbours have signed you off at that place, at Zelyony Road. I found that out. They took you off the register six months ago.

IVANOV. I went there as well. So why should they bother about me? It suits them better this way.

GRANYA (*heatedly*). I went out there, and Mitrevna barely opened the door to me, she kept the chain on, and she says, 'You needn't bother hanging around here, we've signed Ivanov off!' They've got a new tenant in there, presumably. Vitya, go and call Nina in, before she freezes.

VITYA. She won't come.

GRANYA (*glances quickly at* IVANOV). What d'you mean, she won't come? Why won't she come? You just tell her to come right now! I won't tell her a second time!

VITYA (*goes to the door of the adjoining room*). Mama says you've to come in. Before she comes for you herself.

NINA *emerges sidelong, sits down.*

GRANYA. And just stop this carry-on, or I'll give you a good hiding! Fiancée or no fiancée . . . (*To* IVANOV.) She's supposed to be engaged to the Kozlovs' Nikolai, they're on the sixth floor . . . But that won't stop me.

IVANOV *nods. In his present state he will accept absolutely anything.* NINA *is offended.*

It's all right, I was only joking. That's Kolya Kozlov – when she was still just a girl, taking our Vitya out for walks all the time, he used to say, 'There she is, that's my fiancée.' He used to give her sweets. Nina was small, and our Vitka was a big fat lump, just the way Galka's growing now. She could barely lift him up. They even used to call her that in the street – Kolya's fiancée. He's back from the army now, probably he's got a girlfriend of his own now. Stepanovna said he arrived back from the army in a taxi, with some girl.

They eat in silence. The conversation is strained.

Anyway, that's our Nina left on the shelf now. (*To* NINA.) Well? Why aren't you laughing, eh? You know, I've devoted my whole life to you. Eh?

IVANOV. They don't give a damn!

GRANYA. And you'd better keep quiet, just keep out of it.

IVANOV. Fair enough.

GRANYA. You might at least say something to your mother.

NINA. I don't object, why should I? He can have something to eat with us. His things are in the suitcase, I'll bring it. (*Fetches the case.*) They're all here. I've washed and ironed them.

IVANOV. Thanks, you shouldn't have bothered.

Makes to rise.

GRANYA. Sit down. We'll have some tea in a minute.

IVANOV. Anyway, I apologise if I've . . .

GRANYA. Go on, sit down. (*To* NINA.) Since when did you take over? Where did you learn to throw people out? Eh?

NINA. All right, he can have some tea.

IVANOV. Look, I'm sorry if that's how it is. (*Tries to stand up, but* GRANYA *makes him sit down again.*)

GRANYA. 'No, he's not having any tea! No, he can't stay for tea!' What a determined little madam!

NINA. Just because we don't have room, doesn't mean anybody's throwing him out. He can stay with our Aunt Marusya at Chulkovo.

GRANYA. Aunt Marusya has three kids in that little house, and Granny and Uncle Ivan. Aunt Marusya's got enough on her plate without us. You used to go to Aunt Marusya's for the summer, and she needed you there like a hole in the head!

VITYA. We used to pick fruit there, and gather mushrooms . . . And we swam in the pond. Chulkovo's great. And there's plenty of room in the house. Auntie Marusya's out in the fields all day, and Uncle Ivan's either asleep, or at his work. They're never there. Granny's left on her own with us.

GRANYA. Well, well, so that's the radio switched on, is it? There hasn't been a squeak out of you for ages, and now suddenly it's come to life!

VITYA. Sergei, the one that's got no arms, he was always inviting us: come down and see us, he says. His brother's house is lying empty. The whole place! And it's got a stove, and a cellar. And a little shed.

NINA. You could get a job as a nightwatchman there.

GRANYA. Vitya, pour the tea.

NINA. I'll do it. (*Gets up*.) The train ticket costs eight roubles. We always used to take Vitka without a seat reservation.

IVANOV. Anyway . . . in this case . . . Thanks, all the same, thanks. I can go up North and enlist.

VITYA. Chulkovo's up North too. And Mama can bring Galka there in the summer.

IVANOV. Whatever you like. It's up to you, family business.

GRANYA. Don't listen to them, they're just kids.

IVANOV. Out of the mouths of babes . . .

GRANYA. So what do you want? D'you want the red carpet rolled out, like a cosmonaut? It's you that made this mess, you brought it on yourself, you went to jail, and now you think the children are just going to accept you?

IVANOV. It was you that put me in jail, that's the truth of it.

NINA. Mama!

IVANOV. Yes, it was you all right. But I thought, well, I've got a family, I'll be going back to my daughter, to my wife. Like a human being, I thought. A bit of humanity.

GRANYA. And so there is, there will be. Only not right away. If you behave like a man, there'll be some humanity. Like a man, and not a drunken animal. Do you understand?

IVANOV. I do. I just wish you understood me.

NINA. Mama, why are you talking to him?

GRANYA (*to* IVANOV). Do you think I don't understand you? Who was it had to pick you up off the radiator? And I brought you up here, regardless of what other people thought, not even my own children, nobody.

IVANOV. Yes, that's you all right. I know you.

NINA. Mama, why bother with him? Don't lower yourself.

GRANYA. You know me? You know another side of me too. And I know another side of you. I wish to God I didn't.

IVANOV. It'll be all right again, I've promised.

GRANYA. Huh, promises.

NINA. Mama, he's not staying here?

GRANYA. Don't you raise your voice to me.

NINA. He's staying here? Eh? (*Weeps.*) Oh God, what am I going to do? What can I do? Help me, somebody! . . . (*Gets up from the table, reeling.*)

Scene Six

NINA *is standing by the entry. The yard presents a familiar picture: a heap of boxes in the corner, a bench alongside the steps, windows heavily curtained.* NINA *stands quite motionless, wearing felt boots and a shawl.* NIKOLAI *comes past her from the entry, carrying a string bag containing a bottle, various parcels, boxes, packages.*

NIKOLAI. Hi there, fiancée. What grade are you in now?

NINA. None.

NIKOLAI (*oblivious to* NINA's *irritated tone*). No, that's not possible! What, have you you finished school already?

NINA. Yes, I've dropped out.

NIKOLAI (*for form's sake*). So . . . what are you doing now?

NINA. I'm working. A trainee.

NIKOLAI. Where?

NINA. At the grocery store.

NIKOLAI. Well, you've landed on your feet, eh? And you've grown up! You've got it all now. I *was* going to treat you to some sweets, but maybe I'd better not, I don't know what you'd think. Well, I'd better run.

NINA. Best of luck. (*Turns away.*)

NIKOLAI. I'll see you again. I mean, we are neighbours! (*Exits.*)

NINA *remains standing with her back to the audience.*

Scene Seven

A girls' hostel. Four beds, a wardrobe with a mirror, a table in the middle of the room. The furniture is similar to that in a hotel, except that NADYA's dress hangs on a coathanger on the window latch. On the wall above each bed is fastened a rug or wall-mat, and on the night-tables stand make-up bottles, jars, boxes of face powder, etc. NADYA is sitting at the table in a dressing-gown, her legs crossed, wearing mules and chewing something. NIKOLAI enters, having first given a warning knock and receiving no reply.

NIKOLAI. The door was open . . . Hello there, Nadyezhda love!

NADYA. Hi.

Before her on the table is a loaf of bread, sliced sausage, a bottle of milk, and a packet of sugar. There is a kettle on the floor.

NIKOLAI. Is that your lunch? Why didn't you have something to eat at our place?

He takes off his coat and places it carefully over NADYA's Sunday dress, hanging on the window latch.

Too proud, are we? . . . I mean, you just pissed off, you might've waited. So big deal, they offended you. They've done plenty worse to me. I mean they're your folks, your parents, what can you do about them, eh? You always end up going back to them, anyway.

NADYA *carries on chewing, all the while gazing at NIKOLAI, deep in thought. NIKOLAI produces a bottle from the string bag and stands it on the table. He moves NADYA's food aside, and takes out a pie, biscuits, sandwiches, various packets and paper bags.*

What's that junk you're eating? Here, be my guest, the pleasure's mine! Mama made up some sandwiches as well. (*Sits down contentedly.*)

NADYA *knocks on the wall without getting up. There is a gentle scratching at the door, then a faintly embarrassed group of girls file in, in dressing-gowns, one in pyjamas, one in a winter coat and fur hat, and one wearing a muffler.*

NADYA. Help yourselves, it's all yours. Tuck in, it's going cheap!

NADYA *takes a paper bag and empties it out over the table. Sweets shower out in a heap. It is as if a signal has been given, and in an instant the bottle has vanished from the table, nimble fingers have torn the cardboard box-lid off the biscuits, greedy hands have plunged in to divide up the pie, and the jam is being spread.* NIKOLAI *can hardly be seen behind the backs of the young women milling round the table.* NADYA *sits apart, on her own bed. The most striking thing about the girls' violent demolition of the food* NIKOLAI *has provided is their casual ruthlessness, their mischievous waste of, and even contempt for the food. They spread jam over a newspaper, and throw biscuits at the hopper window, so that they land on* NIKOLAI's *coat, which is instantly marked with flour.* NIKOLAI *rushes over to wipe his coat, and at that point they pour wine down his neck.* NIKOLAI *at first tries to join in their merriment, but soon becomes disillusioned and bored, then intensely irritated. Flushed with anger, he starts to protest.*

NIKOLAI. Give over! Stop it, for God's sake, that's enough!

Almost beside himself with rage, NIKOLAI *tries to pinion the girls' arms, to stop them pulling his coat down onto the floor.*

GIRL WITH MUFFLER. Oh, he wants a fight! He's going to hit us! What a thug!

NADYA *meanwhile sits apart, uninvolved, on her bed with her own food packages, drinking milk out of a bottle. Suddenly the doorbell rings. The* GIRL IN THE OVERCOAT, *whose fur hat has slipped to one side, exits to the hall. She shouts from there.*

GIRL IN OVERCOAT. It's somebody looking for Semyonova.

GIRL WITH MUFFLER. She's gone home to Kashira, she'll be back tomorrow morning.

The GIRL IN THE OVERCOAT *disappears, and the others follow her out of the room.* NIKOLAI, *dishevelled, his shirt soaking wet, picks his coat up off the floor and shakes it out.*

NIKOLAI. So, is this how you treat all your guests? That's terrific. I came out here, my mother baked a pie for you. She spent last night mixing the dough. Huh – you can tell a person's character from the company they keep. Mama put sandwiches in for you as well, same as she'd do for any *decent* person. And she let you spend the night with us. You know, after this kind of . . .

NADYA (*in her haughty, metallic voice, as if delivering a proclamation*). Oh, forgive me, Kolya, I'm sorry I've corrupted you!

NIKOLAI (*gasps, astonished*). You've done what to me?

NADYA (*not listening*). I'm sorry I've corrupted you, yes. But you're not my type.

NIKOLAI, *deeply offended, flings on his coat, which he has now dusted down, and circles the room slowly, picking his way through the litter. He rummages around in the debris. Finally, he locates his string bag under the table, shakes it out and puts it in his pocket.*

NIKOLAI. So, that's it then? That's it? Well, I'm sorry. I'm sorry I bothered you.

NADYA *raises her arm, switches on the radio. The rousing march 'The Slav Maiden's Farewell' floods the room, and* NIKOLAI *exits in time to the march.* NADYA *picks up her coathanger from the floor, with her Sunday dress on it, dusts it off and hangs it back up at the window.*

Scene Eight

The yard as before. NINA *is wheeling the pram back and forth by the entry.* VITYA *emerges from the entry and approaches her.*

VITYA. Nina, Mama wants you to bring Galka home.

NINA. Take her.

VITYA. Mama says you've to bring her.

NINA. I'm not coming.

VITYA. Mama says Galka'll get frozen.

NINA. Well, she can just damn well come and get her. I'm not going back home.

VITYA (*reproachfully*). That's you all over. You're not nice.

A silence.

NINA. Anyway she's not frozen. I checked her little nose, and I'll try again now – (*leans over the pram.*) See – it's warm.

VITYA. He's gone into the bathroom, to have a bath.

NINA. So?

VITYA. Mama's changing the bed.

NINA. So who cares?

VITYA. And where am I going to sleep now? (VITYA *asks more as a rhetorical question, thinking aloud, than in a practical sense.*)

NINA. My bed.

VITYA. What about you?

NINA. I'll be by the radiator, in the hall.

VITYA. And what if I tell Mama?

VITYA (*shrugs*). Go ahead.

VITYA. I'll tell Mama everything, you just wait! (*A pause.*) Nina, let's go home. We can stay with Galka, the three of us together. Really! They can have one room and we'll have the other. And that'll be fine. Really truly! We can put a lock on the door, and he won't be able to get in at all.

NINA. Yes, and he'll take a stick, same as he did last time, and batter the door down.

VITYA. Well, we can shut our ears.

NINA. We can't shut Galka's.

VITYA. I'll take my pistol to him. Bang! Bang! I've got a pistol that fires suckers. Phhht! A sucker right between the eyes! (NINA *laughs weakly.*) Nina, let's go home! There'll be cartoons on the TV.

NINA. I don't want your cartoons.

VITYA. Yes, you do! Come on. We'll sit down and watch whatever's on.

NINA. I'm not coming. You take Galka.

VITYA. No! Mama said you had to! (*Runs off.*)

NINA *stands pushing the pram back and forth.* NIKOLAI *appears, empty-handed, turns towards the entry and bumps into* NINA.

NIKOLAI. What's this, are you waiting for me? (NINA *is silent, abstractedly rocking the pram*.) Why aren't you speaking? I mean, that's your fiancé home from the army, as you might say, and you won't speak to him, no welcome of any kind? Well?

NINA *is silent still, rocking the pram.*

I can see you haven't been wasting any time. (*Nods towards the pram*.) Are you married?

NINA. No. (*Turns away*.)

NIKOLAI. Unmarried mother?

NINA. Look, why d'you keep pestering me? It's my mother's little girl. My sister. All right?

NIKOLAI (*whistles*). Your mother's had a baby?

NINA. Yes.

NIKOLAI. But she's old.

NINA. She's thirty-eight, that's not old.

NIKOLAI. Is she married, then?

NINA. No. Well, I don't really know, she's going to, I think.

NIKOLAI. Yes, women are always going to, but the reality's another story.

NINA. No, it's him that wants to get married.

NIKOLAI. And she's not sure?

NINA. That's right. What does she want some useless man hanging round her neck for? Washing and cooking for him, and all that.

NIKOLAI. Well, that means she doesn't love him. When I get married, I won't mess about with my wife. It'll be 'Right, get that bed made! One-two!' (NINA *has to laugh*.) So, have you been out here since morning?

NINA. Yes.

NIKOLAI. I see. A bit of fresh air. That's nice. Anyway, I've been invited out again today. A get-together with the lads, and so forth. I've still got to find time to buy something.

NINA. Is it Boris's you're going to?

NIKOLAI. Why do you ask?

NINA. He's supposed to have some terrific records.

NIKOLAI. No, it's not Boris's place I'm going. Anyway, I'll see you.

NINA. Cheerio.

NIKOLAI hurries in. ANNA STEPANOVNA emerges with a basin of damp washing, and her husband, SERGEI ILYICH, carrying a wash tub. ANNA STEPANOVNA stops beside the pram, takes a look inside, chirping at the baby and repeating, 'Who's a little darling?'

ANNA STEPANOVNA. Hello, Nina dear. God knows, I could dry these at home, but they just wouldn't smell fresh. I've got used to hanging things up outside from the old place. So what are you doing out here? I can see you from the window, walking up and down the whole time. Has somebody offended you? Oh dear, this isn't good, you know, it bodes ill, you mark my words. Come on, Sergei, that's enough of a rest.

They hang out the washing some way off. ANNA STEPANOVNA then hurries up to NINA.

Nina dear, while you're standing here with the baby, would you keep an eye on my washing?

Scene Nine

The KOZLOVS' apartment. The table is laid, and there are guests – KLAVA, TAISA PETROVNA's sister, and her husband, UNCLE MITYA. NIKOLAI enters.

KLAVA. Oh, it's Nikolai the soldier! What a lovely man the boy's turned out!

The guests eat and drink. UNCLE MITYA eats very little, and carefully inspects every morsel, chewing it over, deep in thought, as if listening to some inner rumblings.

KLAVA. Some grow up, some grow down. Me and Uncle Mitya are growing down the way, isn't that so, Nikolai?

NIKOLAI. Nonsense, Auntie Klava, you're still in your prime.

KLAVA. Let me give you a big kiss, my own lovely boy!

They embrace.

FYODOR IVANOVICH. Come on, take your coat off and sit down with us. As you can see, we've got to keep the table laid. I thought the two of you would be coming back?

NIKOLAI. I've got to go out some place now.

FYODOR IVANOVICH. What place is this you're going? (*He is flushed from drinking*) What place? You should have some respect for your own family first, for Uncle Mitya and Auntie Klava, they've come here out of the goodness of their hearts, maybe they'll be able to advise you, since you treat your own parents like dirt.

NIKOLAI (*to his silent mother*). Mama, let's go into the other room.

NIKOLAI *and his mother exit.*

KLAVA. My my, secrets and more secrets.

TAISA PETROVNA *re-enters.*

KLAVA. Secrets, I'm saying.

TAISA PETROVNA (*shrugs*). He wanted a shirt to change into.

KLAVA. She's managed to make a real mess of his shirt. What was it, lipstick?

TAISA PETROVNA. I didn't see. He didn't show me it. He had his jacket on.

NIKOLAI *comes out of the room, heading for the bathroom, carrying his shirt in a crumpled heap.*

Kolya, put that into the laundry bin and I'll give it a wash.

NIKOLAI. I'll do it myself, it's okay.

KLAVA. You see what good care he takes of his mother?

NIKOLAI *exits. A pause.* UNCLE MITYA *shakes his head censoriously. He is annoyed at* KLAVA.

KLAVA. Well, why not? It's true, he looks after his mother, he should look after her, she's the only mother he's got.

UNCLE MITYA *shakes his head again.*

UNCLE MITYA. She's getting carried away, her jaw never stops.

KLAVA. What did I say?

FYODOR IVANOVICH. Let him do it, let him wash it himself. At least he's still got some shame.

KLAVA. All the same, it's a pity for the lad. I mean, you've had your day. But it's a pity for the boy, just starting out in life and getting mixed up with a trollop. You'll get by, it's no big deal, you let them have that room, and you sleep with Granny. You're not young things, you won't blush. Your mother's your mother, you used to live in the same room with her. I mean how did Mitya and I live? Mitya and I, and his mother and Granny Varya, all at the same time – plus Mitya's brother, and his brother's wife. Yes, and then we had Kostya. And all in one twenty-metre room.

FYODOR IVANOVICH. And fought like cats and dogs.

KLAVA. What do you mean? All right, there were fights at times, but Granny Varya always calmed things down. She was some woman, Granny Varya. Eh, Mitya?

UNCLE MITYA. Granny Varya's a wonderful person, not like you.

KLAVA. Huh, look who's talking!

UNCLE MITYA. What d'you want to get involved in other people's lives for?

KLAVA. Well, why do you think they've invited us?

UNCLE MITYA. I don't know why they invited us, but I know why you wanted to come.

KLAVA. Oh, don't talk rubbish!

UNCLE MITYA. Why do you always have to poke your nose into other people's business? You're always the first in, nosying around.

KLAVA. You're in an absolute foul mood because of that chess tournament of yours. You didn't qualify, and now you're taking it out on me. King pawn two! Knight three!

GRANNY. Oh shut up, Klavdia! Nothing suits you. Mitya used to drink, and you couldn't be doing with that. He's got an ulcer, and you gave him a hard time again. Now he plays chess, and you're still not happy. D'you remember how you complained when Mitya was sick, and going on about his illnesses all the time? Eh? You used to say he'd be better drinking like other people, instead of smelling like a chemist's shop!

UNCLE MITYA. Oh, that's great. Now they've turned on me.

NIKOLAI *enters*.

KLAVA. Sit down, sit down beside us, have a seat by the old folks. Take your time. You just wait till you get married, then you'll realise you were running for nothing!

FYODOR IVANOVICH. Sit down, sit with us a while.

NIKOLAI. Papa, I've got to go. Well, okay, I'll have a bite to eat. What the hell, I'm hungry, comrades.

TAISA PETROVNA. Obviously they didn't feed you right at that place. And I made a whole pile of sandwiches.

KLAVA. It's not a matter of what they fed him, but of what gives him an appetite. Isn't that right, Kolya? Let's have a drink.

UNCLE MITYA. Go ahead and eat, don't listen to them. And don't drink. I'm not drinking either, just eating, so you and me'll make two. Let's have some tea.

KLAVA. You'd be better off having a drink with me, Kolya.

They drink.

So. We've heard all about her, we've been hearing about your girlfriend.

NIKOLAI. What have you been hearing?

KLAVA. That she's a smart girl, game for anything, independent, that she works hard on a building site. She's what, casual labourer?

NIKOLAI. That's right.

FYODOR IVANOVICH. She's a painter.

KLAVA. Well, so what if she is just a labourer? That's all the same to you, Kolya, isn't it? You don't choose a wife for her education, or her certificates, right? So what if she can't even read! All you need is a nice lively girl, one that'll run after you, and dye her hair, and pluck her eyebrows and so on. Somebody that smokes and can take a drop of vodka, right?

NIKOLAI. Yes, well, you can take a drop yourself.

KLAVA. Who do you think you're talking to? I'm too old to be spoken to like that.

TAISA PETROVNA. Kolya, that's enough.

NIKOLAI. What are you getting so agitated about? D'you think I'm in some kind of danger? There's no danger, you can relax.

FYODOR IVANOVICH. We're not worried. In any case, we'll soon be getting carried out of here feet first.

TAISA PETROVNA. Kolya, why don't you see what's going on? How is it possible? I mean, you've been in the army, didn't the other lads talk to you?

KLAVA. All they get in the army is refresher courses in patriotism.

NIKOLAI. Exactly.

KLAVA. They teach them all to get married straight off. If you take a girl out, that's a commitment. Grab the first thing that comes along, as soon as you've got your hands on it.

TAISA PETROVNA. That's not the army, he's learned that from his father and me. He hasn't been brought up to anything else. But it's not the same thing as Fedya and me. We came together once and for all, for life. And that's a rare event. You don't find that right away.

UNCLE MITYA. So how then, by trial and error?

KLAVA. Trial and error if need be. You should understand, a man can look around nowadays, take time to think. You didn't think, you just got married. Now it's one word from me, and two from you, and that's it.

TAISA PETROVNA. I didn't want to tell you why this girl's hanging onto you, *why* she went to see you twice in Syzran, and visited me, taking a good look at what we had in the house.

NIKOLAI. Oh, of course, Mama, I'm well aware she wants our flat - our *lovely* polished furniture, the chandelier, Czechoslovakian glass, oh yes, and the carpet.

FYODOR IVANOVICH (*laughs*). Well, you can joke, Kolya, but there's a grain of truth in every joke. A grain of truth, believe me.

NIKOLAI. And a grain of lies.

KLAVA. Well, my God, we'll find you a bride all right! Some good, hard-working girl that doesn't drink or smoke, with her hair in a braid . . . and younger than yourself.

NIKOLAI. Why go looking for her? She's there already, standing downstairs, waiting. She's been waiting for me since first grade at school. Doesn't smoke, drink, she's even got a pigtail, if she hasn't hacked it off.

TAISA PETROVNA. Your fiancée, do you mean?

NIKOLAI. That's her! I mean, she absolutely dotes on me. Everybody used to laugh at her, the way she ran after me. We'd go to play football, and she'd trail after me, carrying her little brother. Totally besotted, what more can you say?

KLAVA (cheered). So bring her up here! Let's meet her!

UNCLE MITYA. Listen, it's time we were going home.

KLAVA. You go, I'll come later.

UNCLE MITYA. No, we're going!!!

KLAVA. Why, why can't you wait?

The doorbell rings.

NIKOLAI. I'll get it. It'll be for me. (Exits.)

FYODOR IVANOVICH. That'll be her from the hostel turning up now to spend the night. Bag and baggage on the doorstep, as they say.

KLAVA. I'll keep her in order.

UNCLE MITYA. And I'll keep you in order now. (Makes to rise from the table.) I'll sort you out.

KLAVA. Oh, Mama!

GRANNY. Huh, she's remembered she's got a mother.

KLAVA. We'll go now, Mitya dear.

NIKOLAI ushers in ANNA STEPANOVNA.

FYODOR IVANOVICH (sarcastically). Ah, it's our dear invited guest!

TAISA PETROVNA. Fedya! Anna Stepanovna, sit down, have a bite to eat.

ANNA STEPANOVNA. No, no, I've no time. Taya, can you lend me a drop of salt? I've brought a glass. I'll give you it back.

GRANNY. Never give back salt or bread.

TAISA PETROVNA. Anna Stepanovna, of course I can, and I'll be obliged to you some time.

NIKOLAI. Sit down, Auntie Anna.

UNCLE MITYA (*pushes up a chair*). You won't offend us, surely, by running away? What's your name?

ANNA STEPANOVNA. Anna Stepanovna.

UNCLE MITYA (*ushers her onto the chair*). My dear Anna Stepanovna . . .

KLAVA. Now he's gone completely soppy.

ANNA STEPANOVNA *reluctantly sits down.* UNCLE MITYA *pushes a plate and a glass towards her.*

ANNA STEPANOVNA. No, thank you, I haven't time. They say an uninvited guest is worse than a Tartar.

FYODOR IVANOVICH. You might as well stay, now you've dropped in.

ANNA STEPANOVNA. I've no time, honest – I've been making rissoles, and the salt ran out. Then I remembered your gran got a packet off me, so I thought it would be easier to borrow from her.

GRANNY. When was this?

ANNA STEPANOVNA. It was last year, one Sunday evening after the grocer's was shut.

GRANNY. I did not.

ANNA STEPANOVNA. And I gave you a packet of yeast as well.

GRANNY. You certainly did not!

NIKOLAI. Granny has a terrible memory.

GRANNY. Yes, and why's that?

TAISA PETROVNA (*returns with the salt*). Here you are, Stepanovna.

GRANNY. Oh, that's right!

ANNA STEPANOVNA. That's right, I did. Well, anyway, I'll have to go. (*Stands.*)

UNCLE MITYA. Sit down, sit down. (*Sits her back down.*)

There is a silence at the table.

ANNA STEPANOVNA. The Gavrilovs' girl's still standing outside.

TAISA PETROVNA. Who is?

ANNA STEPANOVNA. The Gavrilovs' girl, I said, from the first floor – she left the house this morning and she's been standing there the whole day.

FYODOR IVANOVICH. What's she doing that for?

NIKOLAI. I told you, she's waiting for me.

ANNA STEPANOVNA. Really! Ivanov's out of jail. You remember he got put in jail a year ago? And I'll tell you why – he'd come home blind drunk, and Granya didn't want to let him in, so he grabbed a lump of wood and started battering the door down. Galkin tried to drag him away, and he knocked Galkin out, concussion. Galkin wouldn't forgive him – he could've dropped the charge but he refused. Galkin used to be our locksmith, at the Housing Office. He quit not long ago.

GRANNY. I don't remember him.

ANNA STEPANOVNA. Galkin, of course you do. A lump of ice fell off the roof onto him that winter as well. They were clearing snow off the roof, and he was standing down below, to show it was a danger area. And it fell right on top of him. Knocked him out again.

GRANNY. I don't remember it.

ANNA STEPANOVNA. He brought you a toilet cistern as well, trying to sell it, and tripped on the doormat and smashed it. A toilet cistern!

GRANNY. What's he got to do with us?

ANNA STEPANOVNA. It's that Galkin I'm talking about.

GRANNY. He's back out of prison?

NIKOLAI. No, it's Ivanov that's out of prison.

ANNA STEPANOVNA. Their Nina was crying yesterday. Granya took him in, and Nina went out in the morning, and she's still standing there. That's seven hours already she's been stood there, and she won't go home. Sometimes she's standing on her own, sometimes Vitya wheels the pram out to her. I asked her what she was doing, she said she was out for a walk.

KLAVA (*brightly*). She can come up here to us. Why not? Nikolai, go down and get her.

TAISA PETROVNA. Do, Kolya. On you go.

ANNA STEPANOVNA. I was a bit embarrassed to invite her to our place, she didn't want to admit she'd left home. It's Granya that's the problem, she's got no shame. Well, anyway, I'm off.

FYODOR IVANOVICH. Come again, bring us some more news. Give our regards to Sergei, why doesn't he drop in?

ANNA STEPANOVNA. He hardly ever drops in on anybody.

FYODOR IVANOVICH. He could always pop in and see me.

ANNA STEPANOVNA. That's not likely. Anyway, I'll be seeing you.

FYODOR IVANOVICH. Suit yourself.

They all say goodbye to ANNA STEPANOVNA, UNCLE MITYA *even stands for the occasion.*

Scene Ten

The yard. NINA *is standing with the pram.* ANNA STEPANOVNA *hurries past.*

ANNA STEPANOVNA. Well, are you still keeping an eye on my washing?

NINA. Of course I am.

ANNA STEPANOVNA. Hm – with all these jailbirds on the loose, a person can't live in peace. Well, I'm off, bye-bye for now, I'm making rissoles. (*Exits, and almost instantly returns.*) Oh, Nina, this is too much, I can't put up with this! I'm going to call the police! I can't have this, this is a dreadful carry-on! Oh!

NINA. What's up! What is it!

ANNA STEPANOVNA. Ivanov's in the entry, he's sitting there at the radiator. On his suitcase. Somebody should go to the phone-box, get them to come and damn well remove him! I'm going to tell Sergei, he can go and phone. Oh, this is a terrible business! (*Hurries out.*)

NINA *wheels the pram to and fro, absently, for a few moments, then lifts the baby out and exits to the entry. After a while* IVANOV *emerges from the same place, looks around, shrugs, and stands beside the pram. Deep in thought, he takes the handle of the empty pram and begins to rock it, his face expressionless.* NINA *emerges from the entry.*

NINA. Go home. Go on, take the pram up.

IVANOV. I haven't the right.

NINA. For God's sake, go.

IVANOV. I've just been released from detention, you know that.

NINA. Go on, take the pram, and carry it upstairs.

IVANOV. Is that any way to treat a person. One chases him out, another one chases him back. Is it? I'll just leave now and that'll be the end of it.

NINA. My God, he's like a child.

IVANOV. I don't want to, I'm not going back. So thanks for nothing, as they say, that's me finished.

NINA. I'll move out to a hostel, right? I won't bother you. You two can live however you like, without me.

IVANOV. I've no intention of bothering you, if it's me that's the trouble.

NINA. Anyway, just go.

SERGEI ILYICH *emerges from the hallway and turns round the corner.*

That's Uncle Sergei gone out. Honestly, you'd better get out of here quick. Sergei's gone to fetch the police. Go home.

IVANOV. Was it you that called them?

NINA. It wasn't me. (*An afterthought.*) Supposing it was me, what of it?

IVANOV. Well, if you called them, all right, we'll just wait to hear what you say. So what if I wind up in prison? (*Emotionally.*) First it's a children's home, then a hostel. You haven't a corner to call your own there either. They give you a room, that's it, and you can kiss that goodbye the same way. And now it's prison, that's my home. Eh? My God! (NINA *is crying.*) I thought, at last I had some place I could call my own. So, I got drunk, what of it? Does that mean you don't let a person in? Maybe I wasn't going to do it again. Let's say I wanted to apologise. And that was the reason I was knocking at the door. And then that Galkin appears. Trust him to poke his nose in! Shouting, don't you dare hit me, I've got a weak head! And I tell him to piss off. I told him didn't I? I did warn him?

SERGEI ILYICH *returns and exits to the entry. He nods to* NINA *in passing.* NINA *tearfully tries to pull* IVANOV *into the entry, dragging the pram with her other hand.* IVANOV *won't let her wheel the pram, it's important that he explains himself.*

I warned him, didn't I. Go away, I said, or I'll do you an injury. I'll thump you one . . .

NIKOLAI *emerges from the hall.*

IVANOV. I'll hit you so hard, you'll remember the name of Ivanov all right. He was told to clear off. I mean, I'm frightened of nothing. That's what I told him. Your weak head doesn't scare me.

NIKOLAI. Hey, take it easy, old man. Who are you going to thump? Maybe you want to try me, eh?

NINA. Kolya! Oh, Kolya love, leave him, let him go! (*Sobbing.*)

IVANOV. And who the hell are you?

NINA. Kolya, don't go near him, Kolya darling, please, don't touch him! Kolya! (*Flings her arms round him, restraining him.*)

IVANOV. Come on, who do you think you are?

NINA. Run, before it's too late!

IVANOV. Ivanov doesn't run. Who is this?

NINA. Kolya, I'll explain . . . I'll tell you all about it later. Please, Kolya, please, love, don't get involved with Ivanov.

NIKOLAI. I'm not scared of him.

NINA. Oh, God in Heaven, nobody's saying you're scared! I mean, he's a shrimp in comparison with you! He's old, he's weak.

IVANOV. Who's weak? Eh?

NIKOLAI. Yes, well, he's not too weak to beat up young girls.

NINA. Nobody was beating me up. Let's go, Kolya, I've got something to tell you. Come on. (*To* IVANOV.) Didn't I tell you to go home? Eh? Galka's got no pram there, there's nowhere to lay her down. Get away from here, run!

IVANOV (*querulous*). Who is she to tell me to run?

NINA. Look, go away, Father, move!

IVANOV *makes a grand exit to the hallway, with the pram under his arm, and carrying his suitcase.* NINA *releases* NIKOLAI. *She is breathing heavily. She fixes her braid at the back of her head, pulls up her shawl, with trembling hands, and smiles.*

NINA. Now, why'd you have to get mixed up in other people's business?

NIKOLAI. It's always the same – when a bloke's beating up a woman, it's best not to interfere. The woman'll only start swearing at you as well. What were you defending him for? I'd have given him such a doing, he'd have forgotten the road home.

NINA. And who are you to do that?

NIKOLAI. Well, I had to defend you.

NINA. From him? He hadn't even touched me.

NIKOLAI. Yes, you can tell that to the birds. I mean, I heard him: 'I'll do you an injury, I'll thump you one!'

NINA. That wasn't at me.

NIKOLAI. Really? So who was it at then?

IVANOV *emerges from the hallway without the pram, but carrying his suitcase.*

NINA. What is it now?

IVANOV. I handed in the pram.

NINA. And what about yourself?

IVANOV. Well, she won't let me in.

NINA. Then I'll just have to go with you. (*To* NIKOLAI.) Can you wait here for two or three minutes, while I'm away?

NIKOLAI. Of course. (*Shakes his head wonderingly.*)

NINA *and* IVANOV *go out to the entry.* SERGEI ILYICH *emerges soon after.*

SERGEI ILYICH. Hello, Nikolai. Finished your army service now?

NIKOLAI. Hi. (*They shake hands.*) Yes, seems so.

SERGEI ILYICH. So you'll be going out to work?

NIKOLAI. Yes, looks like it.

SERGEI ILYICH. Mm. Well, I suppose so. Yes. Listen, you couldn't lend me a loaf of bread, could you? I went down to the bakery, but they're closed. Didn't make it in time. First she's no salt, next it's no bread.

NIKOLAI. I'll do that, sure.

SERGEI ILYICH. Well, could you run along and get it? Only don't say who it's for.

NIKOLAI *exits.* NINA *reappears.*

NINA. Hello, Uncle Seryozha.

SERGEI ILYICH. We've already met today, sort of. How are you doing?

NINA. Uncle Sergei, did you call the police?

SERGEI ILYICH. What? What police?

NINA. So where were you running off to?

SERGEI ILYICH. To the bakery. Why?

NINA. Auntie Anna told me she was going to send you to call the police.

SERGEI ILYICH. Huh, she wouldn't dare. What was this all about?

NINA. It was because of Ivanov – well, because our Ivanov was sitting in the entry.

SERGEI ILYICH. Oh I see, so we've to call the police? What, did he steal something or what? He's sitting there, so where's he going to go? He'll just sit for a while, and then he'll go. We should give him a bit of bread, and some money, and then he'll clear off. He doesn't have any other option.

A pause.

NINA (*carefully*). So – has Auntie Anna sent you down to look after her washing?

SERGEI ILYICH. What's all this about sending? She sends me to the police, she sends me to the bakery, she sends me to keep an eye on her washing. I'm damned if I'll be sent anywhere!

NINA (*hastily*). That's all right then, I'll look after it. I'm out for a walk anyway.

SERGEI ILYICH. What for? Go on home, go on. Standing guard, huh. Nobody's going to steal it, and she's hired somebody to stand guard!

NINA. Nobody hired me. It doesn't matter, it's okay.

SERGEI ILYICH. No, it's not. On you go home. Dammit, I'll look after the washing myself. It's my washing. On you go, there's no point in hanging about here.

NINA *slowly goes up into the entry.* NIKOLAI *hurries out with the loaf of bread.* NINA *stops.* SERGEI ILYICH, *slightly embarrassed, takes the bread and thanks him, and without acknowledging* NINA, *goes past her into the entry.* NIKOLAI *stands at the foot of the stairs,* NINA *in the porch.*

NIKOLAI (*after a silence*). Well, what is it you want? I've got to hurry to the shop, I've only half an hour.

NINA. What do I want? I don't want anything. It's just that Auntie Anna asked me to keep an eye on her washing, and I wanted you to stay for a while.

NIKOLAI. Oh, you're a crafty one, like a little mouse.

NINA. And you're thick, like an old felt boot. (*Laughs.*)

NIKOLAI. What are you laughing at?

NINA. I'm just laughing.

NIKOLAI. Well, anyway. I'll be seeing you.

Pause.

NINA. Cheerio.

Pause.

NIKOLAI. You know, you could go to our place. Mother's invited you.

NINA (*immediately*). Let's go.

NIKOLAI. Well, I've got to dash out to the shop first. So wait for me.

NINA. Okay.

NIKOLAI. Right, I'll see you.

NINA. Cheerio.

NIKOLAI *disappears round the corner.* NINA *rushes headlong into the entry.*

Scene Eleven

The GAVRILOVS' *flat.* NINA *is rummaging in a wardrobe, while* VITYA *watches television.* IVANOV *is hiding in the kitchen.*

GRANYA. I don't want to speak to you. Not after that.

NINA. Mama, let me get changed in peace.

GRANYA. At least have your supper first. Really!

NINA. I've got ten minutes.

GRANYA. What's this all for? You're not going anywhere. It's late.

NINA. Mama, let me wear your blouse. The sparkling one.

GRANYA. Where do you think you're going? Who gave you permission?

NINA. Mama! Please – it's just next door.

GRANYA. Going out who with?

NINA. With nobody, I'm going to Nikolai's house.

GRANYA. What's this all about?

NINA. His mother's invited me, all right?

GRANYA. What on earth for?

NINA. Well, what if I just go and get married?

GRANYA. You haven't asked anybody's permission, and you're just going like that? Who says you can?

NINA. Mama, it's best if I just go my own way, I can't live here any longer.

GRANYA. And who's stopping you? Are we going through this again?

NINA. Nobody's stopping me, nobody, but please don't you try and stop me either, Mama. Let me have your blouse.

GRANYA. Take it.

NINA. Mama, don't think badly of me, please?

GRANYA. That's all you need, nothing's happened yet, he's not even proposed, and you're rushing straight in as if you were married already.

NINA. I'm going to get changed. (*Exits to adjoining room.*)

Scene Twelve

The yard. NINA is standing in the same jacket, but wearing a fur hat, and leather, not felt boots. She is carrying a handbag. NIKOLAI appears.

NIKOLAI. Okay, let's go. What did you get all dolled up for? Did you nip home?

NINA. What business is it of yours?

NIKOLAI. Do what you like, it's all one to me. It was Mother that invited you.

NINA. Well, then, hold your tongue.

NIKOLAI. The wit's fairly sparkling tonight.

   NINA *laughs happily. They go upstairs to the entry.*

Scene Thirteen

The KOZLOVS' *apartment,* NINA *is out of sight, in the hall.*

TAISA PETROVNA. Come on in, Nina dear, take off your coat and come in. Make yourself at home. You must be frozen? (*A silence.*) Well, I can see you are. It's been cold today, all the same.

NINA *enters, followed by* NIKOLAI.

Oh, what a beautiful blouse you're wearing. Did you really buy that on your salary? (NINA *shakes her head.*) Go on in to the table. I'm making tea just now for the fifteenth time. We've had one visitor after another today. That's our relations just left, which is a pity. They'd have liked to meet you. You must be hungry? (NINA *shakes her head.*) Well, it doesn't matter.

NIKOLAI (*sarcastically*). She's struck dumb at our magnificent splendour. The carpet, the sideboard, the chandelier. We dazzle everybody with these things.

TAISA PETROVNA. Really, Nikolai, why are you in such a bad mood? Don't take any notice of him, Nina. He's not as nasty as he seems.

NIKOLAI. Oh, stop twittering.

TAISA PETROVNA. Sit down there alongside Fyodor Ivanovich, introduce yourself. He'll look after you. I'll go and put on the tea. This is two days in a row we've been entertaining, so the table's a bit of a mess. (*Exits.*)

NIKOLAI. That's quite true; two days' entertainment.

FYODOR IVANOVICH. So, what's your place of work, Nina?

NINA. The grocery store. (*Clears her throat.*)

NIKOLAI (*sarcastically*). She's lost her voice.

FYODOR IVANOVICH. No wonder! Standing all that time in the freezing cold. How many hours were you standing out there, Nina?

NINA. I wasn't standing. I was out for a walk with my little sister.

TAISA PETROVNA (*returning with a plateful of pastry slices*). Well, these pastries have certainly come in handy. When I was baking, I was thinking it'd be the same as usual, we'd eat as many as we had room for, and nobody would want to see any more of them. But here they are, they've come in handy again. We've had a lot of people. I like a lot of visitors. A house without visitors is empty.

NIKOLAI. My, my, you'd have had to chuck them out, and now you don't need to.

TAISA PETROVNA *gestures to her, to pay no heed to* NIKOLAI.

FYODOR IVANOVICH. That little sister of yours – are you looking after her yourself?

NINA. Why? No, with Mama.

FYODOR IVANOVICH. But it was you that brought up your brother. I remember that.

NINA. Not at all. Mama helped.

TAISA PETROVNA. Mama helped! Some people help their mother, but here it's the other way round.

FYODOR IVANOVICH. Anyway, it looks as if you've brought up two kids on your own.

GRANNY. I was the same, we were left orphans, six of us, and I was the eldest. Father just wouldn't get married. And I was fourteen years old. The house caught fire one time, and I woke up – we were on fire!

FYODOR IVANOVICH. We've heard it before.

GRANNY. You've heard it, but she hasn't. Anyway, what could I do – I got everybody up, stood them on the windowsill, and opened the hopper. 'Breathe in', I said, 'And don't fall out!'

FYODOR IVANOVICH. What department do you work in?

NINA. I'm a trainee in the dairy section. (*Clears her throat.*)

FYODOR IVANOVICH. Is it hard work?

NINA. It was worse on the building site. Outside all the time, my nose swelled up, I had a fever, so I left.

GRANNY. I started at fourteen, glueing boxes. I'd set them all down beside me, and we used to complete a full person's norm in a day.

FYODOR IVANOVICH (*to* NINA). Come on, eat up, a working girl's got to eat.

NINA. No thanks, I don't want anything.

FYODOR IVANOVICH. You don't want anything? If you've come into our house, that's it, you've got to do what you're told. I'll give you a little bit of herring. And maybe you'll take a spot of wine, eh?

TAISA PETROVNA. That's enough from you.

FYODOR IVANOVICH. Oh, come on – you'll surely have a drink? Come on, don't be shy. Young girls aren't shy nowadays, they're into everything. Have a drink, we're all at home here, and you're one of us now, Kolya's fiancée, so they tell me.

NIKOLAI *grunts,* FYODOR IVANOVICH's *persistence has more to do with contrasting* NINA *and* NADYA, *for* NIKOLAI's *benefit.*

Anyway, let's have a little drop. I'll pour you some.

NINA (*her mouth full*). I don't want any!

FYODOR IVANOVICH. Oh, come on, let's get past 'I don't want', eh?

TAISA PETROVNA. It's all right, that's enough. It's tea she wants.

FYODOR IVANOVICH. Maybe you'll have a smoke, then? Nina, love?

NINA *looks in wonderment at* FYODOR IVANOVICH.

NIKOLAI. Anyway, I'm off. I wish you all a pleasant evening's entertainment.

FYODOR IVANOVICH (*distracted from his little game*). What are you rushing away for? Your fiancée's here. Sit down.

NIKOLAI. Fiancée yet! That'll be right.

TAISA PETROVNA. Where are you off to? It's late.

NIKOLAI. I told you, I had to rush.

TAISA PETROVNA. Nina's just arrived, and you're leaving? Maybe you could take Nina with you?

NIKOLAI. What d'you want to drive your visitor out of the house for? You invited her, she's your guest.

TAISA PETROVNA. But she'd love to go with you. Why should

she want to stay with us? Isn't that right, Nina dear? You do want to go with Kolya?

NIKOLAI. I don't think anybody's asked me yet . . .

FYODOR IVANOVICH. Young people should be with other young people.

NIKOLAI. Anyway, I'm off.

TAISA PETROVNA. That's very nice! At least be back soon.

NIKOLAI. Yes, well, maybe I won't come back alone. Still want me back soon?

A silence. NIKOLAI *exits.* FYODOR IVANOVICH, *deep in thought, strikes the table with his fist a few times.*

TAISA PETROVNA. There'll be a film on the TV now. Nina dear, you're my guest, and I'm not letting you go anywhere. The men can go out wherever they like, but we two'll just sit here and twiddle our thumbs.

FYODOR IVANOVICH. He'll bring back some other one-night stand.

TAISA PETROVNA. Where to? There's no room for her here. We've no room now. Nina dear, you'll stay with us, won't you?

NINA nods. They all sit round the television set. GRANNY *lies down on the couch and instantly falls asleep.* FYODOR IVANOVICH, *sitting in the armchair, nods off.* TAISA PETROVNA *closes her eyes, and* NINA *also dozes off. Intermittent gunfire on the TV, another patriotic war film. The doorbell rings, and* TAISA PETROVNA *goes to answer it. It is* GRANYA, *standing in the doorway.* TAISA PETROVNA *goes out onto the landing, closing the door behind her.* NINA *strains to hear them, from the other side.*

GRANYA. I'm sorry to disturb you. You've got my Nina there.

TAISA PETROVNA. Yes?

GRANYA. She's got to get up early in the morning . . . so . . .

TAISA PETROVNA. I'm sorry, we're neighbours, but I don't know your name.

GRANYA. Agrafena Osipovna.

TAISA PETROVNA. I think we need to have a little talk.

GRANYA is alarmed.

I know your situation. He's out of jail . . .

GRANYA. Oh, that's no problem.

TAISA PETROVNA. I mean you have to make up your mind –
it's either him or your Nina. She's a grown-up young woman,
it's awkward for her. She doesn't want to stay.

GRANYA. Well, that's all right, he can just go.

TAISA PETROVNA. But why? Look, I understand. You're still a
young woman, younger than me, I'm quite sure. You haven't
had much of a life. Is that right?

GRANYA. Well . . .

TAISA PETROVNA. But Nina's a fine-looking girl, decent,
hardworking. She'll soon get married in any case. And you'll be
on your own again.

GRANYA. So?

TAISA PETROVNA. Anyway, I can take Nina in. We all like her.
You understand? She'll live with us, get used to us. No one'll
harm her. We won't touch her. She needs to study more, too.
Get some decent qualifications, unlike now.

GRANYA. She didn't manage to get an education, of course.

TAISA PETROVNA. So you understand . . . You think about it.
You'll get settled down meantime, he'll find a job, but Nina has
to study. Only how are you going to get along without her?
She's practically like an unpaid nanny to your little girl. I can
well understand you won't manage without her.

GRANYA. There's no need to think like that.

TAISA PETROVNA. Well, I know how difficult it is with a young
baby.

GRANYA. Difficult or not, I'll get by. Of course, she should have
qualifications. And she's clever with her hands, too.

TAISA PETROVNA. I'll tell you what. Let's you and me make an
agreement, my dear. If she's going to stay with us, she won't
come back to you again. Why should she? She'll have a family
here, there's no sense her battling on two fronts. Right?

GRANYA. Well . . .

TAISA PETROVNA. So I'm asking you not to bother her. Don't
come for her, don't phone her up and so on.

GRANYA. Let her come back home just for today. Just today. To get something together for her.

TAISA PETROVNA. No, no, don't bother – she doesn't need a dowry.

GRANYA. Let her come home today.

TAISA PETROVNA. All right, have it your way. But if you're going to ask that right at the start, then that's it, I'm not keeping her. That's the end of it.

GRANYA. I'm not asking. I just thought . . .

TAISA PETROVNA. Well, you know what thought did – if you'll pardon the expression.

GRANYA (*on the verge of tears*). Taisa love, you'll look after her, won't you.

TAISA PETROVNA. What on earth are you saying that for? That makes me sick, that kind of talk.

GRANYA *shrugs*.

TAISA PETROVNA. Well, then, I wish you all the very best.

GRANYA. And the same to you.

TAISA PETROVNA. Only I'm asking you – don't bother her. Don't keep coming to the door.

GRANYA. I understand. So – goodbye for now.

TAISA PETROVNA. Goodbye.

NINA *has been listening to the whole conversation reacting to every turn of events, now giving little noiseless starts, now clenching her fists.* TAISA PETROVNA *comes into the room.* NINA *greets her with an exultant expression, ready to fling herself round her neck.*

TAISA PETROVNA. This table needs clearing. (*Yawns.*) All that eating and drinking.

NINA. I'll take these out, shall I? (*Begins to clear the table.*)

ACT TWO

Scene Fourteen

The KOZLOVS' *apartment three months later.* NINA *is alone, wearing a new coat. She is standing in front of a mirror, having a look at the back and sleeves. This dumb show is interrupted by a ring at the doorbell.* NINA *goes to open it, and ushers in* GRANYA, *with baby* GALKA *in her arms.* GRANYA *kisses the dismayed* NINA *and sits down with the baby at the table . . . She looks frantic, although she continues to smile.* NINA *had managed to whip off the coat quickly, and now takes it to hang up in the wardrobe.*

GRANYA. They've bought you a new coat?

NINA. What do you want? Mama, what is it you want?

GRANYA. Go on, put it on.

NINA reluctantly puts the coat on.

GRANYA. Hm. It's too big.

NINA. So?

GRANYA. How much did they pay for it?

NINA. Mama, honestly – you've come in here . . .

GRANYA. Yes, I'm here, so what? I've got to go into hospital . . . it's just for three days . . .

A pause. The implication is that it's for an abortion.

I might be home earlier, I'll try anyway.

NINA. Oh, I see.

GRANYA. Well, you'll understand now.

A pause.

NINA. You know, I don't have any say here. I can't do anything.

GRANYA. They bought you a coat.

NINA. A coat's different. That's different altogether.

GRANYA. Let's go home.

NINA. No.

GRANYA. I'm afraid to leave Galka with him. He's already taking her out for walks, getting a little nearer to the off-sales each time. Where all that mob are.

NINA. Mama, how can I? I'm here today, but they could ask me to leave tomorrow, don't you understand?

GRANYA. Let's go home then.

NINA. You're only thinking of yourself, you don't think about me. You only need me as a babyminder. But I'm a human being.

GRANYA. But Galka's got to be fed, for a day and a half at least.

NINA. Take her with you.

GRANYA. They won't allow her in.

NINA. Well, I don't know.

GRANYA (sighs). You know, you've become so . . .

NINA. So what?

GRANYA. Look, take her and change her nappy, do. My arms are about dropping off.

NINA (takes the baby). My goodness, you've got so heavy! Who's my lovely little girl, eh? Are you my Galya? Are you my darling little Galka?

She takes GALYA with the bag of nappies into the next room. GRANYA puts some prepared baby's bottles on the table and quietly exits. The front door slams. NINA rushes out with the unfolded nappy, runs out to the hall, comes back in again, sees the feeding bottles, sits down at the table and starts crying. Then, still racked with sobs, she picks up the bottles, and goes into the adjoining box-room to fix the nappy. There is a noise at the outside door, and GRANNY enters. She listens to NINA weeping bitterly, sits down on the settee, sees the discarded coat, and shakes her head, hangs the coat up in the wardrobe. She sits down again, takes a nightdress out of her bag, and tries it against herself, looking in the mirror. The tearful NINA emerges then, cautiously, draws the door tightly shut behind her, locks it, and puts the key in her pocket.

NINA. That's very nice.

GRANNY *says nothing, turns this way and that, inspecting herself in the mirror.*

It's a good thing it has long sleeves. Keep you warm.

GRANNY. I'm too warm as it is in that kitchen.

NINA. Did you get your pension?

GRANNY. Mind your own business.

NINA (*silenced, briefly*). How much?

GRANNY. What?

NINA. How much was it? (*Clears her throat.*)

GRANNY. It's my own money. Supposing it was just three roubles, it's mine.

NINA. That's good. Quite cheap.

GRANNY. Yes, well I can't buy dear. I've got to get ready . . . for the old folks' home. I can't sleep in that damn kitchen the rest of my life. Supposing I take ill. They'll all start wiping their feet on me.

NINA *sighs.* GRANNY *lays the nightdress down, sits deep in thought.*

GRANNY. You think you've got everybody under your thumb here. What were you trying on Taisa's coat for?

NINA. She said she'd make me a present of it.

GRANNY. Huh – nobody ever gives me anything. They'll give me a shroud, maybe, for my grave. Unless they bury me in my old nightdress.

NINA. You shouldn't talk like that, Granny. It isn't nice.

GRANNY. You dry your own tears. It's not right, you know – you've driven an old person out of her own bed. You're crying, but I'm not. Why don't you just bugger off out of here, eh? What are you doing here anyway? You've got no shame. He's not going to marry you, he needs you like a hole in the head.

NINA. Don't you nag at me, Granny. I've enough without you. I don't need you as well.

GRANNY (*not in the least angry*). Huh, now you're talking like a human being, on your own account. Well, you speak the truth, do you hear, don't put on an act for people, or make things up. And I'll tell *you* the truth. You're fed up here, right? And for why? I mean, who are you, to start with?

NINA. I'm Kolya's wife.

GRANNY. So who's taken you to the Registry Office, then?

NINA. That's only a bit of paper, that's all.

GRANNY. So why don't you have one? A scrap of paper, but you haven't got one. That's because he doesn't want you.

NINA. Why's that? He would tell me directly, surely.

GRANNY. Why should he? This suits him nicely. He wants you all right, for all kinds of things, he's not fussy. But he doesn't want you as a human being. No way.

NINA. You can't know that.

GRANNY. Because he doesn't fancy you. You're too young, whatever it takes you haven't got it, you're no good at it.

NINA. You can't know that.

GRANNY. You should've led him on, the way young girls do, the way all women do. You should've made yourself up, had your hair permed. You should have had a laugh with him, joked a bit. You shouldn't have let him see you needed him. You'd have got your feet under the table straight away. Now he's maybe got another girl.

NINA. That's not true.

GRANNY. It is true. He's just sticking with you because he's bored stiff. To tell you the truth, his parents have flung you at him. And he's a young lad, fresh out the army. He's never given it a thought.

NINA. You can't know that.

GRANNY. I can't? Oh yes I can! At first he didn't even want to know you. Then his parents put up a folding bed for him in your room. And chucked his old granny out into the kitchen, for God's sake! And you're delighted.

NINA (*flushed with anger*). You don't know anything, how can you talk like that.

GRANNY. So how should I talk? You're crying, that's just water.

It's me that should be crying. You can go anywhere you like – even to a hostel, or back to your mother. But where can I go? Klavdia's, that's all, and she makes so much damn noise, she doesn't even scruple to shout at her own mother. That's why I can't live with her, on account of all the shouting. She's kind enough, but her tongue goes all the time like the clappers. And now it's even noisier here . . . Oh, anyway, I suppose I'd better put away my nightdress. (*Goes to the door, tries the handle.*) What's this? What's going on?

NINA. You can't go in there.

GRANNY. What d'you mean, I can't? D'you expect me to drag this around in my teeth, is that it?

NINA. Don't go in there.

GRANNY. Give me the key, I'm telling you! You're getting above yourself.

NINA. Later.

GRANNY. Well, you just wait! (*Sits down distractedly.*)

TAISA PETROVNA *enters.*

TAISA PETROVNA. It's pretty cold.

A silence.

Did you buy something?

She goes to the wardrobe, changes her clothes behind the door.

GRANNY. I bought . . . my shroud (*starts crying.*)

TAISA PETROVNA. Listen, you're still . . . (*Struggling out of her dress.*) You're still going to outlive us. Now that's enough.

GRANNY. Well, you just wait, and I'll tell you . . .

NINA *opens the door and instantly vanishes into the next room, closing the door behind her.*

Did you see that? Did you see her? She won't let me into my own room, to put my clothes away. Into my own room!

TAISA PETROVNA. That's the trouble with you two . . . you've nothing to do. You're at it the whole time, squabbling from morning to night.

GRANNY. Don't you lump her along with me.

TAISA PETROVNA. Mama, I'm just in from work. Are we going to eat? Let's just wait for Fedya. Oh, my feet are killing me. So, all right, you sit on your behind all day at work, but then you've got to stand on the metro, and stand on the bus as well – you just get so *tired*.

GRANNY. And I come in, you understand, and I want to put something away in my own chest of drawers . . . my own chest of drawers.

TAISA PETROVNA. Well, we can put it in the wardrobe.

GRANNY. Why should I do that? I want to put it away in my own room. (*Crosses to the door and pounds it with her fist.*) Open up, d'you hear!

TAISA PETROVNA. That's enough, don't start hammering at the door. My head's splitting without that. We've too much stuff here anyway, more than we need.

GRANNY. So, does that mean me? Am I more than we need?

TAISA PETROVNA. Why you? Why does it always have to be you? You take everything to yourself.

GRANNY. And as for her – I told her to go home to her own house.

TAISA PETROVNA *emerges from behind the wardrobe door, lies down on the divan, leafs through the television programmes.*

TAISA PETROVNA. Obviously Nikolai's not keen on this arrangement. Not much, anyway. And we've done our bit, what more can you ask?

GRANNY. That's what I'm saying.

TAISA PETROVNA (*yawns*). For some reason it just hasn't worked out. Kolya does nothing but sleep here. He's cut himself off.

GRANNY. He'll start drinking like that, and going out whoring, he'll keep going out. There's nothing of any interest to make him come home.

She says all this loud enough to be heard behind the door.

What I'd like to know is where he goes.

TAISA PETROVNA (*equally loud*). Well, he's a young lad. Who knows?

GRANNY. She hasn't house-trained him, that's for sure.

TAISA PETROVNA. That's true. (*Yawns.*) Huh, hockey again. (*Now speaks normally.*) Fedya'll be home directly, he'll be a pain in the arse the whole evening.

GRANNY (*towards the door*). And she's locked herself in, yet! (*Goes up to the door, pounds it with her fist.*) Open up! Open up, or it'll be the worse for you!

TAISA PETROVNA. Don't, that's enough.

GRANNY (*retreats*). Well, I'd like to know just what's going on?

A noise at the outer door.

TAISA PETROVNA. That's Fedya coming in. That's him now. Mama, go and heat something up for him, my feet are about dropping off . . .

GRANNY *exits.* FYODOR IVANOVICH *enters.*

FYODOR IVANOVICH. Good evening. There's hockey on tonight. No sign of the young people?

NINA *emerges, as if she has just been waiting for him.*

NINA (*delightedly*). Good evening!

FYODOR IVANOVICH. What, have you been sitting in the dark? Is Kolya asleep?

TAISA PETROVNA. He hasn't come home yet.

FYODOR IVANOVICH. So, have you been asleep then?

NINA *shakes her head.*

Your face is all red.

NINA *shrugs.*

TAISA PETROVNA. She and Mama have been fighting again.

FYODOR IVANOVICH (*waves his hand dismissively*). How many times have I told you, Nina love – you shouldn't take offence at people not right in the head . . . Really, Nina, don't take things to heart so much. I mean, I don't know how many rows I've had with my mother-in-law, I've tried to keep the peace as well. Nothing worked. So I've given up, what the hell, and just stopped paying her any attention.

TAISA PETROVNA. Fedya, how could you! I don't know how you can say that!

FYODOR IVANOVICH. Well, all right then –

TAISA PETROVNA. I mean, really . . .

FYODOR IVANOVICH. Okay, okay.

TAISA PETROVNA. I don't allow people to shout at Mama, and I never have.

FYODOR IVANOVICH. Oh, give it a rest.

TAISA PETROVNA. Now, just hold on, why do you always make me shut up? Why do you do it?

FYODOR IVANOVICH. Me?

TAISA PETROVNA. I won't have people shouting at Mama, raising their voices to her. Nobody, do you hear? Nobody's to be rude to my mother, she's had a lot to put up with in her life, you know! And now she's still got to cry?

NINA. I didn't . . .

TAISA PETROVNA. It's bad enough my mother has to live in the kitchen, to spend her last days there. My heart bleeds for her, but Fyodor Ivanovich and I are saying nothing, we're not saying a word, because what can we do, after all? You've got to give way to the young people. And we're giving way. But the young ones owe us something, too. Even if it's only not to show their bad character.

NINA. I didn't show anything of the kind.

TAISA PETROVNA. God almighty, I'm sick of this. Young people nowadays are so damned clever, is it really that difficult to understand that it's not easy, living together? And if people are openly rude, if they're just going to come right out with it, in this kind of situation, well then, you can't even live in your home!

NINA. But I wasn't rude . . .

FYODOR IVANOVICH. Now you shut up and listen.

TAISA PETROVNA. People don't cry for nothing. Mama didn't even cry when Papa was killed at the Front, and now she's going to cry because of you? That's too much, surely!

NINA. What was she crying about?

FYODOR IVANOVICH. Listen, listen.

TAISA PETROVNA. And in any case I'm going to tell you a thing or two . . .

The doorbell rings.

NINA (*rushes to open the door*). It's Kolya!

NINA *ushers in not* KOLYA, *but* IVANOV. *He looks agitated.*

IVANOV. Hello, everybody. Hello, Nina.

NINA *is stunned, nods. The others remain silent.*

Nina, I want a word with you.

NINA *and* IVANOV *move a little way apart. He whispers.*

So where's my Galka, then?

NINA (*whispers*). What do you mean?

IVANOV (*whispers*). Granya – did she take her with her to the hospital?

NINA (*whispers*). How should I know?

IVANOV (*out loud*). She didn't say anything, she just went off with Galya. (*Whispers.*) She didn't leave any money . . .

NINA. She'll be back tomorrow night.

IVANOV. And what'll I do meanwhile?

The whole of the ensuing conversation is in whispers.

NINA. I don't know, I haven't anything.

IVANOV. Ask them for three roubles.

NINA. What for?

IVANOV. I haven't anything to eat.

NINA. Mama's surely left something. Try the plastic bag hanging up by the window.

IVANOV. Since when? (*Aloud.*) You couldn't let me have a three-rouble note till tomorrow night?

NIKOLAI's *parents exchange glances.*

FYODOR IVANOVICH. I've hardly anything on me. Hold on and I'll see.

Rummages in his jacket pocket, glancing at his wife.

TAISA PETROVNA (*not looking at* IVANOV). We're not a savings bank, you know.

IVANOV. I will give it back.

FYODOR IVANOVICH. I think I've got something here . . . two roubles.

IVANOV. That's fine, that'll do. I mean, I'll give it back. (*Solemnly places the two roubles in his pocket.*) So, until we meet again . . . Huh, family – well, they . . . you know how they treat each other. Thank you for your kindness anyway.

FYODOR IVANOVICH. That's okay. No problem.

IVANOV. Well, I'll excuse myself in that case. (*Exits.*)

TAISA PETROVNA. Well!

NINA. What did you want to give him money for? Oh!

TAISA PETROVNA (*changed tone*). You're a strange girl. We're not beasts, you know. We had to give him it.

FYODOR IVANOVICH. Today we give him, tomorrow he gives us. He'll help us out too.

TAISA PETROVNA. We're always ready to help anyone, Nina. You know that yourself. But you know what happens – you give a person your whole heart and soul, and they give you their arse to kiss. It's not a nice thing to say, but that's how it is.

NINA. But why did you give to him!

TAISA PETROVNA. We give to everybody. We don't ask anything from anybody, but they all batten on us. Because they know what we're like. Everybody hangs round our neck, literally everybody, and we have to carry them all. Why is it we've always got, and they haven't? I mean, we could be as bad as them, we could go around with the arse out of our trousers, and not give it a thought. We could have an easy life, you know, and not give a damn. But we take on the world's burdens. We're ready with two roubles, or a coat, or whatever, anything for peace.

NINA *is about to speak.*

FYODOR IVANOVICH. No, Nina, you listen.

TAISA PETROVNA. It's as if we were the only people in the world that had anything to give. Because nobody but us seems to bother, nobody takes thought, or saves anything. But we never throw anything out, we hold onto everything. So because of that we've got to be the fairy godmothers, and dole out to everybody, right, left and centre. But we need some peace as well. So people aren't tormenting us the whole time, but let us have our last few years in peace. We've never lived just the two of us, Fedya and I, on our own, I can tell you. There's always somebody or other.

FYODOR IVANOVICH (*animatedly*). That's absolutely right. I'll vouch for that. We've always had the mother-in-law.

TAISA PETROVNA. We need to have a serious think about this, Nina. And most of all *you've* got to think. About what your position is in this family, and how you should behave.

NINA. But I didn't say anything.

TAISA PETROVNA. Anyway that's no longer the point. Time's running out. I mean, Fedya and I . . . you understand? I mean, it doesn't depend on us. After all, we can't . . . we can't marry you. (*An involuntary smile.*)

NINA. What d'you mean?

TAISA PETROVNA. Well . . . (*smiles again.*) I mean, it's got to be Kolya. You can't force him, after all. And it's not up to us – without him, we can't . . .

NINA. Of course not.

TAISA PETROVNA. How, of course not? Does that mean Kolya has . . . ?

NINA (*startled*). Kolya has what?

TAISA PETROVNA. I mean, has Kolya said anything?

NINA. I don't know . . .

TAISA PETROVNA. What's to know? Has he said anything to you?

NINA. Sort of.

TAISA PETROVNA. What did he say?

NINA. He did say something.

TAISA PETROVNA. That he'd marry you?

NINA. No. Well, he said something . . . just bits and pieces.

TAISA PETROVNA. Oh, I see, that. That doesn't count. There'll need to be a serious talk with Kolya about this matter. It's got to come out into the open. What his intentions are. You can't drag him by the hair.

FYODOR IVANOVICH. These things have to be gone into willingly.

TAISA PETROVNA. Because we're already being treated as if we were your relatives here, and Kolya seems to know nothing about it.

NINA. Oh, that's just Ivanov . . . He's like that. He was only joking.

TAISA PETROVNA. Because we'll wind up related to God knows who. I mean, Kolya's young, he's hanging around God only knows where, he's maybe making other relatives for us! (*A pause.*) Anyway, Nina, we agreed that none of your relations, while you were staying here out of Ivanov's road, would come to this door.

NINA. They won't, they won't, honestly.

TAISA PETROVNA. Somehow I find that hard to believe.

The sound of a baby crying is heard. NINA *rushes headlong into the other room.*

What's that? Eh? What is it?

TAISA PETROVNA *and* FYODOR IVANOVICH *peer cautiously into the other room, and stand dumbstruck.* GRANNY *emerges from the kitchen, and also has a look.*

GRANNY. Well, well – there it is.

TAISA PETROVNA *and* FYODOR IVANOVICH *return to their seats at the table.* GRANNY *remains standing by the door, as if she's determined not to let anyone close it again.*

TAISA PETROVNA. Well . . . that's interesting.

FYODOR IVANOVICH. What the hell are we going to do now? (*Attempts a joke.*) Maybe we should adopt this one too?

TAISA PETROVNA. Yes, it's a true saying – good deeds need to be able to use their fists. Otherwise people'll sit down and eat you out of house and home.

GRANNY (*into the doorway*). She's got the teat plugged up – she's got it clogged. Turn the bottle up, don't you see? Oh, you're hopeless!

Exits into the side room.

TAISA PETROVNA. You know what's going to happen now?

FYODOR IVANOVICH. Yes, yes.

TAISA PETROVNA. They'll dump her little brother on us next. We'll have a children's home here. Because that drunk's sitting up there, and the children have no place to go!

FYODOR IVANOVICH. Yes, yes.

GRANNY *returns to her post but can't resist prompting her.*

GRANNY. Her nappy's worked loose. Her legs are right out – and it's winter yet! I can't stand this.

Again she exits into the adjoining room.

TAISA PETROVNA. We'll need to do something.

NINA (*appearing at the door*). They've taken Mama into hospital.

TAISA PETROVNA. Hospital?!

NINA. It's only for three days. Maybe less.

TAISA PETROVNA (*stunned*). Well, really!

NINA. And that'll be it finished, then.

TAISA PETROVNA. Well, thank God for that at least.

NINA. It's for three days, that's all. Maybe even less.

TAISA PETROVNA. And why's this landed on us?

The doorbell rings.

NINA. It's Kolya!

She rushes into the hall, they all stand looking towards the door. NINA ushers in a young girl, pregnant, with her face muffled up.

TAISA PETROVNA. Nina, there must be some mistake. What did you bring her straight in here for? Who is it you're looking for? Who do you want?

The girl removes her headscarf. It is NADYA.

NINA. She said she was looking for Nikolai.

TAISA PETROVNA. Nikolai who?

NADYA. Kozlov.

TAISA PETROVNA. What for?

NADYA. On a personal matter.

She wipes her nose with the end of her headscarf.

FYODOR IVANOVICH. Which Kozlov?

NADYA. Yours, of course. (*Stuffs her headscarf into her bag.*)

FYODOR IVANOVICH (*recognises* NADYA). Oh yes – and who might you be, when you're at home?

NADYA. That's of no consequence.

FYODOR IVANOVICH. I see – so that's how it is.

GRANNY *appears in the doorway.*

GRANNY Oh! Long time no see. It's her! Ai-yi-yi . . .

TAISA PETROVNA *sits down on a chair.* FYODOR IVANOVICH *slumps against the wall.*

GRANNY. Hello!

NADYA. Cheers. (*Her manner is rather off-hand and listless.*)

TAISA PETROVNA. And you're who – forgive me, what's your name?

NADYA. Nadyezhda.

TAISA PETROVNA. How come I didn't recognise you straight away?

GRANNY. She's changed.

FYODOR IVANOVICH. She certainly has changed.

NINA *exits to the side room. A silence. It is clear that* NADYA's *appearance has produced such a grave and terrible impression on them all, that they feel an involuntary compassion for her, but they successfully manage to overcome this feeling.*

TAISA PETROVNA (*finding the necessary tone*). Well, just think, eh?

FYODOR IVANOVICH. Yes, you couldn't dream up a situation like this if you tried.

GRANNY. These women again . . .

TAISA PETROVNA (*sympathetically*). Are you hungry?

NADYA. Yes.

TAISA PETROVNA. Take your coat off and sit down. Mama, let's have some supper in here.

NADYA *takes her coat off in the hall, re-enters the room and sits down.* GRANNY *and* TAISA PETROVNA *lay the table, bring in the food.*

Sit in at the table, Nadya. There's bread there, and butter.

NADYA *begins eating, while everyone watches her.*

GRANNY. She's changed . . .

FYODOR IVANOVICH. Certainly has.

TAISA PETROVNA. What month are you in, Nadya?

NADYA. Seventh.

FYODOR IVANOVICH. You don't say! (*Checks himself.*) Yes, Nadya, if you don't mind me saying so, you look . . . well . . . you don't look right, your hair isn't right.

NADYA. I've been in hospital.

TAISA PETROVNA. Nothing serious, I hope?

NADYA. Well, it was a bit . . .

FYODOR IVANOVICH. Well, well . . . so . . . so, what are you going to do now?

NADYA (*shrugs*). God knows.

FYODOR IVANOVICH. Have you registered a husband?

NADYA. A husband? Not officially.

FYODOR IVANOVICH. And you're living in the hostel?

NADYA. Yes.

FYODOR IVANOVICH. They've promised you a room?

NADYA. They've sort of promised – a while ago. Because I'm an orphan, so they said.

FYODOR IVANOVICH. So when are they going to give you it?

NADYA. In about two years from now, probably.

FYODOR IVANOVICH. Well, you should get one through your deputy. As a single parent.

NADYA. Yes, I should. I was flat on my back in hospital nearly two months.

TAISA PETROVNA. You should apply to the building site committee. The local committee women at our place make a fuss about these things.

NADYA. Yes. You wouldn't have a smoke, would you?

FYODOR IVANOVICH. I'm sorry, we don't smoke. Anyway, so who's the father?

TAISA PETROVNA (*interrupting*). We don't smoke. We have a small child in the house.

NADYA. You have?

TAISA PETROVNA. That's right, we have.

NADYA. Since when?

TAISA PETROVNA. Not long since. (*Shouts.*) Nina love, come out here a second!

NINA *appears in the doorway.*

There – this is Kolya's wife. An old flame, you could say.

FYODOR IVANOVICH. An old flame never dies out, eh?

TAISA PETROVNA. She's loved him since first grade at school, and now she's got him. Nina dear, sit down with us for a bit.

NINA. In a minute. I've just got to wash out some nappies.

Disappears into the bedroom and emerges with a pile of nappies, carries them through to the bathroom.

TAISA PETROVNA (*to* NADYA). So then, what brought you to see us?

NADYA. Well . . . I didn't have far to walk. I was passing by, and it occurred to me I knew some people here. I don't know anybody, apart from you.

FYODOR IVANOVICH. That's a likely story. I think you know plenty of people.

NADYA. Not those sort.

FYODOR IVANOVICH. Yes, I've heard that one before.

GRANNY. My, how you've changed – you just wouldn't believe it.

The baby cries. TAISA PETROVNA *suddenly springs from her seat and rushes into the adjoining room, followed by* GRANNY. NINA *hurries in, wiping her hands en route.*

FYODOR IVANOVICH. It's all right, it's all right, Nina love. They've gone in . . . the grannies have run in.

NINA *exits again to carry on with the washing.*

They're all baby-mad, these women.

NADYA. Is it a boy or a girl?

FYODOR IVANOVICH. It's . . . er . . . what d'you call it . . . a little girl.

NADYA. What's her name?

FYODOR IVANOVICH. Er . . . we don't know yet.

NADYA. You haven't made up your minds?

FYODOR IVANOVICH. No.

NADYA. Mine's going to be a boy. Nikolai.

FYODOR IVANOVICH (*slyly*). And the middle name?

NADYA. Nikolaevich, of course.

FYODOR IVANOVICH. What do you mean, Nikolaevich?

NADYA. It's Kolya's.

FYODOR IVANOVICH. Get away with you, that's nonsense! When was it you spent the night here?

NADYA. I travelled to see him at Syzran, you know.

FYODOR IVANOVICH (*scoffing*). Oh come on, that goes for nothing – it could've been anybody's. Give over. Just what are you up to, for God's sake? I mean, it doesn't make any sense.

NADYA. So when did he manage to make a baby then?

FYODOR IVANOVICH. What, d'you think you're the only one that visited him in the army? Eh?

NADYA. Really? You're having me on.

FYODOR IVANOVICH. You think so? So when was it you came here with him to us, eh?

NADYA. Well, anyway –

FYODOR IVANOVICH (*making it up as he goes*). We didn't want to tell Kolya about it straight away, to spoil things for him. I mean, after all, you only come out of the army once. But she lives in our block, everybody knows about it. She suffered too, you know, when Kolya brought somebody home.

NADYA. She did? Well, I suppose so. It'd be surprising if she didn't.

FYODOR IVANOVICH. Anyway, that's how things are. That's why we received you the way we did. You know yourself. You understand now?

NADYA. I just thought you were all nuts. Behaving like wild beasts. I thought, hell, what kind of family's that, I'd be better off staying an orphan. And Kolya also seemed . . . Well, he wasn't his own man, he seemed weak. Not an independent person. A pain in the arse, frankly. Not my type, anyway. And that's what it was . . . Well . . .

FYODOR IVANOVICH. So why have you come to see us now?

NADYA. The other girls said he'd been in to see me. He'd looked in on the girls, but I'd asked them not to say anything to anybody.

FYODOR IVANOVICH. Well, you can drop in on us, if you want. Look in anytime. We're decent people, we'll do what we can. There's nappies there, matinée coats. We won't refuse you. We give to anybody that asks. But as for that being Kolya's, well, come on, I think you're exaggerating a bit there, wouldn't you agree?

NADYA. No, I wouldn't.

FYODOR IVANOVICH (*not listening*). Still, we can always manage a little help. If a person's in trouble, and they've got no relatives, nobody they can turn to. Anyway, you just drop in, whenever.

NADYA. I'll be off now. First I've got to go a place.

FYODOR IVANOVICH. D'you want me to show you where it is?

NADYA. No, I remember. (*Exits.*)

TAISA PETROVNA *and* GRANNY *are listening from the side room.* NINA *enters from the hall, disappears into the bathroom.* TAISA PETROVNA *enters.*

TAISA PETROVNA. Well, let's have a bite of supper now, shall we?

The main door slams. TAISA PETROVNA *and* FYODOR IVANOVICH *strain to hear –* NIKOLAI *enters.*

NIKOLAI. Who's here? Somebody's coat's hanging up.

TAISA PETROVNA. That belongs to Nina, it's Nina's. Come here, Kolya, come in. I've something to show you.

NIKOLAI. Let me get washed from work.

TAISA PETROVNA. Come on, come on. Guess who's in our bed there!

NIKOLAI. In our bed? *(Suddenly alarmed.)* Who is it?

TAISA PETROVNA. Come and see. *(Ushers* NIKOLAI *out.)*

FYODOR IVANOVICH *jumps up, goes out into the hall, carefully closing the door behind him. The front door slams, it is* NADYA *leaving.* NIKOLAI, *and* TAISA PETROVNA *emerge from the side room.*

NIKOLAI. What's she up to?

TAISA PETROVNA. Well, you see, Nina's mother's had to go into hospital. Not for very long. They've nobody to leave her with.

NIKOLAI. Yes, and for some reason or other, you're delighted. So where's she going to sleep?

TAISA PETROVNA. We'll put her on the folding bed.

NIKOLAI. And what about me?

TAISA PETROVNA. The same as always. With Nina.

A pause.

NIKOLAI *(gloomily).* I see.

TAISA PETROVNA. Or we can fix up the armchairs. We can push the armchairs together.

NIKOLAI. What the hell did she bring her here for? That's bloody marvellous.

TAISA PETROVNA. Where have you been?

NIKOLAI. Why do you want to know?

TAISA PETROVNA. You're never at home, that's why.

NIKOLAI. So what am I supposed to do, enjoy myself here with you?

TAISA PETROVNA. And just who *have* you been enjoying yourself with? Are we allowed to know?

NIKOLAI. A few mates, that's all – we were making something. In one of the chaps' garage.

TAISA PETROVNA. Haven't you enough money?

NIKOLAI. God, you want to drag out every bit of information, everything. You keep on and on.

TAISA PETROVNA. Why can't you be like you used to be? Why d'you have to land up God knows where, when you've got your own home here.

NIKOLAI. What's this, d'you mean I'm not allowed out?

TAISA PETROVNA. Why do you have to go out all the time? You've got itchy feet. You've surely sown your wild oats now.

FYODOR IVANOVICH *enters.*

FYODOR IVANOVICH. Kolya, Kolya – East, West, home's best. I'm telling you that as a fact of life.

TAISA PETROVNA. What is it with you, Kolya, why are you deliberately closing your eyes to it all? Are you doing it on purpose? I just don't understand you.

FYODOR IVANOVICH. Well, Mama, it's time we married off our son.

NIKOLAI. What, has something happened?

TAISA PETROVNA. Why should anything have happened? Nothing of the sort.

FYODOR IVANOVICH. I mean, just how long can this go on?

NIKOLAI. As long as it takes, that's how long.

TAISA PETROVNA. No, don't say that, Kolya. That's never been the custom in our family, thank God. This is the first time this has happened to us, and we don't know what to do.

FYODOR IVANOVICH. But we understand. I mean, basically, we do understand. We know what it is, d'you see? I mean, a man's always going to come up against something for the first time, but there's got to be some rules.

NIKOLAI. Now hold on just a minute. You don't know the rules any longer, these rules you're talking about. People nowadays live all kinds of ways.

FYODOR IVANOVICH. Yes, people *may* do, but we do things *our* way. Maybe we're not modern! Out of the last century, eh?

TAISA PETROVNA. I mean, look at you, you're a married man, but you're carrying on like a bachelor.

NIKOLAI. That's rich. How come I'm a married man?

TAISA PETROVNA. Because when two people are living together, they're man and wife.

NIKOLAI. I can't believe what I'm hearing.

TAISA PETROVNA. Look, to get right to the point, I'm sick of this. There's nothing to discuss, I don't want to hear any more nonsense. Nina's living here, isn't she?

NIKOLAI. So, she can go.

FYODOR IVANOVICH. We'll see about that!

TAISA PETROVNA. What do you mean, she can go? How could she look people in the eye? She's had her time, she can just up and leave? Is that it? We took her into our house, then we got fed up with her, and now it's the parting of the ways?

FYODOR IVANOVICH. I won't have that.

NIKOLAI. God almighty.

FYODOR IVANOVICH. Nina, come out here.

NINA *enters, wiping her hands.*

TAISA PETROVNA. Sit down, Nina sweetheart.

NIKOLAI. Huh, it's Nina sweetheart next.

FYODOR IVANOVICH. The fact of the matter is, my dears, you'll just have to go and register your marriage.

TAISA PETROVNA. We want a bit of peace and quiet. And Mama can't sleep in the kitchen the rest of her life.

NIKOLAI. Well, that's fine, I'll sleep in the kitchen.

TAISA PETROVNA. No, it's too cramped here for us, with three generations.

NIKOLAI. As a certain smart young girl called Nadya said.

FYODOR IVANOVICH. Anyway, you'll have to register. That's enough. Dashing about here, there and everywhere, we've had enough of that.

TAISA PETROVNA. And see about buying a co-operative flat.

FYODOR IVANOVICH. That's a great idea. Melkonyan at our place has just been made chairman of the co-operative. Let me know, he says, if there's anything you need. Just the other day!

NIKOLAI. Look, if something's happened, you can tell me, surely. You're holding something back. I know you too well.

FYODOR IVANOVICH. It's just suddenly all boiled up. I mean, your place is here, in your own home, you ought to know that. You've done enough running around the hostels.

NIKOLAI. Not yet, I haven't.

FYODOR IVANOVICH. Well, I'm telling you that's it finished, enough. Nina, you don't have any objection, do you?

NIKOLAI. Oh, she'll vote 'yes' with both hands!

FYODOR IVANOVICH. Why do you have to act like this?

TAISA PETROVNA. You shouldn't hurt people's pride.

NIKOLAI. Well, that's rich. Pride! That's hardly the word here. Nadya's proud. *That's* pride.

FYODOR IVANOVICH. Huh, a lot you know.

TAISA PETROVNA (*interrupting*). Anyway, you can go and apply at the Registry Office tomorrow.

NIKOLAI. Really?

FYODOR IVANOVICH. Yes, once you're registered as a family, then you can get your name down . . . for a car, for a Zhiguli.

TAISA PETROVNA. We'll need to buy Kolya a new imported suit then.

NIKOLAI. Is that a fact?

TAISA PETROVNA. And I've got some dress material, white. Now, hasn't that come in handy!

FYODOR IVANOVICH. We'll get you your own place, you'll be set up then, and we'll be fine here.

TAISA PETROVNA. Only there's to be no funny business tomorrow. You can ask for time off work. And it's maybe better if I call in for you, along with Nina.

NIKOLAI. Oh yes? And maybe I've got other plans.

FYODOR IVANOVICH. Whether you've got other plans, or another girlfriend, we don't know and don't want to know. That can stay shrouded in mystery, nobody's going to say another word about it. And it's no longer your concern.

NIKOLAI. My concern's my business, and mine only. Nobody else's.

FYODOR IVANOVICH. You'd better believe it.

TAISA PETROVNA. And that's exactly why you'll walk right into a trap.

NIKOLAI. What trap? I can take care of myself. Why can't you understand that?

FYODOR IVANOVICH. We understand perfectly well. But you're marrying Nina.

NIKOLAI (genuinely). Why?

TAISA PETROVNA. Kolya, when you grow up you'll realise eventually how much we do understand. But it's got to be Nina, and only Nina, nobody else.

NIKOLAI. Nina, do you want to marry me that much?

NINA is silent.

I mean, I'll tell you the honest truth, I don't want to marry you. So how can you possibly go ahead after that?

NINA. That's up to you, Kolya.

TAISA PETROVNA (outraged). What, you think the girl's in your power? You can treat her any old how?

NIKOLAI. Look, what's all this about? I don't understand why you're all pretending, when it's really quite simple. My God, you're something else. Nina knows all this, I've told her repeatedly. She's said herself that she knows, but this arrangement still suits her.

TAISA PETROVNA. Because she loves you!

NIKOLAI. Not quite, not quite, hold on a minute. It's Nina's own family she can't be doing with, that's why she was so willing to come here.

TAISA PETROVNA. But she's living with you!

NIKOLAI. Yes, she is. That's because she has to, she needs to. But I warned her, isn't that the truth, Nina? It's not very nice for her, to come out with it here in front of you, but it needs to be said, I think. Two people, a young man and a young woman, can live together quite happily, if that's how they want it, if they're normal, healthy adults. That doesn't mean there's any feeling behind it. It's not unusual, a lot of people live like that. Their whole life even. A man needs to live with somebody, to satisfy his animal nature. You can't fight the battle on your own, as they say.

FYODOR IVANOVICH. What rubbish you talk, that's ridiculous!

TAISA PETROVNA. He's just picked that up from somewhere or other.

NIKOLAI. Raising a family isn't a chance business, it's something you have to think about. I've no intention of marrying Nina, I told her that right at the start, and she accepted it.

FYODOR IVANOVICH. Yes, well that's as maybe, but we know you better than that, we know what's been going on, and who's been stirring up trouble. We know the score, Kolya. You think we don't know anything, but we do.

TAISA PETROVNA. It would suit you better to listen to what your father's saying, before it gets any worse.

NIKOLAI. Okay, but I'll go and get washed, my hands are all sticky.

FYODOR IVANOVICH. All right, if you must.

NIKOLAI. My hands are sticky.

TAISA PETROVNA. You see, Nina? Since childhood Kolya's been trained to wash his hands, that's how you should bring up your own children.

NINA *nods, mechanically.*

TAISA PETROVNA. And don't you worry. That's it now, you're on the right track. Did you think it was going to be so easy to get a man married off? You have to get up to all sorts of tricks. Even given them love potions to drink, all that sort of foolishness.

Whispers in NINA's *ear, laughs and spits.* NINA *nods.*

FYODOR IVANOVICH. Is that the Solovievs you're talking about?

TAISA PETROVNA. Yes. Even saying this makes me sick, but they all do it.

Looks over at her husband.

Still, when a man marries, that's him finished. On a leash. He gets used to one place, doesn't like losing it, it's too much effort. He'll stay where he's put, only you've got to meet him halfway, so he has some freedom. You can let him out, it's no big deal, he's not soap, he's not going to melt away. He'll drink beer in the pub, he'll play dominoes there, and whatever else. He'll watch football on the TV And you'll give him a baby. And that's it.

NINA *nods.*

TAISA PETROVNA. The main thing is that he should feel he's the boss.

FYODOR IVANOVICH. And he will be the boss. He's lucky to get you, Nina, don't put yourself down.

NIKOLAI *enters. They all sit at table.* GRANNY *brings out the baby.*

NIKOLAI. What have you brought her in for?

GRANNY. Let her have a look at people for a bit.

NIKOLAI. What's she going to see there? Upside down.

NINA. She sees everything. Anyway, it's time for her sleep, her little eyes are starting to close.

TAISA PETROVNA. We'll push the armchairs together for her at night. After Fedya's watched the TV, he likes to watch from the armchair. Lay her on the bed meantime.

NIKOLAI. I really don't like babies, I can't stand them. I get sick at the sight of them.

GRANNY. Put pillows round her in there, so she doesn't roll off.

NINA *exits with* GALKA.

FYODOR IVANOVICH. You get sick at the sight of other people's kids. But you can't see enough of your own. When you were a little boy, we went to see the city lights, and the fireworks. The cannons made so much noise, you were clinging onto my knees like grim death. You were shaking all over, cowering down, tears in your little eyes. It was so funny.

NIKOLAI. So why did you take me there, if I was frightened?

FYODOR IVANOVICH. Because I was going to root the fear out of you. I took you right underneath the cannon.

NIKOLAI. You wanted to make a man out of me? Totally fearless?

FYODOR IVANOVICH. You could say that.

NIKOLAI. That's all bullshit, as a certain girl used to say.

FYODOR IVANOVICH. You wait until Nina's had your son, we'll see what kind of father you turn out.

NIKOLAI. So what the hell, I won't make a good teacher. What can I teach anyway?

FYODOR IVANOVICH. Well, everyone sees where they've failed in their own lives, and they want their son to make up for it.

NIKOLAI. Make up for what?

FYODOR IVANOVICH. Well – everything. So that he'll forge ahead, develop his talents, if he has any talents. In music, for example. So he won't spend his life telling lies.

NIKOLAI. You used to beat me with a belt for telling lies.

FYODOR IVANOVICH. So I did.

NIKOLAI. And because of that I began to lie so well that you never suspected. And I know damn well when other people are lying. You two lie all the time, for example.

TAISA PETROVNA. And what do we lie about, I'd like to know, go on, tell us!

NIKOLAI. Everything.

FYODOR IVANOVICH. I can't believe my ears, I'm speechless.

NIKOLAI. Don't pretend you don't.

TAISA PETROVNA. You just remember what sort of mess we got you out of.

NIKOLAI. What you got me out of? Away from Nadya, do you mean? Is that it?

TAISA PETROVNA. What's Nadya got to do with it? We've saved you from messing up your life, you just think.

NIKOLAI. There was nothing to save me from. That's almost funny.

FYODOR IVANOVICH. I mean, basically, you're still a nobody. You see nothing and know nothing, like a blind man.

NIKOLAI. You don't say.

TAISA PETROVNA. Without us you'd fall flat on your face.

NIKOLAI. Yes, well that's where you're mistaken. I'm not going down the tubes anywhere or anytime. Nobody's going to have me for breakfast, so get that straight. I'll stand on my own two feet. I'll do my own thing.

FYODOR IVANOVICH. Yes, rubbish – that's your thing. Rottenness. That's what destroys a man. Drunkenness and all that carry-on. And that's just where you're headed.

NIKOLAI. Well, that's where you're severely mistaken. I know what I'm doing, and I'm not giving it up. I'll hang onto it with both hands.

FYODOR IVANOVICH. Yes, and what do you want to hang onto that one for? She's nothing but an unstable mess! She'll blame God only knows what on you, and you're happy.

NIKOLAI. I don't know what you're talking about.

The doorbell rings. They all fall silent. FYODOR IVANOVICH *goes to open it and ushers in* ANNA STEPANOVNA.

FYODOR IVANOVICH (*brightly*). Well, it's our dear visitor dropped in to say hello again – look who's here. So what's new? Sit down, Stepanovna.

ANNA STEPANOVNA. I've only popped in for a second. Is Nina here?

FYODOR IVANOVICH. Nina!

NINA enters.

ANNA STEPANOVNA. Well, my God almighty, you should see what's going on downstairs. On the first floor!

FYODOR IVANOVICH. You see, I was right. She's brought some news again.

ANNA STEPANOVNA. Nina dear, Ivanov's got the whole flat full of people, he's brought them all in from the off-sales. There's two dockers there, and the old man from the first landing. That's as much as I saw. They've got the door wide open. They're watching hockey on TV, would you believe, and drinking and God knows what all. Granya's in hospital, of course, she came to see me this morning with Galka. By the way, where is Galka?

TAISA PETROVNA. She's here with us, and where are we going to put a baby?

ANNA STEPANOVNA. Well, that's right, I mean, Granya wanted to leave her with me. But why should I take her, when the house is full of her own folk? Isn't that right? I says to her, Granya, make use of your own people, let them do their bit for you. It's better when people help their own. It strengthens good relations – peace and friendship, you know? All the same, God knows, your own folk aren't your own these days, there's very few on good terms with their kin. They all want their own space, and that's not right. My Lyubochka and her husband, Volodya, are clearing off from us as well, they've built a co-operative flat. My son-in-law Volodya's a good lad, but that's because he's mean. We'll still come to you for meals, Mama, he says. They're putting by one hundred roubles a month each, saving up for a set of furniture. These days an unfurnished flat counts for nothing. Well, anyway, Nina, what are we going to do? How are we going to get rid of them?

NINA. Get rid of them? Why should I get rid of them? They're his guests. They came to see him. He is in his house, after all. Why should I get rid of them? I can't do that.

ANNA STEPANOVNA. That's all well and good, Nina dear, but these people are like children. He'll let them have something, and he'll take it back, and he won't even notice. Before he can blink, they'll be carrying out the furniture. Those kind of people have got just about enough brains to lift the first thing that comes to hand and sell it. That old man from the first landing, old Senya, sold his old dear's milk churn not long ago, for a rouble. I mean, they don't give a damn that it's somebody else's house. All you'll need to do is take them by the hand and bingo! They can just about make it round the corner to the off-licence, for a drink.

TAISA PETROVNA. Nina dear, you'd better go just the same and straighten things out. Kolya, go with her, make sure there's no carry-on.

NIKOLAI. Let her go herself, she can manage. Besides, what's somebody else's place got to do with me, who am I to them? No, when she needs to, Nina's not frightened to go anywhere, she's not shy.

FYODOR IVANOVICH. Count me out, is that it?

NIKOLAI. Yes, count me out. That's all you can remember about Nadya, that's imprinted on your mind. But she had a poisoned finger then, she couldn't wash the dishes.

TAISA PETROVNA. Anyway, Nina love, I think you and Anna Stepanovna can do what's necessary. Somebody's got to do it. On you go, on you go.

ANNA STEPANOVNA. Yes, it'll take two minutes to show the whole lot of them the door, and that's it. Let's be going.

NINA. In a minute, Auntie Anya.

Exits to the adjoining room, they are silent. FYODOR IVANOVICH *switches on the TV.* NINA *quickly emerges with the baby, and the string bag with its feeding bottles.*

Let's go, Auntie Anya. I've just got to fling on my jacket.

GRANNY. Where've you taken Galya? Where are you taking her? Can't I sit with her a while?

NINA. That's about the lot, I think. I don't think I've forgotten anything. I've left the clothes you gave me there. You can chuck out whatever you want. So – cheerio, I'm off. And you, Kolya, you should go to a hostel.

TAISA PETROVNA. What's all this, Nina? We're not letting you go anywhere.

FYODOR IVANOVICH. And he's not going to any hostel.

NINA. You should go, Kolya. You'll find it interesting.

NIKOLAI. Don't you worry.

NINA. Anyway, cheerio, I'll be seeing you.

FYODOR IVANOVICH. Look, you just throw those people out, and then come back, d'you hear? Don't pay any attention to him, he's off his head.

NINA *and* ANNA STEPANOVNA *exit.*

TAISA PETROVNA. Well, Kolya, you've done it now. God only knows what you'll do next. You did it, it was you that drove her out, nobody else. Have you no conscience? Or what have you got in place of a conscience, eh? How is Nina going to show her face in the street now?

NIKOLAI. Same as always. Anyway, whose business is it?

FYODOR IVANOVICH. It'll be Stepanovna's business, if nobody else's.

GRANNY. They'll be giving us all our blessings on the benches, you won't be able to go out.

NIKOLAI. So what's all the shame? I don't understand this. We lived together a while, and then split up, so what? I mean, you lived with somebody in your block. When you were younger.

TAISA PETROVNA. What!!!

NIKOLAI. I know you did, for a fact. Anyway, you had somebody before father. It's no big deal.

FYODOR IVANOVICH. You . . . snivelling creep!

NIKOLAI. Yes, and don't start a row. This isn't the time to discuss these things. Besides, it's no secret.

FYODOR IVANOVICH. And just who told you this filth?

NIKOLAI. Somebody told me, that's all.

TAISA PETROVNA. Klavdia, most likely.

NIKOLAI. Well, so you lived with him, so what? It doesn't matter.

FYODOR IVANOVICH. Go ahead, that's right, bad mouth your own mother.

NIKOLAI. No, I respect that. I really do. But you should have some respect as well. I did my thing, you did yours.

FYODOR IVANOVICH. Don't you dare compare yourself with us! My God, what a bloody cheek!

NIKOLAI. Yes, well, I'm a human being, same as you.

FYODOR IVANOVICH. That's just the point, you're not the same. You've no shame, but we have. Your parents have run themselves ragged for you their whole lives, and you're just going to dump God knows what kind of wife on them, with God knows whose child. Is that what you want, is that what you're bringing down on us?

TAISA PETROVNA (*gently*). You've just no idea about loyalty, Kolya son. I'm sorry, but as a man, you're nothing. That's almost three months now you've been living with Nina, and you've sent her packing. And what was that other one? You think that was true love? That was just a moment's passion. Made-up eyes, dyed curls, and that was it. But if you'd seen her without her eyes made-up, you'd have run a mile. And after the wedding you'll see precious little of that make-up. You'll see her bare face, the one God gave her.

FYODOR IVANOVICH. Besides which you've still got to find out whose the child is. You can't tell for seven years, so the peasants say, then you've just got to look and you can tell whether it's yours or not. And you're already making plans. It only takes a minute's work to make babies, you know. So what are you so bothered about?

TAISA PETROVNA. That's not love, Kolya, it's blind passion. It soon fades. You'll rub your eyes one minute, and there it is – just pure ignorance, no sort of culture. Just made-up eyes.

GRANNY. He should have seen her. She looked horrible enough without eye make-up. They were black enough without it.

TAISA PETROVNA. Anyway I'm sure he's already seen her. Have you seen that Nadya of yours, how she's looking these days?

NIKOLAI. No, I haven't.

GRANNY. Oh, she looks terrible. Her big eyes sunk right in, her lips black . . . she can scarcely put one foot in front of another.

TAISA PETROVNA. Well, she doesn't look quite *that* bad. All women feel a bit like that . . . There's nothing especially remarkable about it.

NIKOLAI. That's because she poisoned herself!

GRANNY. Poisoned herself!

NIKOLAI. Her flatmate at the hostel told me. I did go there, you know.

TAISA PETROVNA. Well, that's it. That means the baby'll be born a freak. That's the end.

NIKOLAI. They even had to send her to the hospital.

TAISA PETROVNA. And you know what that means. No arms, or two heads!

NIKOLAI. Well. So what?

TAISA PETROVNA. Oh, so you don't care what kind of child you have? You're so hard, you're like a stone.

FYODOR IVANOVICH. Kolya, you're taking on a whole mess of trouble for yourself, and you'll be stuck with it your whole life.

NIKOLAI. What are you all shouting for? I'm standing here looking at you, and thinking, what are they shouting about? I just don't feel like arguing with you. I mean, you're really weird!

TAISA PETROVNA. So it's all settled for you, is it?

NIKOLAI. As it happens, yes.

TAISA PETROVNA. Are you going to be bringing her back here again?

NIKOLAI (amused). Why should I do that?

FYODOR IVANOVICH. So what are you going to do then? Find a corner to rent some place? Well, let me tell you, if that's the case, I'm not your father any longer, I don't want to know you.

NIKOLAI. Does that mean you're not going to help? Oh, this is too much! (Starts laughing.)

FYODOR IVANOVICH. What are you laughing at? Do you want the belt?

NIKOLAI (laughing). This is really too much. The belt belongs in the past, Papa.

FYODOR IVANOVICH. We'll see about that.

Tries to take the belt out of his trousers, but his hands won't obey him.

TAISA PETROVNA (shouting). Making a fool of your father, who's brought you up, who's devoted his whole life to you, who helped you with your music lessons!!!

FYODOR IVANOVICH (*still struggling with his belt*). I'll show him, I'll give him music! I'll show him right this minute!

Whips out his belt and starts to beat NIKOLAI. GRANNY *rushes between them.* NIKOLAI *falls down helpless with laughter.*

GRANNY. Don't touch him! He's your only son – your only son! Leave him alone, I'm telling you, you rotten bugger!

She is shielding him with her body. FATHER *throws the belt into a corner, stands breathing heavily.* TAISA PETROVNA *sits, stunned,* FYODOR IVANOVICH *walks up and down, from corner to corner,* GRANNY *sits* NIKOLAI *on a chair, stands over him.*

FYODOR IVANOVICH. You think we've had an easy life, eh? You think there's never been any differences between me and your mother, eh? We've had the lot. I'm a normal man too, you know. I've got some life in me as well, some feelings, but there comes a time when you've got to call a halt, take stock of your life, and just switch off.

TAISA PETROVNA. Your father's not made out of wood either. He's made his mistakes. But he put them all behind him for your sake, for your sake alone. And he came back to me.

GRANNY. Yes, they got together again. God knows what for.

FYODOR IVANOVICH. I can't count the number of times I changed my mind at that time. But I decided, no. Absolutely not. I have a son growing up.

NIKOLAI. Yes, I know about that, Mama even went to your boss at work about you.

FYODOR IVANOVICH. All right, if you know that much, you can maybe appreciate it then. You're a grown man now, you can understand that nothing'll hold a man back, no boss, no parents, nothing. Same as yourself. But a man will listen to his conscience. You're doing your own thing, I can accept that. But we're Kozlovs, do you understand? Everything we do, we do for the family, for our own. Beating our brains in, your mother and me, and it's all for you. Who else would we do it for? We don't need it ourselves.

NIKOLAI. Fine. Now I want to say something. I just want to

bring a little light to bear on this matter. (*Pause.*) In fact, I share your point of view totally. I'm in complete agreement with you.

A pause.

TAISA PETROVNA. Well, that's fine. Bravo!

FYODOR IVANOVICH. What are you saying?

NIKOLAI. I'd nothing like that in mind at all, not remotely. But it was you, making my mind up *for* me, assuming that was what I was going to do. I'm not getting married at all, and that's that.

FYODOR IVANOVICH. How d'you mean?

NIKOLAI. Well, I would have gone after Nadya, but when her girlfriends there told me what the score was, I bailed out straightaway. Poisoned herself – I mean, that's heavy. That could stir up all kinds of trouble, that could mean a term in prison. You're better not to get mixed up in that kind of business. A suicide attempt, that's how it's described. She's something else, her, and so proud.

TAISA PETROVNA. Yes, well, she's not that extraordinary, not really. If you want to know the truth, I'll tell you. She came here to us, to wait for you.

NIKOLAI. So what did you do?

TAISA PETROVNA. We showed her out, after doing the decent thing.

NIKOLAI. You did the right thing then.

A pause. They have all come round now. GRANNY *sits down. Order is restored.*

FYODOR IVANOVICH. Anyway, why don't you get married to Nina?

NIKOLAI *shrugs.*

TAISA PETROVNA. He's said, it's too soon for him.

FYODOR IVANOVICH (*slowly*). Well, I'm really surprised at you. I never expected it.

NIKOLAI. Never expected what?

FYODOR IVANOVICH. This. I mean, there we were fighting,

and you're just watching and thinking, well, okay, let them get upset for a bit, and I'll just enjoy it. That's so funny – there they are beating their heads against the wall.

NIKOLAI. Well, you wouldn't let me get a word in.

FYODOR IVANOVICH. You managed to get your oar in when you wanted to.

TAISA PETROVNA. Actually, it wasn't very nice. You could have spared a thought for us. I mean we were only thinking of you.

FYODOR IVANOVICH. You're still young, Kolya, and look at the mess you've created already. You've almost driven two young women into an early grave.

NIKOLAI. Here we go again.

FYODOR IVANOVICH. I mean, did I bring you up like that?

NIKOLAI. Like a stuck record.

FYODOR IVANOVICH (*quieter*). The word 'conscience' means nothing to you.

NIKOLAI. Let's watch the hockey.

They sit watching TV.

FYODOR IVANOVICH. Mama, bring me a glass of water, to take my pill.

He is clutching his head. TAISA PETROVNA *goes out of the room, steps into the hall, and immediately returns closing the door behind her.*

TAISA PETROVNA. Nina's standing out there. In the hall. With Galka in her arms.

The whole of the following scene is experienced by the KOZLOVS *like a bad dream. They fall silent.* GRANNY *stands up.*

GRANNY (*exits to the side room*). I've had enough of this.

NIKOLAI. I told you – this pride thing, it's all rubbish. She's out to get me.

FYODOR IVANOVICH. Somebody loves you at least.

NIKOLAI. Lots of people love me.

GRANNY crosses the room, carrying a bundle.

GRANNY. I'll be seeing you. I'm off to Klavdia's.

TAISA PETROVNA. Mama, you can see what's going on. I'll take
you back when everything's settled.

GRANNY. Huh, I'm nothing to you – a trunk full of bedbugs.
You won't take me back.

TAISA PETROVNA. Don't get angry. I'll come for you.

GRANNY. Yes, meanwhile, I'll be seeing you. (*Exits.*)

Above the darkened stage a swing is illuminated. NINA *begins to swing
backwards and forwards on it, slowly and sadly, the baby in her arms.*

FYODOR IVANOVICH. For God's sake, get me some water.

TAISA PETROVNA. I can't. I can't move.

FYODOR IVANOVICH. You get it, Kolya.

NIKOLAI. Papa, it's the third period.

FYODOR IVANOVICH *goes out into the hall and immediately
returns.*

FYODOR IVANOVICH. That isn't Nina, that's Nadya standing
there with a baby. You get every damn thing mixed up. (*Sits
down, clutching his head.*)

TAISA PETROVNA. Granny must've let her in, surely? Why's the
baby there?

The door slowly opens, and a muffled figure enters holding a baby.

NADYA. I've come to stay here with you. It's nice here, you've
got two rooms. Furniture.

NIKOLAI. Have you really had a baby? It's got nothing to do
with me, nothing at all. I can prove it, I can count up.

NADYA. I've come to live with you. My baby's been born without
a head, I can't feed him.

TAISA PETROVNA. That's because you took poison.

NADYA *slowly and sadly also mounts the swing, where* NINA *is
already sitting.*

TAISA PETROVNA. Don't pay any attention to them. If you
don't pay them any attention they'll go away. (*Animatedly.*) Will
the hockey be over soon? I want to go to bed.

NIKOLAI. It's finished. (*Gets up, and stretches, but is forced to crouch
down as* NADYA *swings over his head.*)

TAISA PETROVNA *stands up and walks with her knees bent, while the swing spins out of control around her. The swing comes down lower.* FYODOR IVANOVICH *gets down on all fours and crawls into the kitchen.*

NIKOLAI *sinks his head deeper into the armchair and freezes into an almost horizontal position, drawing his legs up, ready to repel the flying swing.*

The curtain falls.

THREE GIRLS IN BLUE

Characters

IRA, a young woman, aged thirty to thirty-two.
SVETLANA, a young woman, aged thirty to thirty-two.
TATYANA, a young woman, aged twenty-seven to twenty-nine.
LEOKADIYA, SVETLANA's mother-in-law, aged seventy.
MARYA FILIPPOVNA, IRA's mother, aged fifty.
FYODOROVNA, the owner of the dacha, aged seventy-two.
PAVLIK, IRA's son, aged five.
ANTON, TATYANA's son, aged seven.
MAKSIM, SVETLANA's son, aged eight.
NIKOLAI IVANOVICH, a friend of Ira's, aged forty-four.
VALERA, TATYANA's husband, aged thirty.
A YOUNG MAN, aged twenty-four.

The action takes place at a dacha in the Moscow countryside, in Moscow, and at Koktebel, on the Black Sea coast.

ACT ONE

A child's voice is heard.

PAVLIK. Mama – what's two take away one? Mama, do you want me to tell you a story? Once upon a time there were two brothers. A middle-sized brother, a big brother, and a tiny little brother. A teeny-weeny little brother. One day he went to catch a fish. So he took his little pail and he caught a fish. And on the way home the fish began to croak, so he cut it up and made a fish-cake.

Scene One

The verandah of a dacha. There are two doors, one leading into the room, the other outside. IRA is preparing a lemon drink.

IRA. How are you feeling, Pavlik?

PAVLIK (*off-stage*). A little bit fine.

Enter FYODOROVNA. She is wearing an ancient dressing-gown and yellow wellingtons. Tucked under her arm is her cat, ELKA.

FYODOROVNA. You haven't seen her kitten, have you? The kitten's disappeared. You didn't take it in and feed it, by any chance?

IRA. No, I didn't. I already told you.

FYODOROVNA. That's three days now, and no kitten. Maybe your boys've killed it, eh? (*Peers into the room.*) What's he doing in bed in the middle of the day? Come on, it's time you were up! Why's he lying there with his face tripping him?

IRA. He's got a temperature of thirty-nine point three.

FYODOROVNA. Hm – caught a chill, I suppose. Well, it doesn't matter what you tell them, they'll sit in that river right to the bitter end. Then it's the mother that has to suffer. Boys will be boys. They were in at the raspberries yesterday. There's fruit-buds scattered all over the place. And my claw-hammer's lying on the doorstep, now who d'you think did that? They'll have killed that kitten. Not a sign of it since Thursday. That's three days. I thought she'd been keeping it herself, up in the loft. So I crawled up into the loft and there she is, searching for it, and miaowing. So where's your little baby gone, Elka, eh? 'Miaow!' No, it's not 'miaow', it's those bad boys. But I'm keeping an eye on them.

IRA. We weren't here on Thursday. We went into Moscow for a bath.

FYODOROVNA. So you gave him a good bath, and that's how he took ill. You gave him that bath, and he's down into the river the selfsame afternoon, washing his sins away! That's all he needed! Well, I didn't want you here in the first place, and I was right. Three boys on one plot, that's asking for trouble. They'll burn the house down next, like as not. They've lured that kitten away. They had their eye on him, I noticed that a while ago. They either tempted him down out the loft with a drop of milk, or else they trailed a bit of paper in front of him.

IRA. Look, Fyodorovna, I've told you already – we weren't here on Thursday.

FYODOROVNA. Maybe it was Jack again, next door's dog. He'll have killed him. That dog'll have torn him to pieces. It's hardly a dog, bloody great hulking brute. Maybe that kitten's been scared, your boys've been chasing him, and he's jumped into next door's. That's just what they'd do.

IRA. Maksim and Anton, possibly.

FYODOROVNA. Maybe it was, but so what? It won't get my kitten back. It was them did it, I'm certain. They were out to get him. Same as those Ruchkins, that's their place just opposite, they bought that Igor of theirs a rifle, now that was really clever of them. Anyway, to cut a long story short, Igor Ruchkin bought a rifle, and started shooting the stray dogs. And he killed my dog Yuzik. He was out in the field, harming nobody, my Yuzik. I didn't say a thing, just picked Yuzik up and buried him. What can you say to people like that? That

family's notorious, the whole of Romanovka knows about them.
Well anyway, a week went by, then another week, and their
Lenka Ruchkin got blind drunk, and drowned. Charged down
and dived head-first into the river, in two feet of water. I mean,
really – what can you expect?

IRA. Pavlik's got a temperature of thirty-nine, and those two,
Maksim and Anton, they're tearing around under his window,
kicking up a racket.

FYODOROVNA. And I've got balsam planted under that
window! I'll give them a piece of my mind! There's celandine
planted there as well.

IRA. I keep telling them: run about in your own half, boys. And
they just turn round and say: it's not your house, so there.

FYODOROVNA. Ah, well – you can get away with murder, if
you've enough cheek. You see that house up on the hill there?
That's where the Blums live. You see it – looks like a two-storey
shack. It's got all Blums in it. And God knows how many times
the downstairs Blums have been to court, to try and get Valka
Blum evicted. He occupied one room and boarded up the door
into the other half, after Isabella Blum died. Isabella Blum used
to work for me at the nursery school. She taught music. She
was a rotten music teacher, she could hardly put one foot in
front of the other. She'd turn up, gasping for breath, and cry
into her soup – she'd nothing to wipe her mouth with. She'd
say: 'I used to play concertos, Fydorovna, and now I can't even
play *The Sun Shines on the Motherland* without messing it up,
that's the truth.' I believed her all right, I'm not deaf. Anyway,
there was a famine that year, 1947 it was. And one of my
teachers started pilfering stuff, she couldn't stop herself. I had
to keep them all in line, I can tell you. She had a grown-up
daughter, a cripple since childhood, that was the reason. She
was taking apples off the kids, and bread – our nursery was a
kind of sanatorium for under-nourished kids, you see. So
anyway, there she is stuffing all these things into her stocking,
she keeps the stocking in her locker, and the cleaner says to
me: Yegorova's got apples, and bits of bread in her stocking. So
we confiscated it all, and filled Yegorova's stocking with wooden
blocks instead. And she went off home with this stocking. So
that was them, they had wooden blocks for tea. She quit the
next day. Isabella Blum was dying in hospital at that time. I
used to visit her, and it was me that buried her. Valka Blum

broke into her room right there and then, and moved in with his whole family, he still had his kids then, three of them. And nobody could prove a thing to the police. I mean, he was a Blum, they were all Blums. And to this very day Nina Osipovna Blum – she's a doctor – bears a grudge against him. Just the other day they were getting their pension, and Nina Osipovna shouts to him in the corridor, he'd been in to sign before her, and she says: 'Yes, that's just your style, you think you can get away with anything!' And he says: 'I'm seventy years of age, what do I want to get away with?' (*To the cat.*) Well, well, so what've you done with your little baby, eh? Usually she has her litter, the kittens are all accounted for, she starts bringing them out of the loft, and after a couple of days there's not a single one left! She loses all her kittens. It's that Jack, that's what. Back and forth, in and out, like the waves at the seashore. There were three cats here last winter, and by the summer there's only Elka left.

IRA. What do they mean, 'It's not your house?' So whose is it, then? Is it theirs, maybe? They've plonked themselves down here and they're paying nothing, but I've had to rent this place. And I'll inherit my share, the same as them. I've got rights to that half as well.

FYODOROVNA. Yes, Vera's still alive, she's still hanging on. And I told you it would be expensive here, but you agreed just the same.

IRA. I'd no other choice, in my position – I was at my wits' end.

FYODOROVNA. Well, you're always at your wits' end about something or other. But I've got my own heirs to think of. Little Seryozha needs new shoes. And d'you think *she'll* buy them? No chance. It's me, Granny on her pension, I'll have to buy them. Fifty a month, that's all I get, then there's the insurance, the electric. I bought him a heavy nap coat, black it was, and a yellow ski-suit, woollen gloves, a pair of imported trainers, made in Vietnam. I bought him a satchel, and gave her money towards his schoolbooks. And all that out of a pension, fifty roubles a month. Now it's hiking boots for Vadim, and a rabbit-fur hat for the winter. And d'you think she cares? No, she wants a Zhiguli car, that's what *she* wants. I had two thousand put away, money that Mama had left me, and one of my lodgers last year, Seryozha, his name was, he stole it. And I'm looking at him and thinking – what's he keep going up into the loft for? Then when they left, I looked behind the chimney-stack . . . fifteen years that money'd been lying there, and that was it gone – two thousand roubles!

IRA *has meanwhile taken her son a drink, returned, fetched a thermometer, gone in to take his temperature, re-entered, and wound an alarm-clock.*

FYODOROVNA. Actually, it was six thousand that Mama left us – myself, my sister and my brother. So that robber Seryozha got away with six thousand! I went to Moscow, to where he lived. And right there on the street, I see it – they've bought a car, a Zhiguli! With my six thousand! I wasn't going to say anything – I mean, what's the point, with people like that – I just said: 'Well, how'd you like my Zhiguli?' Anyway, Seryozha's father went red as a beetroot and started mumbling: 'I don't know what you're talking about, I don't know what you mean'. Then Seryozha himself turns up, rubbing his hands, grinning, afraid to look me in the eye. I mean, they'd bought that car with an old woman's savings. How am I supposed to account for that now, to my brother and sister? My brother was going to come over from Dorogomilovka, and fix up a toilet for me. And he'd promised to help my Vadim buy *his* Zhiguli: he's giving him seven thousand, and that included the money I'd been keeping for him, and now they've whipped that off me! My sister arrived, she brought meat with her, two whole kilos, and some bones for Yuzik, but by that time Yuzik'd been killed. She brought me material for a summer frock, she brought a jar of tomatoes, a big five-litre jar, and she brought ten packets of soup. And they're still lying there, untouched. And Yuzik's gone! Yuzik's mother was a genuine sheepdog, God knows what his father was. His mother the sheepdog, well, she'd got loose, she used to run about all over the place, I just let her. And then last spring that Igor Ruchkin shot her. She was running around, like I say, and last March one day I found her in the Pioneer camp, in one of the huts. I went there to get a door, I'm taking the door off its hinges – and there she is, this sheepdog, stretched out with five little puppies – real little butterballs, they were – lying beside her. Anyway, I started giving her bread to eat, I've got no teeth of my own now, so I had to soak the dry slices for her. And that Igor Ruchkin shot her. Three days after that I went and got one of the puppies for myself. They'd already started to crawl, crawling around blind, they were, starving. Well, that was Yuzik, that little pup.

The alarm-clock goes off, and FYODOROVNA *starts up. The cat springs out of her arms and runs off.* IRA *hurries into the adjoining room.*

FYODOROVNA. Ira, how much do you earn?

IRA. A hundred and twenty roubles.

FYODOROVNA. So how were you going to manage to pay me that kind of money for the dacha? I mean, two hundred and forty roubles?

IRA (*enters, holding the thermometer*). So – what d'you suggest?

FYODOROVNA. What?

IRA. What should I pay you?

FYODOROVNA (*hastily*). Oh, what we agreed, of course. I'm just wondering how you're going to find that kind of money.

IRA. I'm wondering that myself.

FYODOROVNA. Maybe I can get you a lodger, one of the people from the rest-home. There was a woman here, asking. She spends the whole day in the rest-home on the hill, she'd only be sleeping here. She's got some man or other up there in the rest-home.

IRA. I can manage without.

FYODOROVNA. Well, I could let her come. A bed on the verandah, she and her husband could sleep out here – twenty-four days, that'd be twenty-four roubles. Or maybe he's not her husband, I don't know.

IRA. Don't bother. I've only just managed to get rid of my mother, so I don't need that.

FYODOROVNA. Anyway, I told her I'd ask, but I couldn't guarantee anything. I mean, what's twenty-four roubles these days? She'd probably give more.

IRA. Huh – what's a hundred and twenty-four roubles these days!

FYODOROVNA. I told her that as well. I said: you can keep your thirty-six roubles, her divan won't hold two. For instance, who's to say you might not suddenly want to have a lie down, a bit of a kip in the afternoon, and there are kids around the place, she's got a kid, and those other two have kids as well. Three boys, it's like a whole platoon! That's what I told her. Then she asked me, she says: 'You couldn't find room on your plot for my beehives?' She's got three beehives.

IRA. God almighty.

FYODOROVNA. I mean, what's she want with beehives? First it's a bed, then it's her husband, next it's beehives! By the way, have you got a husband?

IRA. I did have. We're divorced.

FYODOROVNA. Is he paying alimony?

IRA. Yes. Twenty-five roubles.

FYODOROVNA. Huh. Well, that's how it goes. Valya Blum proposed to me a while back, he gets a pension as well, seventy-two roubles. His three kids are grown up, and he's only got two rooms, whereas I've got half a house. I mean, he's seventy, and I'm in my seventy-second year. And I can still manage to water my apple-trees, takes thirty buckets a day. It was Marya Vasilievna Blum that did the matchmaking. I wore my good tan shoes, put my teeth in, put on my dark-blue raincoat, and my dark-blue shawl with the roses on it – it was the only present my daughter-in-law ever gave me. It's hanging up in the wardrobe, I'll show you it. I mean, here I go about any old how, but I've got an astrakhan fur coat, it's been in my daughter-in-law's cupboard since God knows when, along with a pair of boots, sheepskin-lined. One of these days I'll drop in to see you in Moscow, like the Fairy Queen. I'm saving them all for better times. My daughter-in-law's mother's forever bragging, she'll say: 'So how much have you got in the bank now?' And I'll say: 'And how much have you got? Into five figures now, I suppose'. And she'll say: 'Well, there's no point trying to hide it – that's about right. And some'. She wears diamond earrings to her work, she's a cashier at 'Supersave'. A couple of Georgians came up to her once, and one says: 'Listen,' he says, 'my mother's desperate for a pair of earrings like yours'. So she got the message, next day she turns up, she's not wearing the earrings any more. I mean, they could've whipped them out by the roots! Anyway, what do I want with Valka Blum, I can't be bothered with men. That's more than I could take, running after a clapped-out old ruin. I didn't even like my husband.

Enter SVETLANA, TATYANA *and* VALERA.

VALERA. And here's the old trout herself, large as life! Hello, Granny!

FYODOROVNA (*not listening*). So what? I just didn't like him. The minute I'd had Vadim I went straight home to Mama. I don't even know where he's buried.

VALERA. Hey! Granny Alya!

FYODOROVNA. (*feebly*). Oh, no.

VALERA. So how's it going, me old love, eh? (*Sets down a bottle on the table.*)

FYODOROVNA *wipes the corners of her mouth with two fingers.*

FYODOROVNA. Well, you've got company, I see, I'd better be off.

SVETLANA (*she is as thin as a rake, but speaks in a deep bass voice*). No, stay. Come and join us, Fyodorovna. For a bit of company.

TATYANA (*giggling*). Stay, stay – you're not going anywhere, Granny.

VALERA (*pompously*). Please be seated.

FYODOROVNA. Well, that's why the priest got married – for a bit of company. I'll just take a spoonful, though – I'll go and get my little dessert spoon. (*Exits.*).

VALERA. Huh!

They all sit, VALERA *remains standing.* IRA *gets up and closes the door to the adjoining room.*

VALERA. We're relatives, even though we've not seen much of each other. Off the same litter, so to speak.

TATYANA (*giggles*). What a thing to say!

SVETLANA. What d'you mean, litter?

VALERA. Litter! (*Raises his clenched fist.*) Like when a sow gives birth to a whole bunch of piglets. That's called a litter. A litter of piglets, I saw it myself in the local rag, some place I was working once. There was this slogan: 'A thousand tons of litter from every sow!' I thought it was pigshit – I thought they were raising pigs for the manure! No kidding! They had to explain it to me. Litter. Leaner and fitter.

TATYANA. Really! There's people sitting here and you're going on about manure! (*Giggles.*)

IRA *eventually gets up from her seat, sets out the cups and starts slicing the bread.*

SVETLANA. Oh, Tanya! We clean forgot. We've got some cheese. Mine's wrapped in cellophane, yours is in paper.

TATYANA (*giggles*). All right, get it then!

SVETLANA *hurries out.* IRA *exits to the adjoining room and closes the door firmly behind her.* TATYANA *addresses* VALERA.

What did you take my purse again for?

VALERA. Well, I had to get a bottle, hadn't I.

TATYANA. I'm not keeping you in food and drink, you know.

VALERA. Once a mug, always a mug.

TATYANA. Yes, well, *I'm* no mug, and don't you think it.

VALERA. Look, you can only sort these things out over a bottle.

TATYANA. Yes, and supposing she won't agree.

VALERA. Oh, give it a rest! You can fix anything with a bottle. And anyway, it was you that asked me to come, so here I am, I've arrived. So I've run out for a bottle, so what? It's for your sakes, you silly buggers.

TATYANA. But what did you take my purse for, eh? Creep!.

VALERA. Look, have you any idea what it's like for a man to be in debt the whole time?

TATYANA. I've had eight years of your debts and your bloody alimony payments. All your wheeling and dealing.

VALERA. So how am I supposed to get by on a hundred and thirty a month, less alimony, thirty-five roubles?

TATYANA. You've only yourself to blame, it was your own drinking that caused the smash.

VALERA (*enraged, hisses*). You just watch it!

VALERA. And you've had kids and all!

VALERA. Who's had kids? Me?

TATYANA. Yes, you, who d'you think? Like it says in the Bible, you've begat, Isaac begat Jacob.

VALERA. Now you listen to me! Every time a baby's born, a part of a man dies, right? It's the same every time. And no man wants that. There's even a book about it – it's called *You Only Live Twice*. You get it? *Compris?*

TATYANA. What are you talking all this crap for? Bloody waste of time coming here.

VALERA. Yes, right, *certainement*. (*Laughs.*)

IRA *emerges carrying a chamber-pot, and* TATYANA *giggles.*

IRA. I'll be back in a minute.

VALERA. You can empty it in our toilet, feel free.

IRA *exits.*

TATYANA. It's always the same – the minute you want something out the shops, vodka or something, it's my purse that gets snatched.

VALERA. Here we go again – harping on about her bloody money!

TATYANA. Why don't I just sue you for alimony myself?

VALERA. Huh! And the best of luck! How much d'you think you'd fall heir to, eh? Bugger all! Yes, I've worked it out, you know. I get a hundred and forty-three roubles, so it's 33 per cent of that. Three into a hundred and forty-three goes four times, carry two . . . that's forty-seven roubles, and a couple of kopecks.

TATYANA. Forty-seven roubles, sixty-six kopecks, actually.

VALERA (*spitefully*). Yes, and then divide that by two, okay? Twenty-three roubles and a few coppers. And that's *monthly*! I'm giving you more than that now!

TATYANA. Yes, twenty-five.

VALERA. Right, so.

TATYANA. Look, I'm sick telling you: you eat and sleep here, somebody's got to pay for the flat, and the electricity!

VALERA. What, are you going to charge me for sleeping next? Have I got to pay for it, eh?

A pause.

TATYANA (*blinking*). And what about your washing? I mean, I've got to send that out to the laundry.

VALERA (*cheerfully*). Okay, a package deal, including nights – I'll give you a rouble a throw! (*Uncorks the bottle.*)

They pour out the vodka, clink cups, and drink. TATYANA *giggles and stretches.* SVETLANA *enters with the cheese.*

SVETLANA. My old Leokadiya's still sitting up in there. She's scared in case it rains, I'm sure. She thinks if she lies down she'll choke.

VALERA *offers to pour* SVETLANA *a drink. She at first covers her cup with her hand, then gives in.* TATYANA *giggles.* SVETLANA *drinks.*

TATYANA. That roof's bloody well full of holes. (*She pronounces 'bloody' like 'blurry'.*) It's a bloody nightmare, one winter and it's like a sieve.

SVETLANA (*wipes her mouth with her hand and sniffs the cheese*). Yes, well, it was you that let the house get into this state. Unfit for habitation. It's just rotting away, and it's all your fault.

TATYANA. Now you look! On the contrary, if it wasn't for us this place would be a pile of rubble! Any house'll start to rot if nobody's in charge of it. We've kept it in one piece. Valera's at it hammer and tongs, he's carried up bucketfuls of earth onto that roof.

SVETLANA. Yes, maybe so, but it was you that let it get like that.

TATYANA. No we didn't. We just happened to bloody live here, that's all. And if you were living in somebody else's house, well, you'd think twice about it and all. That roof'll take four hundred to fix. We'd be better renting something in the village – we'd get two summers' worth out of that. Four hundred roubles! (*She giggles.*)

SVETLANA. Well, you were using it, weren't you? So you should pay.

TATYANA. Yes, and you're using it now, so *you* pay!

SVETLANA. It was you that made the holes in it.

TATYANA. We weren't dancing on it, you know. It's showing its age, that's all. I mean, if you'd been living here, would you have got it fixed?

VALERA. Here? Not bloody likely.

TATYANA. You wouldn't fix somebody else's roof, I'm sure.

SVETLANA. My old Leokadiya's sitting in there, hunched up under an umbrella, waiting for the flood.

VALERA. Is she your mother, this old creature?

SVETLANA. She's my mother-in-law, a legacy from my husband. That's her son. He died, and she was living with us at the time, so she stayed on for old time's sake. I basically work night-shifts anyway, so it means Maksim isn't left on his own. I can't pick and choose with relatives in my situation.

VALERA. So who's Maksim?

TATYANA. Maksim's her son, of course.

VALERA. Oh yes, the young lad. That's the one that was fighting with ours earlier on?

TATYANA. I work days, she works nights. When she's got to work at weekends I have to watch the boys . . . it's like hard labour.

VALERA. Anyway, it's good that Anton has somebody to play with here. Otherwise those Ruchkins would be taking over, raising hell . . . Hey, have you heard the latest? What is it that's got whiskers and stripes?

SVETLANA. I don't know.

VALERA. Your mattress!

TATYANA *giggles, covering her mouth, embarrassed.*

SVETLANA. They're nothing but hooligans, them.

VALERA. And the Blums are the same, little buggers, the ones upstairs, anyway. Seven or eight year's old and they're smoking already.

SVETLANA. Well, I never thought you two would con me into coming to a dump like this.

TATYANA. Well, I get on okay here . . . It could be worse. I mean, you just try and rent a dacha here. They're all owned by the Planning Authority. And you've got the river, the woods, the airport. Plus, you're getting it for free.

VALERA. Same as the Planners!

SVETLANA. Yes, and the bloody roof leaks! Suppose it rains the whole summer?

VALERA. So? You'll get the rain for free as well!

TATYANA. No, she's right enough, Valera – there's no getting away from it, we'll just have to put up some roofing felt.

VALERA. Roofing felt my arse! Hey, I'm allergic to manual work. Yes, and brainwork makes me throw up.

TATYANA. Well, we could at least thatch it, cover it with straw.

VALERA. So where are you going to get straw this time of year, idiot? The beginning of the summer? It's all been used for fodder.

SVETLANA. And what are we supposed to do with the kids?

VALERA. Panel-beaters, that's the thing – that's *real* money. They're the guys that stick your Zhiguli back together again, after it's had an overhaul. Yes, I think I'll go and be a panel-beater.

TATYANA. Oh yes, I'm sure they're just waiting for your services.

VALERA. Watch it, you.

TATYANA. I mean, what kind of husband are you, eh, what sort of man? The rain's coming in, and your own son's got bronchial asthma, for Chrissakes!

VALERA. Yes, well, he needed toughening up, but you wouldn't have it!

Two boys, ANTON *and* MAKSIM, *appear in the doorway.*

MAKSIM. Auntie Ira's locked herself in our toilet!

VALERA. Look, clear off, you kids, go and play! Don't keep hanging around here. Go climb a tree. Hey, your wounded comrade's out there somewhere. Up a tree. So on you go, piss off, that's an order.

The boys exchange glances and disappear.

You see? Kids love me. And dogs. And drunks, by the way.

TATYANA. Yes, they can spot one of their own a mile off.

VALERA. I'll toughen them up, I'll come down regularly, and train them.

TATYANA (*ironically*). That'll be right.

SVETLANA. I don't know how you conned me into this. I mean, it's bad enough I've got to crawl round after your Anton: Anton, pet, it's dinner-time, Anton, sweetheart, wash your hands. He's got me running around like a blue-arsed fly, chasing after him.

TATYANA. Well, don't bother. He'll come soon enough when he's hungry.

SVETLANA. Oh, terrific, I'm at his beck and call, re-heating his dinner. I mean, what am I here, the bloody skivvy?

TATYANA. He can heat it up himself, he's not a baby. He does it at home. He gets home from school, he's got his key round his neck, and he makes his own dinner.

SVETLANA. Yes, well, I'm not letting him near the gas-cooker. It's bad enough for grown-ups, it can blow up in your face, and it means kids start fooling around with matches. Definitely not. Anyway, you can do what you like, but I'm not staying here with no roof.

VALERA. Look, hold on, hold on. Hey, Svetlana, let's have another drink – let's get acquainted, eh? (*Affectedly.*) My name's Valera, as I believe you've known for some time. (*He takes her hand, gives it a squeeze.*) You're going to find me a pretty handy guy, I can feel it in my bones. We just need to get our hands on some roofing material.

They pour out more vodka and drink. IRA *enters.*

VALERA. Hey, Ira – too good for us, eh? You want to watch that.

TATYANA. At last! How long, oh Lord, how long! Come on, Ira, come over, do sit down.

SVETLANA. We're cousins, for God's sakes. Come on, let's drink to our meeting.

IRA. No, I'm sorry, I can't . . . My little boy's ill.

TATYANA. I mean, the three of us . . . we're . . . (*Hesitates.*) . . . second cousins.

VALERA. You've got to take a drink, Ira – keep you from falling ill.

SVETLANA. We had the same great-grandmother, and the same great-grandfather.

IRA. I can't remember that far back. I had a step-grandfather called Filipp Nikolaevich.

TATYANA. I can't remember any of mine. They all stayed behind in the village.

VALERA. It's a shame you can't remember. We could've gone to your village and stayed with them. For free.

TATYANA. Yes, well, you'd need to shower them with presents, cast-offs and stuff. Rucksacks-full, huge bundles.

VALERA. Oh, come off it – nobody wants dead relatives' cast-offs these days.

TATYANA. No, these days you need to take little Crimplene suits for their kids.

IRA. I've got my husband's surname. But my maiden name was Chentseva.

SVETLANA. My married name's Vygolovskaya. Papa's surname was Sysoev. Mama's was Katagoshcheva.

IRA. My father's name was Chentsev, but he's been dead for ages. Mama took my stepfather's name – Schilling.

VALERA. What's that, English?

IRA. No, he was one of those Russified Germans.

TATYANA. Well, my mama and papa had the same surname – Kuznetsov, both of them. So both sets of grandparents were Kuznetsovs as well!

VALERA. Yes, namesakes, please note – they weren't related. Now *my* surname – I'll spell it out if you like – is Kozlos Brodov, Kozlos! (*Pause.*) Brodov.

SVETLANA. What, with a hyphen?

VALERA. No. What for?

TATYANA. And mine's Kuznetsova!

VALERA. But Anton's a Kozlosbrodov!

TATYANA. Yes, well, we'll change it, don't worry. We'll slip somebody a tenner when the time's ripe and get it changed.

VALERA. You just mind your mouth! So . . . anyway . . . I vote we propose a toast in honour of patronymics – I don't mean all the biological relatives, just present company!

Enter FYODOROVNA *in a dark blue silk raincoat, a dark blue shawl with a rose pattern, light tan shoes, and a gleaming set of false teeth. She is holding a dessert spoon.*

FYODOROVNA. Hello, how nice to see you. Look, I've pulled up some greens here. Just what's come up in the garden, and rinsed it in the rain-barrel. So eat up, it's full of vitamins! A watercress salad.

VALERA. And this is for you, m'dear. (*Pours some vodka into her spoon.*) Panteleimonovna, isn't it?

FYODOROVNA (*drinks, pulls a face, and starts munching her salad*). No, no – I'm Fyodorovna. It was my husband – his middle name was Panteleimonovich. His father was a well-to-do merchant, he owned a mill and two bakeries. There were twelve of them in that family: Vladimir, that was my husband, then Anna, Dmitry, Ivan, Nadyezhda, Vera, Lyubov, and their mother Sophie, I can't remember the rest. But it was their father, he was Panteleimon, Vera Panteleimonovna's the only one still living, down in Drezna, in an old folks' home, God bless her. So you're their grandchildren, sort of. I don't really remember any of them myself. Vladimir was a pilot, but I couldn't tell you where he's buried. We got divorced. Your mama would remember some of them, Ira.

VALERA. Yes, well, you're all phoney grandchildren, that's what I say. I suppose this Vera had kids of her own, then?

FYODOROVNA. Yes, and outlived the lot of them. As to where *their* kids are, I haven't a clue.

SVETLANA. Were there a lot of kids?

FYODOROVNA. Well, there's you three off three of them, but if there's any more off the other nine, then God knows where they're hanging out now.

VALERA. So, in fact – this house doesn't belong to anybody!

SVETLANA. There could be another twenty grandchildren.

FYODOROVNA. No. It was one child each then, even for us. Same as yourselves. I had Vadim, then went home to Mama. I just happened to wind up with a husband, I didn't love him. And when Vadim was born, I didn't take much care of him either. I remember the next-door neighbours' house caught fire, and I had to grab Vadim up in the middle of the night, wrap him in a blanket, and run out and lay him on the ground, then I went off to fetch buckets of water. By the morning the whole place was burnt down, our fence as well, but it didn't reach the house. Anyway, it suddenly struck me – where the hell's our Vadim? And he'd been lying there on the ground all night. I tell you, I was a real live wire in those days! Vadim's got his own boy now, Seryozha, a clever little lad.

VALERA. So, do you see much of them, Granny?

FYODOROVNA. Them? No, not at all. There used to be a big difference in kids' ages in the old days. The oldest could be maybe sixty, say, and the youngest forty. For example, you could have another kid in fifteen years' time.

VALERA. Over my dead body!.

SVETLANA. I wouldn't want to hang a stepfather round a kid's neck, frankly.

IRA. You have enough trouble with one, before they're up on their feet. You just keep praying you'll live to see it!

VALERA. Yes, well, you want to toughen him up. Cold water every morning, ears, neck, and face. That's what I've been doing with Anton.

TATYANA. Who's going to do that in the winter, you silly bugger?

VALERA. If it wasn't for Tatyana I'd have him toughened up by now, I can tell you. Out in the cold. The windows open. Cold showers . . .

SVETLANA. Well, you'll have all these facilities here now. It's cold showers all right. I'm not on duty today, so Tanya and I can cover everything up with plastic tablecloths, or polythene sheeting. You can't get a bloody thing dry anywhere here . . . there's no use talking. Thanks a bunch, Tatyana, you're a real pet, inviting me down here to be an unpaid babysitter for your Anton, while you're taking it easy at work, yes, and with no bloody roof over our heads! Besides which, I've got exactly the same right as you to live in this dacha – I don't need your permission.

VALERA. Hey, hey – I'm pouring another round! Last orders, folks! (*Pours a round of drinks.*)

IRA *exits to the adjoining room.*

VALERA. By the way, Fyodorovna – you haven't any of that medicine left? You know, that stuff you make with marigolds.

FYODOROVNA (*guardedly*). What d'you want it for?

VALERA. A sore throat.

FYODOROVNA. No, Valera love, I use a gargle made with burdock. D'you want me to pick you some?

VALERA. No, what about that lemon extract they give the cosmonauts – whatsitsname?

FYODOROVNA. No, Valera. What's it for anyway?

VALERA. It's for toning up your metabolism. Haven't you got any kind of infusion?

FYODOROVNA. You mean spirit-based?

VALERA. Yes, that's it.

FYODOROVNA. As a matter of fact I have, but it wouldn't do you. Tincture of iodine.

VALERA. What about something a bit sweeter?

FYODOROVNA. I'll see what I can find. (*Exits.*)

IRA (*enters, decisively*). Well, I don't care what you think, but I've got a right to live in that half of the house as well. My mother's got all sorts of documents, so don't think you can just do what you like. Just because you plonked yourself down here first, I'm supposed to pay two hundred and forty a month in rent?

SVETLANA (*hastily*). Nobody said anything of the kind. We'll swop rooms, then.

TATYANA. We'll move in here, and you can go next door – no problem!

VALERA. You see? What did I tell you? You can fix anything over a bottle. And that's everybody happy.

IRA (*agitated*). Fyodorovna actually phoned my mother up, and told her there was nobody living in that half of the house, and that the place was going to rack and ruin with nobody looking after it. So I came down here, scrubbed the whole place out, white-painted all the window-frames, washed the windows . . . I turn up here a week later with all my stuff, I've got my fridge, the kids in a hired van, and lo and behold – you're occupying the rooms I've just cleaned! Bloody wonderful! (*She slumps down, her head sagging, exhausted.*)

VALERA. Well, there's no use crying over spilt milk. It's the law of the jungle!

IRA. You've made a mug of me.

VALERA. Stupid women. Bloody idiots. They don't know when they're well off. Right, come on, look lively! Clean that place up and give it back to Ira. They haven't made that much of a mess. You move in over there, and I'll get a barrow to cart your fridge across.

IRA. No. I haven't the energy to move now. I suggest we stay put, but we've all got the same rights. We split the rent, and you chip in eighty roubles each. Otherwise you're living rent-free in my bit of the house.

VALERA. Okay, fine. We chip in eighty roubles each, then what happens? What's in it for us?

IRA. I mean, why should I have to pay, when you're all staying here?

VALERA. Right, suppose we *do* pay? What's the score then?

IRA. I stay where I am, you stay there.

SVETLANA. No, I don't think you quite get it. We'll just go ahead and pay the whole lot, and move in here.

IRA. Oh, that's terrific. Me and a sick child and no roof over our heads?

TATYANA. Right, okay – how about this? We'll fix the roof, Valera can fix it, and meantime you let our kids and old Granny in under *your* roof.

IRA. What, on the verandah?

SVETLANA. No, inside. In the room. It's cold out here.

IRA. And what about us? Pavlik's got a temperature of thirty-nine point six!

SVETLANA. So what do we always do in these cases? I mean us professionals? We isolate them, put up some sort of screen, blankets, whatever. We wash the walls with chloride of lime.

IRA. It's not as if it was even raining.

TATYANA. It'll come down any minute, you just watch.

SVETLANA. We'll put up screens round him. The main thing now is to keep him warm. It'll be warmer with us in the room.

IRA. And we'll split the expenses three ways. Eighty apiece.

TATYANA. But there's the roof to be mended – you've just said yourself – four hundred roubles. You're a hard woman, Ira, I don't understand you. You pay eighty, and we've to pay two hundred and eighty each?

VALERA. Other people would take six hundred for that job. But because it's for ourselves . . .

IRA. Wait, hold on, I don't get it . . . You pay two hundred each . . . But I'm paying two hundred and forty, plus I'm having *how* many people in that one room?

SVETLANA. Look, the roof's common property. It's yours as well!

IRA. How come it's mine?

VALERA. This is getting us nowhere. Hey, come on, girls, let's chip in a rouble each, before the off-sales closes! Me and Tatyana are already down four roubles here for this stuff.

IRA. I haven't got any money. Besides which, you don't even let me use your loo!

VALERA. Because you're too stuck up, Ira. You should be more sociable.

TATYANA. Valera built that toilet with his own hands eight years ago. I mean, you're living in the landlady's half, it's up to her to provide you with one.

SVETLANA. What a bloody stupid conversation. Use it if you like. Just watch you don't fall down the hole.

IRA. Fyodorovna hasn't got a loo herself. She says: 'just use the hen-house'. And there's a vicious cockerel in there. . .

VALERA. Eh? You mean old Vaska? Yeh, that one'll peck your arse all right.

IRA. Yes, well, I'm frightened of him. (*Sits down, dejected.*)

VALERA. Hey, come on girls, we're wasting time here. The off-sales'll be closed.

SVETLANA. Anyway, we've just got to get on with it.

IRA. Oh, yes? So for a start your boys can just beat up my Pavlik, can they? I mean, they held him down in the water, and took off his pants. That's what made him ill.

SVETLANA. Huh, I'll get them in here right now, and we'll just find out who took whose pants off. Right this bloody minute! (*Marches out, her face flushed with anger.*)

FYODOROVNA (*enters, holding a medicine bottle*). Here we are, here's something sweet, Valera, like you asked for.

VALERA (*takes the bottle*). Nice! A hundred and fifty grammes at least!

FYODOROVNA. It's brewed from poison-ivy root. (*Offers him her dessert spoon.*)

VALERA (*affectedly*). Thank you. Mm – sodium benzoate. Sodium hydrocarbonate. It's all full of chemicals nowadays. Ammonia and aniseed drops. I know what the aniseed's like. Cough mixture. What's the use of that? It's like sugar syrup. The hell with it.

FYODOROVNA *is still holding her spoon.*

VALERA. Wait, hold on. (*Sniffs the bottle.*) What sort of shit's this? It's got no smell. Some mysterious potion, eh? Ah, what the hell, here goes nothing! (*Drinks it down straight from the bottle.*)

TATYANA. My God! You're a bottomless pit.

VALERA (*startled*). Ugh! What in God's name was that!

FYODOROVNA. It's harmless. Even kids can take it. You've just drunk too much, that's all. It says on the bottle – one dessert spoonful.

She snatches the bottle back from VALERA *and pours out the remains into her dessert spoon.*

See, this is how you should take it.

Drinks it down with relish, wipes her mouth with her hand.

VALERA (*groans*). Ugh! It's revolting! Ugh!

FYODOROVNA. It'll do you good. You'll be coughing and spitting away in no time.

VALERA. What the hell for?

FYODOROVNA. It's an expectorant, that's what for . . .

VALERA. Eh? Bloody hell! Shit! (*Rushes out through the door.*)

FYODOROVNA. Huh – my entire stock, right down him!

TATYANA. Where's he buggered off to with my purse? He'll spend my last two roubles.

FYODOROVNA *exits to see what is the matter with* VALERA.

IRA. Oh, Tanya, I don't know what to do, I'm just so lonely. I feel like I'm nobody. Nobody needs me. When you came here, I thought we'd make it up between us, I mean, we're supposed to be cousins.

TATYANA. And what about you?

IRA. I'm on my own. I've never had a brother or a sister. All I've got's my little son.

TATYANA. You've got your mother.

IRA. Mama? Huh, some mother *she* is.

TATYANA. Well, I tell you, if I had my mother down here, I'd soon get shot of *that* idle creep. (*Nods towards the door.*) When she comes to see me from Sakhalin it's like one long holiday, everything's nice and cosy, just like home again. They got posted to Sakhalin after she remarried, of course.

IRA. Oh God, I wish, I wish, I wish it was like that for me!

TATYANA. Mama . . . That's the first word a human being speaks, and the last.

IRA. Yes, well, my mother hates me. She just doesn't love me.

TATYANA. Oh, cut it out, Ira. I don't like that kind of talk. You must be some daughter, if that's the case. I mean, your mother's your mother. Anyway, I've got your number, I know what sort you are – you're just waiting to sink your claws into people.

IRA. So maybe I need claws, just to hang on.

TATYANA. Anyway, you needn't come whining to me. A mother brings forth in pain, right? She has to raise us, feed us – what more do you want? She washes for us. Everything that we do now. Plus we go out to work as well. As if it would ever enter my head to hate my little Anton! Dear God, I could kiss every little toe on his feet! I'd kill for him, I really would!

IRA. And I'd kill for my Pavlik as well. So you can understand what it's like when somebody tries to drown your son.

TATYANA. Oh, give over. Cut the melodrama.

IRA. What if it was your Anton under the water, eh?

Both women are now furiously angry.

TATYANA. Oh, for God's sake, who told you that rubbish? It was his own bloody fault, most likely. Stayed in the water until he was blue with cold, then made the whole thing up.

IRA. Two against one.

TATYANA. He's like an old man, that kid of yours, he's not a real boy. Reading all the time. Regular little bloody bookworm! Well, you wait, it's his kind that always get picked on, you'll see.

IRA. Okay, that's enough. You piss off out of here. Bitch.

TATYANA (*remains seated, dejected*). It's going to rain, that's all we bloody need. Anton's coming up for eight. He's got to have a summer in the fresh air. I mean, it's just his bad luck, he was sick the whole winter. Caught pneumonia. That stupid bugger pouring cold water over him – I'd like to kill him! Anton was ill for two months, I had to take two months' unpaid leave. I didn't put him in hospital – my mother phoned up: 'Don't put him in hospital whatever you do', she says. She lost her first kid, a boy, in hospital, they just let him drop. He'd have been my elder brother. Ira, for God's sake, let Anton sleep in your room.

IRA. Huh, you wouldn't let me into yours when I asked you, when I was crying and everything.

TATYANA. But he's just a kid, Ira – a baby!

SVETLANA *marches in, eyes ablaze.*

SVETLANA. So, now I've got the whole story! That Pavlik of yours, it turns out, bit my Maksim on the shoulder! And that's an infected wound! A septic laceration! Your Pavlik's going straight to a remand home, I'll damn well see to it! And Maksim didn't say a word to me about it, he wouldn't, he was too scared. Because he knows how I'll react! Maksim's been delicate ever since his father died! He used to pass blood in his motions, diarrhoea! They even checked his stool for dysentery! I'm not whining about it, he's just got bowel problems. And

I'm run ragged the whole time, that's why I switched to the night-shift. And now all this bloody carry-on!

TATYANA. Look, that Maksim of yours'll heal up in no time, like a dog. My God, I mean, he beat my Anton's head off a rock yesterday, did you know that? I get home at night, and there's this bruise on his forehead. Eh? D'you want to pack your little Maxie off to a remand home? You didn't take a sample of *his* saliva, did you?

SVETLANA (*in despair*). I treated his wound – it was an accident, I mean, they're just kids.

TATYANA. Oh, of course, you're our senior nursing officer.

SVETLANA. And incidentally, Maksim said it wasn't him that held Pavlik under the water, it was Anton! Maksim was standing on the bank!

TATYANA. Yes, giving the orders!

FYODOROVNA *enters with her cat. She is now in her everyday shabby clothes.*

FYODOROVNA. She's lost her kitten, you haven't seen her kitten? She keeps yowling, you can't get any peace. I'm trying to sleep, and I've got to put up with that.

TATYANA. And Pavlik bit Maxie, because Maxie shouted at him: 'We're not letting your mother come here any more, she's not to come here!' That's why Pavlik bit him, and quite right, too. I'd bite somebody for *my* mother.

A pause.

FYODOROVNA. Her milk's started to come, you see. That's why she's yowling. Or maybe she wants a tom, eh? 'Miaow!'

IRA. Svetlana, you wouldn't take a look at Pavlik, would you? I'm not happy about him at all.

SVETLANA. I'm sure it's nothing, nothing drastic, anyway, I'll have a look. (*Her whole demeanour is transformed.*)

IRA. Here's a fresh towel! And there's a wash-hand basin just behind the door. (*Takes down the towel from a clothes-line.*)

SVETLANA *exits.*

FYODOROVNA. Elka! Here, kitty, kitty, Elka! (*Looks under the table.*)

TATYANA *also has a look under the table.* IRA *waits for*
SVETLANA, *her cheeks flushed with worry.* FYODOROVNA *is clearly
reluctant to leave.*

TATYANA. Look, Fyodorovna, I've got some soup left over from
yesterday. The boys didn't finish it. Most likely Anton just
toyed with it, playing with his spoon, same as usual. I'm going
to cook today anyway, fresh stuff, with some bones. So I can
give you half a pot-full, if you like.

FYODOROVNA (*thinks it over*). I'll take some, it'll do the cat. I'll
fetch a bowl.

TATYANA. What d'you mean the cat, for God's sake! I made it
for the kids. That cat of yours isn't the queen, you know! (*They
exit.*)

SVETLANA *enters, holding out her hands.* IRA *rushes towards her with
a towel,* SVETLANA *is in her white gown, with a stethoscope round her
neck.*

IRA. Here you are, take this. (*They exit.*)

PAVLIK's VOICE (*off-stage*). . . . And then the octopus started to
wave its legs and said, 'Oh, let me out of here, it's too hot!' So
he let the octopus go, and it flew away. It swam around for a
bit, and it flew through the air for a bit, and then they caught it
up in the sky . . .

*For a while the verandah is deserted. Then there is a knock on the outside
door, and* NIKOLAI IVANOVICH *enters, carrying a holdall and a
telescopic umbrella. He is wearing a very expensive woollen tracksuit, with
a white plastic zip, and white piping – what successful Soviet man wears
these days instead of pyjamas.*

NIKOLAI IVANOVICH. Have I come to the right place?

No one answers. Enter SVETLANA *and* IRA.

SVETLANA. Well, anyway, he's got an acute respiratory infection.
It's going the rounds, all the kids are getting it. His
temperature'll remain high a few days, and you'll have to give
him sulfadimetoxin, right? One tablet now, another whole
tablet in the morning, and then a half-tablet twice daily. That's
a strong dose to begin with, and you'll need to watch him, he'll
have a high fever. Once his temperature starts to fall, keep an
eye on him, change his clothes frequently and make sure he's
dry.

IRA. I haven't got any sulfadimetoxin. What'll I do?.

SVETLANA. Well, I haven't any.

IRA. Svetlana, what'll I do? Haven't you anything else?

SVETLANA (*pompously*). Personally, I only use herbal medicine
myself. And all I've got is some lime flowers, honey and lemon.
I'll give you that if you like. Between you and me, quite frankly,
I don't hold with drugs. Except maybe in special cases.

IRA. So what am I going to do?.

NIKOLAI IVANOVICH. Excuse me? I'm sorry to butt in, but
there's an excellent English remedy for 'flu called Keating's . . .
(*Stammering a little.*) no, Beeching's Powder. That'll have him on
his feet in three days. I caught 'flu in London, the hotel put me
onto this stuff, and I brought back a supply.

SVETLANA. No, I couldn't recommend anything like that. I've
no knowledge . . . (*In her professional manner.*) The important
thing – are you listening? – is to reduce his fever, encourage
him to sweat, give him some lemon juice. Do you have a
lemon?

IRA. Yes, I have.

SVETLANA. And I'll bring you some lime flowers. The new
flowers'll soon be out, but these are from last year. (*Exits.*)

IRA. Anyway, I have got a lemon.

NIKOLAI IVANOVICH. So, I've tracked you down at last. What's
the matter? Why weren't you at the Orient at eleven this
morning, eh? It was only thanks to the postman I found you at
all. Have you read the papers yet?

IRA. No, why?

NIKOLAI IVANOVICH (*obviously hinting at some circumstance or
other*). Something interesting in the *Weekly News* maybe?

IRA. How should I know? (*She is embarrassed, doesn't look at
NIKOLAI IVANOVICH as she begins preparing the lemon drink.*)

NIKOLAI IVANOVICH. Look, I've been chasing around all over
the place! My car's in for a minor repair. That's okay, I'm fit
enough. But this morning I ran practically the whole way to
meet you – and my *Weekly News* wasn't there! My mother-in-law
kicked up hell, literally, you've no idea, because I'd given it to
you. She binds them all together specially, she saves them for

my daughter. I mean, bloody hell! Alyona'll arrive back, and her collection'll be incomplete! As it happens, at this precise moment in time, Alyona's on holiday with her mother, actually they're at Koktebel. (*Then teasingly.*) So, d'you mind if I ask what was it in the thing that caught your eye?

IRA. I don't know.

NIKOLAI IVANOVICH. Well, hand it over anyway, I haven't dreamed all this up just for the hell of it. My mother-in-law'll make a meal out of this, believe me. I mean, just yesterday she said to me: 'You see, Nikolai, for once in your life you've had to take the train, and straightaway some good-looking girl's got her eye on you!' I mean, she's a decent enough woman, my mother-in-law, but she just doesn't like any sort of funny business.

IRA *has poured boiling water into a vacuum flask, she now adds sugar.*

NIKOLAI IVANOVICH. Well, I can see there's somebody ill here, and I've got some oranges here. (*Takes a paper bag out of his holdall, puts it on the table.*) Okay if I sit down? (*He sits.*) I've been through the whole of Romanovka with a fine-tooth comb – where the hell's my *Weekly News*? I had a vague idea of the area – you mentioned it was near the pump, and the name on the door was Chentseva. The post-office supplied the rest. My car's in for repair, you see. Nothing serious, but I've had a fair bit of running around. So this morning, I practically ran to the off-sales, only to find no *Weekly News*! Anyway, I've found you now, thank God, otherwise all hell would break loose. I can just hear my mother-in-law: 'You get that *Weekly News* back, I don't care how you do it!' She's no idea what she's getting me into, though, if you know what I mean. I haven't run a marathon like that for years. Especially not chasing after a girl. I mean, you're about twenty-five, and a crazy person!

IRA. And you're the man on the train! The *Weekly News*, of course – I'll get it now. (*She rummages through a pile of papers, gives it to* NIKOLAI IVANOVICH.)

NIKOLAI IVANOVICH. So – was there anything interesting in it?

IRA. I haven't read it. I haven't had time. Anyway, you can go now, I don't have time for you either.

NIKOLAI IVANOVICH (*stands up, lays the* Weekly News *on the table*). That's okay, read it if you want. My car's in for repair, you see. Brakes gave out. (*Laughs.*) Crazy. Anyway, I've tracked you down at last. And from now on I'm not letting you out of my sight. I can keep my mother-in-law sweet now – I'll tell her I managed to buy a spare copy at a kiosk!

IRA *takes the vacuum flask into the adjoining room.*

SVETLANA. So where's your little boy? (*Peers into the room.*) Goodness, what a big strapping lad, eh? Has he got a temperature?

IRA's VOICE (*off-stage*). Forty.

NIKOLAI IVANOVICH. Well, it's not that bad. I wouldn't be alarmed at that. Could be worse . . . I told you I had a real dose of it in England? Anyway, we'll get over it. We'll just have to sweat it out of him. That young woman, the doctor, was quite right. Herbal medicine's really making great strides nowadays. But I'll get hold of that drug for you right now. So, anyway, I've had to run around all over the place. My God, when that paper of mine disappeared! My mother-in-law collects them for my daughter. They enjoy reading them. You know I've got a daughter, by the way? Nice-looking girl, too. Big for her age. Yes, tracking you down's like a whole detective story!

IRA's VOICE. Pavlik, please take your Analgin.

PAVLIK's VOICE (*shouts*). No, I don't want it!

NIKOLAI IVANOVICH. What are you giving him Analgin for? That . . . whatsitsname . . . Keating's . . . Beeching's! You take three doses . . . Ah, well done, he's taken it. You should be good to your mama. And drink up your lemon stuff, too. Oh, look at the face he's making. That's it, that's the ticket. You'll soon get better.

IRA *enters.*

NIKOLAI IVANOVICH. Here, Mama, listen – peel the boy an orange. You know, when you didn't show up at eleven, I started to comb the whole place looking for you, immediately. I thought, something's happened. I mean, we'd agreed to meet at an exact time, and I thought, well, she's a decent, straightforward girl.

IRA. Look, I don't have time just now – later. We'll talk later, I haven't got time. He's got a really high fever.

NIKOLAI IVANOVICH. So when's later? When'll later be? Kids

get sick all the time, you don't want to lower the boy's resistance, you shouldn't make a fuss. Life goes on, after all. You're not in mourning! You shouldn't give in to him. He'll have to stay in bed for a little while, it's no big deal. Let him know you've got visitors. He's doing fine in there on his own.

IRA. No, you'll have to clear off. I've *told* you, I can't see you just now!

NIKOLAI IVANOVICH. Look, you shouldn't show your feelings like that. That'll only have a negative effect on him.

IRA *exits to* PAVLIK's *room, closing the door behind her.* SVETLANA *enters then, and opens the door. She is holding a bicycle tyre and inner tube.*

SVETLANA (*indignant*). Well, well – guess what I've just found out? And there's witnesses here, that's even better. I'll have you know it was his father bought him this bike, it's the only reminder he has of his father! Now you just tell me, in front of witnesses – I want an answer – what did Pavel slash his tyre for? This tyre – it's all he's got left from his father! You look, Pavel, you did this with a knife, didn't you! I'll give you knives, you little bugger!

IRA *abruptly closes the door.* SVETLANA *starts to cry.*

Maksim's crying now. I can't stand hearing kids cry, I really can't bear it . . .

NIKOLAI IVANOVICH (*soothingly*). Look, hold on a minute. Give it to me. Thanks . . . (*Inspects it.*) Well, I'm afraid there's nothing for it but to chuck this inner tube away. It's beyond repair, I can guarantee you that. Same goes for the tyre, you can bin it as well.

SVETLANA *nods, wiping away her tears.*

NIKOLAI IVANOVICH. I'll try and find you a similar item by this evening. My daughter's bike's lying around somewhere at home and it's the same basic construction. She got a new one a while back, a folding bike. She's a big girl now, this height. (*Indicates very tall.*)

SVETLANA *nods, sits down.*

NIKOLAI IVANOVICH. My mother-in-law never throws anything out – a vintage bike, she'd say, keep a thing for seven years . . .

SVETLANA. Maksim told me: 'If I get my hands on that Pavlik, I'll bash him!' Pavlik, that's what he said. And I'm shouting at him: 'No, you can't bash him, he's younger than you!' But I haven't got the energy to trail round everywhere after them. I've got two of them on my hands as it is, somebody else's old granny, you've got to understand. Look at this! See? (*She holds out both hands, turns them palms upward, then down.*) They're trembling! So you listen, Pavlik – (*Faces the door.*) from now on, you're on your own, I'm not helping you, and you'd better be prepared to run! (*Exits.*)

NIKOLAI IVANOVICH *casually drapes the tyre and inner tube round his neck, and partly opens the door into* PAVLIK's *room.*

NIKOLAI IVANOVICH. Boo! You won't run away, will you? With a mother like yours? You just go out and face the enemy with whatever comes to hand – pick up a log, or a stick, a bit of old firewood. And if you can't find anything, just poke his eyes out! Hey, I wasn't expecting *that* reaction! (*He gestures with two fingers, nods, and salutes with his hand at his nose.*) That's it, that's the answer!

IRA *enters, closes the door behind her, and stands leaning against it.*

NIKOLAI IVANOVICH. We ought to introduce ourselves – I'm staying up there, above the quarry. You know the 'Moscow Nights' estate? Belongs to the Planning Authority. I commute here from Moscow nearly every day. (*Shouts towards the door.*) My name's Kolya. And what's your mama's name, by the way? Let's get introduced, eh?

IRA. It's Ira, Ira.

NIKOLAI IVANOVICH. Pleased to meet you, Ira. Maybe we could have a cup of tea, eh? I'm absolutely parched.

IRA. The water in the flask is only for Pavlik.

NIKOLAI IVANOVICH. And is that all there is? Haven't you any more water? What about the kettle? Let's have a look . . . no, you're right enough, there's none. (*Picks up the kettle and shakes it.*)

IRA. We've no water. And I haven't time to go running to the pump.

NIKOLAI IVANOVICH. Where's the buckets, then? I know

where the pump is. Okay? I've got my orders, I shall now carry them out.

NIKOLAI IVANOVICH *exits, in good humour with the buckets. In the doorway he bumps into* SVETLANA, *who is bringing some honey.*

SVETLANA. And there's something else, wait till you hear this. Anyway, here's some honey. Make up a horseshoe-shaped compress with it, and place it round his neck – with boys his age you shouldn't put a compress over the thyroid, it can have a bad effect on him later. Now, there's something else! Your precious Pavlik, little and all as he is, shoved my Maksim off his bike into that heap of scrap metal at the corner!

IRA. Oh, yes, and why is Maksim always running into people with that bike of his? He knocked a little girl down in the playground yesterday. Her grandmother was in tears. And he's never done ramming Pavlik with it!

SVETLANA. It was only a game! Or else it was an accident! Maksim's not a softy. D'you know what Maksim means in Latin? The best!

IRA. No, it doesn't – it means the biggest. Maximum.

SVETLANA. The best! I picked it out of a woman's magazine! It means the best!

IRA *is silent.*

SVETLANA. The fact remains, Maksim went flying into a heap of rusty tins – that's nasty. That's how you get tetanus. For God's sakes, it burst the tyre, so what could it do to a child? (*Makes a threatening gesture in* PAVLIK's *direction.*) You just wait, you little monkey! Little bugger. You've let Pavlik run wild, and you'll regret it one of these days. (*Begins to cry.*) My God, they think because Maksim's got no father, they can treat him how they like.

NIKOLAI IVANOVICH (*enters, out of breath*). Well, that pump's pretty far away for the weaker sex, eh? (*Sets down the buckets.*) I haven't carried water in buckets for ages, since I was a lad. By the way, Ira, is this your own house?

IRA (*annoyed*). Yes! It's my property! It belonged to my grandmother's aunt.

SVETLANA. Huh! *Her* house? Don't you believe it! Tanya'd be chewing the carpet if she heard that! Her house indeed!

NIKOLAI IVANOVICH. Anyway, your grandmother should draw up an application to have the water-main extended onto her holdings.

IRA. She lives miles away. She's been in a home for the disabled in Drezna for the past eight years.

NIKOLAI IVANOVICH. Well, couldn't you sign for her? I'll give you a hand with it, I've got a good mate on the district council here.

SVETLANA. First it'll be the water, then they'll rake in the whole lot! Her property, my arse! (*Exits.*)

NIKOLAI IVANOVICH. Ira, put on the kettle, would you? I'm dying of thirst. Running all over the place after a woman. My wife and daughter have been away for six weeks now. Onto their second voucher. My mother-in-law's staying here, at the dacha. In Moscow I eat out of tins, basically, whatever I can find. You finish work in the evening, and the shops are closed, *en masse*. So I've started coming down here, what the hell, at least my mother-in-law'll give me something fresh, without preservatives. I've got so many bloody ailments, you know? So anyway, she and I went looking for strawberries yesterday. And that's how you came to bump into me on the train! The mother-in-law says: 'What a bold girl! Asking a strange man for his newspaper, just like that! Of course, she obviously fancied you, Nikolai.' Anyway, she thinks I shouldn't have given you my *Weekly News*, just for that reason. 'And it's obvious you fancied her as well,' she says, 'if you gave it to her. I had to assure her: you'll get your *Weekly News* back! So, my mother-in-law knows what's going on. Incidentally, why did you approach me? Did you fancy me? Tell the truth.

IRA. What, can't I just ask to see someone's paper?

NIKOLAI IVANOVICH. You're some girl, you really are something else! Crazy! I think I'm in love! (*Towards the door.*) Hey, Pavel – tell me something. Where's your papa?

IRA. Leave the child in peace. You're becoming a pest.

NIKOLAI IVANOVICH. Oh, yes, of course, of course. So – you've no papa, eh?

IRA. That doesn't mean a thing.

NIKOLAI IVANOVICH. And what does Mama do for a living?

IRA. I teach Gaelic. For a hundred and twenty roubles a month. Paid by the hour.

NIKOLAI IVANOVICH. Good for you! You've got your toe on the bottom rung, we'll push you right up the ladder!

IRA. I also know Manx.

NIKOLAI IVANOVICH. Well, it's not my field, but I'll help if I can, have a look round. If those lingoes exist, there must be opportunities.

IRA. And Welsh. Oh, yes, and Cornish, too.

NIKOLAI IVANOVICH. Really? And you've barely just graduated.

IRA. Actually, Cornish is almost a dead language.

NIKOLAI IVANOVICH. Never mind, we'll take steps to revive it! I'll tell you what, Ira – why don't you come back with me to the dacha and I'll hand you out some of that whatsitsname . . . Keating's . . . that medicine. You'll have to lock Pavel's door, so your neighbours don't get up to anything. Yes, and we shouldn't forget that tyre and inner tube. The mother-in-law's rushing out to some briefing next door just now, so she's not likely to notice if I nick a wheel and bring it here.

IRA. These aren't neighbours, they're my relations. Second cousins.

NIKOLAI IVANOVICH. Well, that's how it goes.

IRA (towards the door). Pavlik, I'm running out to get some medicine. I'll lock you in, okay? Your pot's under the bed, and there's tea with lemon in the flask, Don't spill it. (To NIKOLAI IVANOVICH.) His hands are shaky.

NIKOLAI IVANOVICH. D'you think you can peel an orange, kiddo?

PAVLIK's VOICE. No!!!

NIKOLAI IVANOVICH. Peel some oranges for him, Mama. Do a whole pile. Give him a treat, I'll hand some more out to you. I can get as many as I want, honestly. Privileges of rank. (Laughs.) For the moment.

IRA. Pavlik, do you want me to call Fyodorovna, to keep an eye on you?

NIKOLAI IVANOVICH. You better take something warm, Mama. A travel rug or something.

IRA. It's okay, I'll put on my raincoat.

NIKOLAI IVANOVICH. Yes, but you'll still need a rug. I know the terrain round here, it can get very misty.

IRA. I don't have a travel rug.

NIKOLAI IVANOVICH. D'you have a blanket or something?

IRA (confused). Yes.

NIKOLAI IVANOVICH. That'll do nicely!

IRA. Hold on. Pavlik's calling for me. (Exits.)

NIKOLAI IVANOVICH. He's a sensible chap, your little lad, don't worry. We'll be back soon. Half an hour or so. Forty minutes – forty-five at the most. I'll bring him back my slide projector with some slides. My daughter'll be away for another month yet . . . My mother-in-law's in conference . . . You can have a look at the slides. The Changing of the Guard. I took them myself, I'm pretty good with a camera! (Makes a 'thumbs up' gesture.)

IRA (entering). It's no use. I can't come with you. He'll be starting to sweat any minute, and I'll have to change his night-shirt. Fyodorovna won't manage.

NIKOLAI IVANOVICH. What a shame! That's a real pity. Oh well, fog or no fog, I'd better go and fetch the stuff – the patient needs it. Now, where's that tyre and inner tube . . .

IRA. Do you want a blanket?

NIKOLAI IVANOVICH (bitterly ironic). What do I need that for on my own?

VALERA (pops his head round the door). Strategic reconnaissance! (Vanishes.)

NIKOLAI IVANOVICH. You want to keep your door locked, with neighbours like that! (Exits.)

VALERA enters.

VALERA. You're pretty stuck up, Ira, and that's a fact. (He produces a bottle, and sits down, pleased with himself.)

IRA. Look, please go away, he's just getting down to sleep.

VALERA. You know, whenever I look at you, I'm reminded of a
parquet floor, before it's been sanded down. That's only twice
I've seen you, and both times I've thought the same thing. I
went to a funeral once with my sister. By train. And she tipped
her handbag out on the table, jars of this and that, started
painting and powdering. Made herself unrecognisable, she did.
You'd have needed a wet cloth to get it off. That's a real
woman, though! (*Uncorks the bottle.*)

TATYANA *enters*.

VALERA (*hastily*). I've come to see her about the roof. I'll explain
in a minute.

TATYANA. Oh yes, had a few in the off-sales?

VALERA. What d'you mean? I was bringing this for you.

TATYANA. So where's my two roubles? And give me my purse
back, for a start.

VALERA *returns her purse, she peers inside it*.

So where are they?

VALERA *taps the bottle*.

Two roubles for that? That was one-fifteen.

VALERA (*indignant*). Plus the restaurant surcharge.

TATYANA. D'you mean you got that in a restaurant?

VALERA (*serious*). Now, about the roof . . .

TATYANA. Bare-faced drunken liar. You'll wind up sweeping the
streets, that's what'll happen to you.

VALERA. Don't be so bloody stupid! You're talking through your
hat. (*Pours out a glass, starts drinking.*)

TATYANA. Listen, Ira, I've got something to tell you. I've found
out it wasn't Anton that held him down in the water, Anton
told me the truth. He's on his own for days on end. It's that
little bugger Maksim that gives all the orders. Anton always tells
me everything, and when I came home from work he ran to
meet me, didn't say a word, just buried his face in my hands,
and I could feel my hands wet from his tears. Anton had asked
Maxie for a book – one of your books, incidentally, *Mary
Poppins*. Maxie'd finished with it, but he wouldn't give it to
Anton. 'Only if you become my slave', he said. He had to get

down on his knees in front of him, with his hands by his side. And I said to him: 'Maksim, you've just finished this book about nice, kind people – didn't you learn anything from it?' Anyway, *Mary Poppins* is your book, Ira – would you please lend it to Anton?

IRA. Go ahead, take it. Tell him I said so.

TATYANA. Actually, if you must know, they weren't going to give it back to you at all! Not until you hand over a new tyre and inner tube.

VALERA. Well, just don't let them in here, right?

TATYANA. Right. Look, your Pavlik would be better off playing with Anton, I'd rather *they* were pals, than have that Maksim creature. And I'll do the cooking for you, I'm cooking for her just now, but I'd rather do it for you. I'll do the shopping. All you've got to do is feed Anton, she doesn't feed him, just throws him the scraps. And I'll make it up to you. I'm due some leave in November.

VALERA (*importantly*). And I've got leave in December. (*Pours out another glass, drinks.*) One of the Decembrists.

TATYANA. So, is that a deal?

Enter FYODOROVNA.

FYODOROVNA. I was just telling poor Svetlana, it's going to rain any minute. Tatyana, you'd better put the buckets and basins out. It'll be coming down cats and dogs in a minute. And where are you going to sleep tonight, eh? Come on, I've got two buckets in the larder, and there's a tin bath under the porch.

TATYANA. Ira's letting us sleep with her.

IRA. On the verandah.

Enter NIKOLAI IVANOVICH.

FYODOROVNA. Come on, Valera, up you come. You can give me a hand with some bits and pieces.

She sits down at the table, wipes the corners of her mouth with her fingers.

NIKOLAI IVANOVICH. There was some medicine needed here. And I've managed to get it.

IRA. Thanks. You shouldn't have bothered. He'll be sweating it out in a minute, and we're getting ready for bed now. (*Exits to* PAVLIK's *room*.)

VALERA. Have a seat. Let's get introduced. I'm Valery Gerasimovich. Motor mechanic to trade. Temporarily redeployed on car-washing duties. Have a drink, it's my treat.

NIKOLAI IVANOVICH. You should keep your voice down, there's somebody ill in the house.

VALERA. You Ira's husband, then?

NIKOLAI IVANOVICH. Got it in one.

A pause.

FYODOROVNA. Well, best of luck to you, it's time you were in bed. Tatyana, give me a hand here.

They lift VALERA *up by the arms, to lead him out.*

VALERA. Hey, Ira! Never give in, okay?

TATYANA. Come on, on your feet.

VALERA. That's life – dog eat dog! Survival of the fittest!

TATYANA. Look, if you're not going to stand on your own two feet, I don't know . . .

VALERA. There's only two ifs in this world: if you don't drink, it'll only turn to vinegar anyway . . .

TATYANA *picks up the bottle from the table, and they lead* VALERA *out.*

NIKOLAI IVANOVICH. And I've brought some more medicine! (*Carefully places a bottle of cognac on the table.*)

IRA. Look, would you please go away!

NIKOLAI IVANOVICH (*tuts*). Temper, temper. And I've brought a new tyre and inner tube as well! (*Produces the tyre and inner tube from his holdall.*) I sweated cobs to get these off. And here's that English medicine. Okay?

IRA. God almighty, you're giving me a pain in the head!

NIKOLAI IVANOVICH. Look, it's starting to rain. Well, no matter, I've got an umbrella. You know what I really like, is when it's raining, and you're indoors somewhere. It's like out there's the rain, coming down, and you're still warm and dry.

Gives you a feeling of security. Look, don't cast me out, eh? Don't shout at me. I've missed you so much!

IRA exits. NIKOLAI IVANOVICH puts the kettle on the gas, warms his hands at it.

NIKOLAI IVANOVICH. You know, the funny thing was, my mother-in-law still hadn't gone out, she was pottering around for ages. I had to sit tight and wait, like a peeping Tom.

IRA (*re-enters*). You know, they'll get soaked. They've no roof at all their side. Just go home, please. They'll be arriving here any minute. We came to an agreement about it. Now please go, and hurry!

Outside in the yard, FYODOROVNA can be seen trotting past, with a tin bath over her head, making her way to the other side of the house.

NIKOLAI IVANOVICH. Yes, some mighty events are under way, I can feel it. We won't get any peace here now. Why don't you come down to the meadow tomorrow evening, to the little bridge? Around ten or so, okay? We'll make a bonfire and I'll bring some kebabs. Shashlik, d'you fancy that? And some Georgian wine to go with it. I've fallen head over heels, you wouldn't believe it. Stabbed to the heart by your beautiful eyes!

IRA. Look, what are you doing sitting there! People running around mad, and you're stuck there, rooted to the spot. They won't even let me use their toilet! And now I'm supposed to put up with them, and a sick child on my hands as well! Go away, please, Nikolai Ivanovich! Hurry, they'll be here any minute.

NIKOLAI IVANOVICH (*sadly*). You know, Ira, you frighten me!

IRA hurriedly pushes the table and chairs against the wall. NIKOLAI IVANOVICH exits. IRA stands in the doorway, puts out her hand to feel the rain. She shudders. A procession then appears, with FYODOROVNA at its head, still sheltering under her tin bath; next comes VALERA, with his jacket collar turned up. VALERA is also carrying two folding beds, and a rucksack. Behind him, TATYANA brings ANTON and MAKSIM, with her raincoat spread out over them: the boys are carrying a saucepan and a kettle. SVETLANA brings up the rear, with LEOKADIYA on her arm, and holding an umbrella over her. In her free hand, she carries a suitcase. Not one of them looks at IRA.

FYODOROVNA. We'll find a place for you all, don't worry. Sixteen square metres, my room is, warm and dry.

They exit, IRA *closes her own door, bolts it shut, and begins moving the furniture back to its original place. She switches out the light, and exits to* PAVLIK's *room.*

PAVLIK's VOICE (*off-stage*). Mama, d'you want me to tell you another story? Once upon a time Grey Wolf got into the city hospital, and they grabbed him by the tail and took him to see the doctor. That's where they used to do operations on all the wolves, to cut up their livers, and see if any of their dinner had got stuck. Then they sewed their tummies up again, and it really hurt. And he liked it there. They gave him his dinner there, meat and cabbage it was. He was so crafty – he ate lots and lots of cabbage. But the wolf had a huge liver, a ginormous one, and that's where his dinner went. But this wolf was an English wolf, and so he had wings. Teeny-tiny little wings, growing out from here . . .

End of Act One

ACT TWO

Scene One

IRA's *flat in Moscow.* MARYA FILIPPOVNA, IRA's *mother is on the telephone.*

MARYA FILIPPOVNA. Hullo. It's me again . . . Is that you? . . . Why haven't you phoned me? It's been ages . . . Eh? . . . Oh, all right, I'll call you again this evening. (*Hastily.*) Just make sure you come to my funeral. Right, I'll call you later.

Replaces the receiver, thinks for a moment, then dials another number.

Hullo? Have I got the right number? Could you ask Kondrashkova to come to the phone, please? . . . So when will she be back? . . . Isn't Yelovsky there now? Or anybody at all, from the old staff? . . . This is Marya Schilling here. Who is that speaking? . . . Well, that's the first I've heard of you . . . You must be new there . . . Or rather, you haven't heard of me. Anyway, I'm sorry to bother you – we're obviously not acquainted . . . I'm sorry . . . No, no, not at all!

Replaces the receiver. She remains seated a few moments, smiling, then dials another number, purposefully.

Hello? Listen, I've definitely made up my mind to go into hospital. No, don't hang up, don't hang up, please . . . You know how things are, there's nobody here. Ira's rented a dacha at two hundred and forty a month. She got a hundred of it off me, to pay the deposit. She won't need to give it back now. Anyway, listen to me, I've decided to go into hospital. I don't know where it'll be, but I'll let you know as soon as I find out. I've been putting it off for six months now, but I'm going to take the plunge. They can cut me up in bits, if they want . . . She'll do nicely out of it, she'll be left a two-roomed flat, she'll be able to bring men in . . . Yes, and she won't have to pay back that hundred roubles . . . Don't hang up! You just hear me out! . . . I'm telling you, I've made up my mind to go in.

Ira needs my help, but what sort of help can I be to her? Pavlik's sick all the time, she lets him catch cold, and she's not feeding him right. The child needs proper nourishment, and she's not giving him it. I'm about at the end of my tether with them . . . And I've got my admission papers now. Well, all right, I'll phone you again from the hospital – that's if they don't haul me off straight away to the operating table. I won't be phoning after that. So, if I don't call, you'll know I'm on the table. But I'll try and give you a call just before the operation . . . Well, of course, they have to get people ready, take blood samples, and so on. But they'll cut me up urgently, mine's an urgent case . . . I can't put it off any longer, I've been hanging on for six months now. No, I haven't been down to the dacha, Ira doesn't want me there, and I don't even know how to get in touch with her . . . A telegram. Yes, but I don't know which hospital. And how do you send a telegram from hospital? She comes here to bath the boy now and again, once a week, but that's two weeks now and no sign of them . . . I don't know, maybe they're dead. I'll leave a note for her, to tell her to phone you . . . But if Pavlik's sick, and she happens to be sick there as well, she might not get back here for another week, that boy of hers'll be crawling by then . . . And she won't take him swimming. She's scared of the water, terrified, has been since childhood . . . I tell you I've got myself in a right old mess. If Pavlik's fallen ill, chances are she won't even turn up to bury me, now there's a thing!

The door opens, and IRA *enters along with* PAVLIK, *a scarf round his head, and a woollen cap on top.* IRA *leads* PAVLIK *past* MARYA FILIPPOVNA, *who turns to face them, continuing to speak very distinctly, until* IRA *and her son disappear into their own room.*

Anyway, you know what the position is, I'm inviting you to my funeral. You'll maybe be the only person walking behind my coffin. Don't bring Mikhail, he doesn't like these things. You can bury me in that dark English costume I have, it's hanging up in the wardrobe in a gauze bag. Don't forget my medal. And my blue shoes are wrapped in tissue paper in a box underneath the suit. My blouse and all the other things you'll find in a big pink boot-box, underneath the shoes . . . No, Ira knows nothing about this, she doesn't want to know, she won't listen to me. Anyway, I'll phone you again, just before I die. I've got some money put aside for the funeral, and a wake, in my savings-bank account, and I'll have a will witnessed in the hospital itself, before the operation. And it'll be in your name!

So bear that in mind! . . . Hang on, hang on, you'll make it to the doctor's, you'll only have to sit in a queue anyway. I sat there for four hours, day before yesterday, to get my blood-pressure checked, which needless to say had gone up! So don't bother. Misha'll wait for you . . . Anyway, it's summer, so what if he is dressed, he's not going to expire, it's not a fur coat he's wearing . . . Well, just sit him down! . . . Don't keep interrupting! Listen, I want to be buried at the Vaganskov Cemetery, the same as my mother. The grave's in her name, Chentseva-Schilling, and the plot's No. 183. Right? Are you making a note of this? . . . Well, do so . . . Look, put him down on the chair, for God's sake . . . You run and get a pencil and I'll talk to him . . . Hello, Misha? . . . Put him on to me . . . Hello, Misha? How are you keeping? . . . He can't hear me. Misha! Plug in your hearing aid! He's got a hearing aid, there's only four like it in the whole of Moscow! Misha! Ah, she's got the message, she's put it in his ear now . . . Hello? It's me, Marya! What are you going to the doctor's for at this late hour, you'll be too late, they only consult till three o'clock, and you'll have to sit there for four hours anyway! . . . God, he doesn't understand a thing these days. Hardening of the arteries. Misha, it's Masha, Masha Schilling! . . . Eh? He's not in his right mind. Doesn't remember. Which doctor are you going to? . . . They're taking him to see a urologist. Oh, he's started to talk. It's really worrying him. You're doing well for your age! Hello? I said you're doing very well! I'll make him laugh now – hello, Misha? Hey, Misha, come up and see me some time – there's a bottle of vodka here! God, he can't hear again. Deaf as a post. Hello, I'm still here! Is that you? . . . You've found a pencil? Right, take this down. Plot No. 183, Schilling, Aleksandra Nikiticha, Schilling, Filipp Nikolaevich. That's it. What time have you got to be there at? . . . Well, you've plenty of time still. So – I'll draw up the will and leave everything to you, and you can bury *me* . . . No, *you* can bury me! (*Jokingly.*) That's right, you'll bury *me*! (*Laughs.*) Anyway, I'll look in this evening . . . You'll manage a cup of tea? . . . No, I'm not going in today now, I'll go tomorrow. I can hang on another day, I've waited six months after all . . .

IRA (*enters*). Mama . . .

MARYA FILIPPOVNA. That's six months I've waited, so what's another day.

IRA. Mama, Pavlik's ill.

MARYA FILIPPOVNA. So, how are things with you? How are you coping?

IRA. Mama!

MARYA FILIPPOVNA. Don't shout, I'm not deaf . . . That's Ira just turned up, out of the blue . . . No, don't be silly! She'll be leaving straight away, same as always. Don't hang up. (*To* IRA.) D'you realise your mother's slowly dying here? . . . No, I'm talking to *her*. Well, all right . . . I'll take a run over, if you can call it that. Ira can get all the details from you. (*To* IRA.) It's Nina Nikiforovna, she phoned to see how I am, she's worried about me. (*Into the receiver.*) I'm just letting her know that other people phone me more often than she does. And that's my own daughter. Listen, I still haven't got to the important part. How's Lenya? . . . Oh, my God! Run then, run, if you can call it that. (*Replaces the receiver.*) They can just about stir their stumps, these days.

IRA. Mama, I've had to bring Pavlik home, he's sick.

MARYA FILIPPOVNA. And have you given any thought to the fact that *I'm* ill? Have you thought of that? Why haven't you been here the past two weeks? Two weeks is just too big a slice out of my life, in my condition. I could be dead.

IRA. Look, just sit with him a minute, will you, while I run down to the chemist's. And the bakery.

MARYA FILIPPOVNA. I'm going into hospital. I've got my admission papers.

IRA. So what's the rush all of a sudden?

MARYA FILIPPOVNA. It's got to be done some time.

IRA. You can surely wait a bit longer. I mean, I'm tied hand and foot here!

MARYA FILIPPOVNA. Huh, I knew it! That's two weeks now you haven't brought him for his bath. The child's covered in spots. If anything happened to me, the first you'd know about it was when they broke down the door!

IRA. Oh, give over, you're perfectly healthy.

MARYA FILIPPOVNA. So what's this then? (*Rummages in her handbag.*) An admission card, eh? Why have you got such a spite against me?

IRA. This is only for an examination, it says.

MARYA FILIPPOVNA. Oh yes, and you know what they're looking for, do you?

IRA. Look, please wait fifteen minutes, just till I go down to the bakery.

MARYA FILIPPOVNA. The doctors'll be on their way home!

IRA. It's a hospital, they don't *go* home! Which hospital are you going into?

MARYA FILIPPOVNA. What's it to you?

IRA. Mama, don't be so selfish. Look what I've brought – a jar of goat's milk. And eggs. Some soup in a jar for you and him. And some rissoles in a pan here. Give him something to eat and put him to bed, he's tired.

MARYA FILIPPOVNA. It's you that's got him like this! Look how thin he is! And his long johns, full of holes. Who d'you like better, Pavlik – Mama or Granny? Huh, he's forgotten me, or else been made to. I'll read you your favourite story-book, shall I? *Mary Poppins*? Did you bring my *Mary Poppins* book with you, Ira?

IRA. I gave it to somebody. A loan of.

MARYA FILIPPOVNA. It's not yours to give.

IRA. It *is* mine. I bought it in Kamenets, along with *One Hundred Years of Solitude*.

MARYA FILIPPOVNA. So where's *One Hundred Years of Solitude*, then? I haven't seen that for ages either. Everything gets given away, and I'm still alive here! You're spineless, that's what you are. You trust everybody, you let everybody take advantage of you! You'll never know where anything is, whether it's your books, or your own mother's grave!

IRA. Oh, that's enough. What d'you want me to do? Drag Pavlik along with me to the chemist's? He can't be left on his own, he'll start crying. All right then, I'll feed him myself, and put him to bed, he'll fall asleep, and then we'll go to the chemist's and the bakery.

MARYA FILIPPOVNA. The damned cheek of her! (*Wiping away tears.*) I'm sitting here, worried sick, and she couldn't even be bothered to phone, not to say how Pavlik was, or ask how I was. You just wait, one of these days you'll be sorry! I mean, I am *dying*, if you must know!

IRA. We've all got to die sometime!

MARYA FILIPPOVNA. And just when are you going to pay me back my hundred roubles?

IRA. In the autumn, I told you.

MARYA FILIPPOVNA. Why don't you ask the child's father? It's his job to provide financial support.

IRA. He's providing it.

MARYA FILIPPOVNA. Well, go and ask that other one . . . The one you've been knocking around with.

IRA. Oh God . . . (*Starts to cry.*)

PAVLIK's VOICE (*off-stage*). Damned cheek of her!

MARYA FILIPPOVNA. You see? You see what you're teaching him?

IRA. Pavlik, we'll have something to eat in a minute, we'll get washed and have a sleep, then we're leaving. We'll walk down to the river, and into the woods. We'll go and pick mushrooms.

MARYA FILIPPOVNA. Yes, Mama spends plenty on other people, but she wouldn't think of bringing her own mother a bit of chocolate.

IRA. I haven't any money.

MARYA FILIPPOVNA. And I'm short a hundred roubles! What about my funeral? How's that to be paid?

IRA. You've got money in your savings-bank.

MARYA FILIPPOVNA. That's for something else.

IRA. Auntie Nina'll do what's necessary.

MARYA FILIPPOVNA. Yes, and I'm not leaving it to you.

IRA. Suits me fine. (*Exits to PAVLIK's room.*)

MARYA FILIPPOVNA (*makes another phone call*). Hello? I'd like to speak to Kondrashkova, please . . . Oh, yes, I see – obviously I didn't understand . . . she won't be in today at all . . . Oh, it's you again! . . . This is Marya Schilling again, the pensioner you spoke to . . . Yes, would you please relay a message to

Kondrashkova tomorrow that there's no panic now, it's been
sorted out, I was trying to find my family, they'd gone and got
lost on me. They'd taken off to a dacha somewhere, and there
was no phone. Tell Kondrashkova that everything's rosy now,
Mrs Schilling's fine. I'm so happy I could laugh out loud . . .
(*Wiping away tears.*) You'll tell her, won't you? . . . I won't be
here tomorrow . . . So I won't be able to phone again . . .
Anyway, all the very best to you . . . I've got to run out to the
chemist's for them, her little one's not well . . . Best wishes to
you too – long life and happiness! . . . I'm so glad! They're
here at last! Yes, it turns out they were ill, and they couldn't get
a message through to me!

IRA *enters.*

MARYA FILIPPOVNA. They're all I have, they're the only thing
in my life . . . You're such a kind person, it's a shame we've
never met. I would have introduced you to my daughter, she's
practically got her Ph.D . . .

IRA. Mama!

MARYA FILIPPOVNA. That's her calling now. I'm coming, I'm
coming. (*Replaces the receiver.*) What are you shouting for? Go on,
go out if you want, do what you like. On you go to your . . .
chemist's! I'll give him something to eat, and put him to bed,
my little sweetheart. On you go, enjoy yourself. Somebody
phoned here, looking for you. I noted it down somewhere, I'll
find it later . . . Mikhailov, was that it?

IRA. Nikolsky?

MARYA FILIPPOVNA. No, more like Mikhailov.

IRA. There's nobody by that name. You should write these things
down, Mama.

MARYA FILIPPOVNA. Well, I think I'll remember it, and then I
just forget. You know, you can't imagine it, I cry the whole
night sometimes, I keep thinking Pavlik's dead.

IRA. Oh, that's enough.

MARYA FILIPPOVNA. And here he is! My little sweetheart!

IRA. I've also brought some sausages, I've put them in the fridge.
And there's some cooked buckwheat in a packet.

MARYA FILIPPOVNA. But what about yourself, why won't you
have something along with us? You must eat! You're so pale!

IRA. I've got to run. There's all hell going on down at that dacha. The other half's got no roof.

MARYA FILIPPOVNA. Has it fallen down?

IRA. It's sprung a leak. And now it's pouring rain.

MARYA FILIPPOVNA. Raining? . . . I hardly ever go out. I just sit here and have dreams about you.

IRA. Well, anyway, I invited them into our place, and Pavlik's lying there ill, temperature between thirty-nine and forty degrees! Can you imagine? And those people really don't want to be a bother . . .

MARYA FILIPPOVNA. You let everybody walk all over you. You asked them in, but not me, you'd have done better to invite me. Your mother stuck here all on her own . . .

IRA. Oh, yes, and spend the whole summer listening to your whining.

MARYA FILIPPOVNA. Don't you shout at me, you neurotic!

PAVLIK's VOICE. Mama, what's neurotic mean?

MARYA FILIPPOVNA (shouts). Neurotic, that's what! She's neurotic!

PAVLIK's VOICE. Neurotic!

IRA. Right, that's it, we're not staying for lunch, we're leaving right now!

MARYA FILIPPOVNA. You see? Neurotic, that proves it! Grudges a plate of soup even, for her old mother. Well, on you go, run away, go on! D'you think I can't see what you're after? We'll stay here and have something to eat in a minute or two, we'll have a sleep, we'll read for a while, I'll do your job for you again, I've got the bit between my teeth now . . . What did you do with my *Mary Poppins*? You've given away the whole house just about, the boy's got nothing to read . . . What kind of daughter do you call yourself after this, eh?

IRA *hurriedly exits.*

MARYA FILIPPOVNA. Oh, Granny's got such a sore tummy, it hurts. It really does . . . Maybe a hernia . . . Maybe something else . . .

Scene Two

IRA's *verandah at the dacha. The sound of a key in the lock.*
FYODOROVNA *enters and switches on the light. She is followed,*
circumspectly, by the other lodgers, carrying bundles and folding beds, i.e.
SVETLANA, TATYANA, *the two boys. On the end of the procession,*
framed majestically in the doorway, stands LEOKADIYA, *holding up an*
umbrella. They all look very dishevelled. The boys immediately run off.

FYODOROVNA. Now look, I'm opening this place up for you at
my own risk, because we're all crammed together in there. You
can stay one night here meanwhile, then we'll see . . . I need to
get a decent night's rest myself. She won't be back till
tomorrow night at the earliest, she's not planning to leave early.
And if Pavlik's still coughing, she'll maybe take him to the
doctor, she was intending to take him. So that'll be another
day. One down and two to go.

SVETLANA. We're like refugees here.

TATYANA. More like bloody partisans.

FYODOROVNA. So, will you be wanting into that other room?
The door's locked.

SVETLANA. I don't know. Possibly.

FYODOROVNA. I don't have a key.

SVETLANA. Then we won't. We're not going to break in. The
boys'll sleep on the couch . . . I'm on night-shift . . . Where'll
you go?

TATYANA. No, Anton and I'll sleep on the folding beds . . .
Otherwise Maxie'll start a carry-on. He'll pinch Anton. He can
sleep on his own for now.

SVETLANA. But what about you? You're not getting a decent
night's sleep, if you're standing guard over them the whole
time. You need your sleep. Otherwise you just fly off the
handle at people.

TATYANA. Anton keeps shouting.

SVETLANA. Oh, give over. Kids used to be locked up the whole
day on their own. My mother would go out to work, and I'd
spend the whole day with the cat for company. And that's how
I grew up.

TATYANA. Yes, and you can see what good it's done.

Meanwhile they have unpacked their things, and got LEOKADIYA *settled.*

FYODOROVNA. Anyway, you can stay there meanwhile, and when Ira comes back I've got to go to Moscow, to arrange a memorial service for my mother. It'll be her anniversary soon. I'll stay the night with my brother at Dorogomilovka, and you can have my room then. That's another day and a night notched up.

SVETLANA. Well, if you ask me, Ira won't be back in a hurry. I can feel it in my bones. We were cramping his style here. Putting him off his stroke.

FYODOROVNA. That's some toilet he got built for her! He's worth hanging onto for that alone.

TATYANA *giggles.*

FYODOROVNA And she gave him nothing but dirty looks. She's already got a boyfriend in Moscow, a fine chap, Ph.D., she was telling me.

TATYANA. Well, anyway, at least we've got a new bog now.

FYODOROVNA. Yes, a freebie. And all for a pair of beautiful eyes.

SVETLANA. What, call her eyes beautiful? Give her a good scrub in the bath-house, then maybe they'd be beautiful.

TATYANA. Big eyes, certainly, like organ stops.

SVETLANA. Have you noticed how she never laughs?

FYODOROVNA. Well, what's she got to laugh about?

SVETLANA. Not even at the pictures?

TATYANA. She's got a tooth missing, that's why she doesn't laugh. When I broke one of my teeth it took me all my time to laugh as well. Or if I had to, I covered it up with my sleeve. (*Demonstrates.*)

SVETLANA. Anyway, what've we got to laugh about? But we still laugh.

FYODOROVNA. He's a well set-up man. Even got hold of a carpenter somewhere! I've been trying to get that carpenter of ours, that Volodya, for six months now. Never has the time, he says, keeps sending up here for wine, and making excuses. I've been on at him six months now, to cut me some fence-posts and knock them in. Thirty-five posts at five roubles apiece – plus the wine, that'll come to two hundred! Then Vadim turns up, and he's worn holes through his socks, I can see them, so I had to buy him two new pairs. She never buys him nothing, just sends him to his old mother, to show off the holes. I could sit down and weep, I tell you, when I see that. Anyway, he starts rummaging around, he's looking for his bike. 'Why's it all rusty?' he says. So why wouldn't it be rusty, it's been lying there under the house for five years! He makes me weep, I've got to get away from him. He's so demanding, always wanting something or other. But he's a big shot in the construction business. And she's an inspector or something. Swarthy-looking, she is, hair black as coal. Her whole family's the same. Descended from beetles, I reckon. Anyway, they're buying themselves a car, a Zhiguli, so they can drive out to their own plot, they've built a shack on it. They won't come and see me, though, that's because Vadim married her after a fortnight just. He had a really nice girl, too, went out with her for three years, then goes and gets married to this one. 'Is she from Kazan', I ask him, she's that dark. 'No, she's from Ryazan', he says. Vadim thinks this place is his, and he's getting as much out of me as he can, I've got to pay for the insurance, repairs, repainting. Meanwhile what am I to subsist on, eh? Well, I'm not telling him we've got a toilet now. They can find out for themselves. The minute Vadim spots the toilet, he'll tell me not to let this place out for less than three-twenty, no, three-fifty. I'll have beehives here. Holiday-makers on bunk-beds. Oh, yes, my loves . . .

SVETLANA. Yes, it took him just three days to organise the toilet. That's what's needed, a real man!

TATYANA. He's a creep, actually.

SVETLANA. Mm! This neighbour of mine, Shura, she comes to me and says: 'Oh, Svetlana dear, you've got to introduce me to some man, anything in trousers, I don't care what.' She wants me to introduce her to one of my patients. Her husband and three-year-old son were killed in a taxi, and she survived.

TATYANA. Well, you can introduce me as well! That Valera of mine's not worth a button these days, because of the drink. Far as I'm concerned, he's played out.

SVETLANA. Yes, listen, I wish your Anton wouldn't keep bragging in front of Maksim all the time – every second word it's 'Papa' this, and 'Papa' that. 'Papa's coming.' 'Papa'll do it.' Drop him a hint, I mean, he's big enough to understand, it hurts Maksim's feelings.

TATYANA (*stretching*). Oh well, it's been quite a while now since our Papa was down here, Anton's been missing him. It's time we took a trip home, had a bath.

FYODOROVNA (*raising a finger*). Listen, d'you hear that? She's bringing all them tom-cats here again. They were clattering around in the attic the whole night.

TATYANA. Really? And I'm thinking, who's that turning the whole place upside down?

FYODOROVNA. They come for her, for my Elka. She's already forgotten that little kitten of hers. Seven of those toms there are, peering out of the strawberries. I don't like that kind of thing . . . I don't like the female sex, nor the male sex, nor cats neither. Randy lot of buggers.

Scene Three

The kitchen in NIKOLAI IVANOVICH's *house.* IRA *and* NIKOLAI IVANOVICH *are sitting at table, she in a dressing-gown, he in a towelling bathrobe.*

NIKOLAI IVANOVICH. You better eat. What about some pineapple in its own juice? Let's see, what else is there? Instant coffee, Nescafé granules. There's nothing in the house. No, hold on – what about some caviar on a sandwich? (*Spreads caviar on some bread.*)

IRA. Pavlik hasn't had caviar for ages.

NIKOLAI IVANOVICH. I'll give you a jar to take home. Would you like some port wine? The genuine article, from Portugal. There's some real jasmine tea as well, and some rose-scented stuff. It's bizarre, there's no food in the house, not even eggs. It's just as well you thought to pick up some bread.

IRA. I went out on the pretext of going to the bakery. So, that's where I went, then phoned you from a call-box.

NIKOLAI IVANOVICH. How are you feeling? Eh? How's your head?

IRA. I've forgotten I had a head.

NIKOLAI IVANOVICH *chuckles, pleased with himself.*

IRA. Is this her dressing-gown?

NIKOLAI IVANOVICH *nods.*

IRA. And that's her shower-cap in the bathroom.

NIKOLAI IVANOVICH. She's got three of them.

IRA. And perfume . . . I used some of it on myself. And a manicure set. Everything's so clean and shiny.

NIKOLAI IVANOVICH. Have another sandwich. Have two. And drink up. It's my mother-in-law that keeps everything spotless. 'I'll be at the dacha the whole week, Nikolai,' she says, 'And I'll head back to town on Friday, okay?' Advance notice. So she won't burst in on anything, you know?

IRA. I see.

NIKOLAI IVANOVICH. Yes, that was some night, walking around till three in the morning, and then you said: 'Take me now, right under this fir-tree!' I'll never forget the way you said that. Your faithful hound, that's me. Woof! Woof! There was nothing for my mother-in-law to clean up that Friday. I'd been tearing off to the dacha every day, like a mad thing. She maybe flicked away a bit of dust, but I think she had her suspicions. Woof! On you go, stroke my fur!

IRA. What's the time?

NIKOLAI IVANOVICH. It's just three o'clock. In five hours' time I'll be flying out on a business trip, and I'll have something to remember now. (*Stretches.*) I'll be gone a week.

IRA. I've got to dash.

NIKOLAI IVANOVICH. Nonsense! We'll have something to eat in a minute, then we'll have another little lie-down. You can't leave.

IRA. Are you nuts? It was eight o'clock when I ran out of the house . . . Well, I suppose Mama's accustomed to it by now. I used to run off for three and four days at a stretch. She'll have put the chain on the door now, most likely, so's she'll hear what time I come in. And in the morning she'll ring round all her cronies and tell them about my escapades. They're all so concerned about me.

NIKOLAI IVANOVICH. Actually, my mother-in-law's pretty tolerant. She'll put up with anything. Ever since I walked out on them – it even got that far – I'm above suspicion! She doesn't suspect a thing. I'm not married to them now anyway. I walked out, tried to start a new life with this other woman . . . Even bought a two-room flat, a co-operative. Then my daughter Alyona comes to see me, she says: 'Papa, we can't live without you'. I mean, she's my first consideration. She's fifteen. And in time that flat'll be hers. So it all turned out for the best. D'you want to see her photograph?

IRA. No, thanks.

NIKOLAI IVANOVICH. That's her picture up there! You're looking right at it. (*Laughs, complacently*.) There's pictures of her everywhere.

IRA. Mama had to keep me on the straight and narrow from the age of fifteen.

NIKOLAI IVANOVICH. You were obviously a good looker! My Alyona's fifteen now. Nice pair of knockers, good bum! He'll be a lucky man that gets her . . .

IRA. That's when I started running away from home. I used to sleep in railway stations, the telegraph office, anything but go home. She treated me like absolute shit!

NIKOLAI IVANOVICH. Poor you! Anyway, let's go, my little sweetheart, I'll kiss it better . . .

A pause.

Well, come on.

IRA. Some nights there wasn't even a place to sit down in the stations. And it's cold in winter. Everybody sitting around, freezing. How people can just sit around in the cold like that. Kids as well, sitting or sleeping. Such pale little things. I felt so sorry for them, those kids. I felt like killing all those grown-ups!

NIKOLAI IVANOVICH. And they'd be making a pass at you, I can just imagine.

IRA. What?

NIKOLAI IVANOVICH. Dirty old men – didn't they try to pick you up?

IRA. Well, anyway, one morning I just went home and said: 'You can stop worrying now – I'm a woman.' She was frying up some potatoes. And she said: 'I've known that for a long time.' Then she burst out crying.

NIKOLAI IVANOVICH. So who was he? Let's have a bit more detail. What happened exactly?

IRA. I . . . I don't remember him. I just did it to spite my mother.

NIKOLAI IVANOVICH. Poor little thing! Hey, drink up! . . . Come on, finish it off . . . That's the stuff!

IRA. My mother was so vexed, howling right into the potatoes, and I just stood there and laughed.

NIKOLAI IVANOVICH. You know, it's funny, but I've never seen you laugh. Come on, give us a smile!

IRA. No, I don't feel like it.

A pause.

NIKOLAI IVANOVICH. So, tell me what it was like. You know, how you felt . . .

IRA. I told you, I don't remember. Now leave off.

NIKOLAI IVANOVICH. No way! No chance! I'm your faithful dog, remember! Grrrr! I'll bite, you know. I went out on the tiles one time in Nakhodka, just like you. With some old bird name of Lyubka. I had twenty-five roubles in my wallet, I remember that clearly. And she was a real old bag, I tell you. So I gets up in the morning: 'Hey, Lyubka,' I says, 'where's my quarter note?' And she says, 'Piss off, while you're still in one piece.' And I was feeling really rotten. I walked down the street, howling, till I reached a phone-box, and called an ambulance. Next thing the police arrive. So I showed the policeman my party card, paid-up member and all that . . . I didn't have anything else . . . he literally couldn't believe his eyes. I'd had three books published at that time . . . Well, pamphlets, really. Descriptions of technical innovations, that sort of thing. I mean, he just clutched his head. We've been searching for you for three weeks, he says. Your family's reported you missing.

IRA. Well, I've got to go. That's it, okay? I've had a great time, but Pavlik's at home, and my mother's sick, she'll have to drag herself out of bed to let me in . . . She's ill, but she refuses to go into hospital even for a check-up.

NIKOLAI IVANOVICH. No, I'm not letting you leave. You're too tired, for a start. We'll go and have a lie-down. Your mother'll have gone to sleep, she won't wait up. Anyway, everything looks better in the clear light of day. I'll get you up at seven, drop you off on my way to the airport. It's all one trip. We've got to make the most of what time we have left!

IRA. Look, next time you're down at the dacha, you can come with us into the woods to pick mushrooms.

NIKOLAI IVANOVICH. No, that's more in my mother-in-law's line – I'm not that keen on mushrooms, they don't agree with me.

IRA. Pavlik and I love it. Out in the early morning, with the dew still on the grass . . . The morning mist. Round about four o'clock, it's just beautiful.

NIKOLAI IVANOVICH. Anyway, how d'you like your new toilet? Suit you all right? Pass muster? I mean, have you tried it out yet?

IRA. Oh yes, it's a big hit. They're all ecstatic.

NIKOLAI IVANOVICH (a self-satisfied laugh, then seriously). I got them to put a lock on it specially. Just a simple lock, sort of a latch. So Pavlik won't do anything stupid. Don't be giving the key to anybody.

IRA. We never lock it anyway.

NIKOLAI IVANOVICH. Well, you ought to. They'll mess it up! You know what the toilets are like in Germany? Absolutely gleaming. You could eat your dinner in them. They've even got a sort of embroidered lap-bag for newspapers.

IRA. Fyodorovna's in charge of things down there, she's already been to Zelenograd, and bought a seat for it.

NIKOLAI IVANOVICH. No, seriously, you want to take a firm line on the question of the lock, in my view – as a matter of principle. I mean, they wouldn't let you use theirs, would they.

IRA. Anyway, theirs is an absolute shambles. You wouldn't want to set foot in it, it's dreadful.

NIKOLAI IVANOVICH (*deeply moved*). Just remember, Ira, that toilet is my personal gift to you!

IRA. I do remember it, every day – and more than once!

NIKOLAI IVANOVICH. Yes, well, just so you don't forget. Anyway, have you any other sort of domestic problems? In your private life?

IRA. Not really. You gave them the bicycle tyre and inner tube. You've fixed up a toilet for me. That's the lot! Oh, yes – you couldn't maybe help them repair the roof, could you? Before their half collapses.

NIKOLAI IVANOVICH. Well, I can't promise. (*Cheerfully.*) But when it's all yours, well . . . I mean, why should I fix something that's common property? They'll grab it all for themselves, and you'll be back to square one again. I'll tell you what – once they've finally let it all go to ruin, you'll be able to buy it off them at half price. I mean, I'll help you with the paperwork. It's a highly desirable place for a dacha.

IRA. Well, I'll still have to wait until great-aunt Vera dies. And she's only seventy-four.

NIKOLAI IVANOVICH. So? Your great-aunt Vera'll die sometime. Comes to us all in the end, as my old man used to say – which in his case happened sure enough. And in my old dear's. So I was left on my own.

IRA. Anyway, I've got to go. You know, against expectations, you've turned out a really nice guy. (*She kisses his hand.*)

NIKOLAI IVANOVICH. Oh, come on . . . really . . .

IRA. Look after yourself. I've got to go. Where is it you're going?

NIKOLAI IVANOVICH (*hastily*). It's a business trip.

IRA. I'd better not hold you up.

NIKOLAI IVANOVICH (*seizes* IRA's *hand*). Ira darling, stay! My angel! Stay with me another two hundred minutes! I'll miss you so much. You're like a moth! That's what I'll call you from now on, my little moth! Please stay. And I'll take you home at seven, tomorrow morning.

IRA. No, take me home now, please. I've no money for a taxi. As you can imagine!

NIKOLAI IVANOVICH. I'll take you! And I'll get a signal to you. I'll miss the plane! And we can spend another day of our lives together, my darling moth, my little night-bird. I'll phone you from the airport, you'll come to me, I'll pay for the taxi, and we'll go to a sauna, then some restaurant out of town. Okay?

IRA. No, I don't think so, I've got to do the washing tomorrow, Mama won't do it. And there's the shopping, for the whole week. She'll kick up hell in the morning, believe me.

NIKOLAI IVANOVICH. Look, I've got a mother-in-law . . . but I'm not beholden to them. My passport says I'm divorced. You understand what that means?

IRA. Just take me home now.

NIKOLAI IVANOVICH. But we've made an *agreement*, Ira love. Oh-seven-hundred hours! So let's go to bed now, right? Are you tired? Is that it?

IRA. It's just as well you've got a car.

NIKOLAI IVANOVICH (*solemnly*). I'll have to change it. Trade it in. D'you follow me? Come on, Ira!

IRA. No, you listen to me.

NIKOLAI IVANOVICH. What do you mean?

IRA. I had a boyfriend once. *Had* a boyfriend, past tense. We used to meet once a week on Fridays. That was his regular day for me. I would phone him up and he'd say: 'Same as usual, then'. Or else he'd say, 'Sorry, can't make it today, give me a buzz next week'. It was me that had to call him all the time, you see? One good thing about him was that he lived right next to a metro station, very handy. Even so, I was forever missing the last train. And frankly, on what I earn, I can't afford taxis! Anyway, at first I was too shy to ask him for the fare, but then I thought, what the hell! I mean, what could I do? So I asked him. And that's when it all slotted into place: he could have me for the price of a taxi. I was a taxi fare! Anyway, it all fell apart soon enough. Either he didn't have that kind of money, or maybe I just got fed up taking the initiative. And I've been thinking the whole day – it's really stupid – I'll have to find five roubles somewhere for a taxi!

NIKOLAI IVANOVICH. So did he give you more? I'm jealous!

IRA. No, that's it. I've got to go.

NIKOLAI IVANOVICH. Listen, I'd give you five roubles without even thinking about it, I'd see you out, put you in a taxi, I'd even take you home in it and come back! That's how men should behave. And that's the way I am, always have been.

IRA. One of my girlfriends told me her husband kisses her feet.

NIKOLAI IVANOVICH. Right, give me your foot, this instant.

IRA. No, don't be silly. You're not my husband.

NIKOLAI IVANOVICH. But you're my wife! My darling very own wife! Don't you love me?

IRA. I love Pavlik.

NIKOLAI IVANOVICH. Well, that's your right, you're a woman.

IRA. That's the most important thing for a woman, loving her child. A child means everything to a woman. Her family, and her love. It's all there.

NIKOLAI IVANOVICH. Anyway, the time'll come when some young girl loves your Pavlik. But you've got to love a *man*! That should be your hobby, my little night-moth, my little bird!

IRA. Look, let's go. It's time I was going, I need to get some sleep. Mama won't let me sleep on in the morning, no way, she sends Pavlik in; go and clap Mama on the head, so she won't sleep in. One time he even hit me on the head with a spoon!

NIKOLAI IVANOVICH. You'd be better having a lie-down here! And I'll drop you off on my way.

IRA. I'll walk.

NIKOLAI IVANOVICH. Look, it's high time you put a stop to all this. I mean, you should always have enough money for taxis. If you don't have your own transport. You need to look to the future – at least further than the end of your own nose! Listen, why don't I take up your case, eh? I'll work you into our system – I mean, with your knowledge of languages, you'd be in line for all kinds of perks. My assistant Nina, for instance, she's just a liaison person, but she's already been twice to Czechoslovakia.

IRA. With you?

NIKOLAI IVANOVICH. What's this, starting to get jealous, are we? I've got my unofficial wife to do that for me. Look, don't

be jealous, my little bird. I really do love you. And I'm surely
due some happiness in life.

IRA. I've got a headache.

NIKOLAI IVANOVICH. Then we'll cure it! We'll make it better.
We'll fix it right now! Come on, Mama, up you come.

IRA. Okay, I'll go. Give me five roubles.

NIKOLAI IVANOVICH. I'll give you six! Six roubles! Just don't
leave me. You're my only happiness, Ira. You wouldn't believe
the kind of life I lead. Running around like a blue-arsed fly. My
wife's been having it off behind my back the past three years.
Alyona smokes, the local girls down at the dacha were lying in
wait to beat her up, because some boy or other had given her
the eye, and we only just managed to head them off. I'm afraid
to say . . . (*Falls silent, deep in thought.*)

IRA. My head's splitting.

NIKOLAI IVANOVICH. Hey, my little night-moth, my little bird,
you should have diamonds, a car, your own bought flat away
from your mother, I mean, just look at you, just take a look at
yourself – you're like a beauty queen! You should change out of
all that stuff you're wearing, yes, and what's underneath! You
should have gold, platinum! (*Delightedly.*) God, when I think
what bitches most women are! (*Laughs, shakes his head.*)

IRA. I'm not letting you go on this trip. I'm definitely not letting
you go.

They exit.

PAVLIK's VOICE (*off-stage*). Mama, look how the stars twinkle.
One minute they're tiny, next minute they're really big. Mama,
I'm going to tell you a fairy story. The moon flew down into
hospital to have her tooth fixed. It'd got broken and wobbly, so
they put it back in. Then she flew in my window and whispered
something into my ear. She says there are lovely birds flying up
in the sky – sparrows, crows, woodpeckers, and rooks. And she
says she can fly very fast, faster than the birds. But she's only
got a tiny little tail. And she can run very fast as well, she can
fly and run. And she can crawl a little bit. And she can use
scissors, she's got hands, only she can't be bothered.

Scene Four

A telephone-box at Koktebel. IRA *is agitatedly dialling a number.*

LIFEGUARD's VOICE. Will all bathers please return to the safety zone!

IRA (*rushes out of the phone-box*). It's engaged! Maybe they've hanged themselves on the cord, or something!

A young man wearing Bermuda shorts and a cloth cap with a yellow plastic peak, nonchalantly shuts the thick foreign-language paperback he has been reading and enters the phone-box.

YOUNG MAN (*on the phone*). Hullo, Mam! How are you doing? We're here in Koktebel now . . . Yes, that's right. Yes, we've got fixed up quite nicely . . . We're studying the ants on the doorstep, Sasha and Natasha and me, right on the porch! They've had a look at the sea, gone absolutely nuts over it! Filled their sunhats full of pebbles off the beach and lugged them home . . . Yes, it's okay: we've got nicely fixed up, and there's not too many people here yet. There's one cafeteria open, and one restaurant. We had a try at getting in there, but it's no great shakes. They'll be opening a milk bar soon, they're cleaning the windows already. They'll have kasha and cottage cheese, just the job. Meanwhile we've bought some bread and milk, and we've got some tinned stuff. Rose-petal jam, would you believe? They've got strawberries in the market, seven roubles a kilo! No kidding. We bought the kids a hundred grammes each. They made short work of them! It's three to a room, so I'm sleeping out under a canopy. Pure luxury! . . . I'm telling you, the fresh air, the mountain scenery . . . Incidentally, before I forget, can you send some warm things for the kids? It's pretty urgent – you know, sweaters, jackets, trousers . . . And I need my green jacket . . . You'd be better sending them poste restante, I don't know the landlady's address, and anyway she's got thirty-five people bedded down in there . . . the parcel might go astray. What do I need an umbrella for? Well, okay, send it if you like. Anyway, it's really great here, really splendid. So, that's it, then – my money's run out . . . Everything okay with you? Right, okay, 'bye . . .

Hangs up and emerges from the phone-box. He stands abstractedly a moment. then nods. Counts the money in his hand. IRA *goes into the phone-box. She tries to keep her voice down, so the* YOUNG MAN *won't overhear her, but in vain.*

IRA. Hullo? Mama? . . . Thank God you're there. Listen, I haven't got much money, I'm calling (*Lowers her voice.*) from the dacha . . . From the *dacha*! I told you already, the roof's leaking. The *roof*, for God's sake! (*Lowers her voice again.*) It's pouring rain down here. Everything's wet through . . . It's not raining where you are? That's strange. It's chucking it down here. I've got to keep emptying out the buckets. (*Lowers her voice.*) *Buckets*! Yes, Yes, I'm staying on here! How's Pavlik? Tell me quickly, though . . . Fine, give him some warm milk and soda last thing at night. No, I'm not coming home today! I'll call you again same time tomorrow. So don't be on the phone!

MARYA FILIPPOVNA 's VOICE. So where's that bread of yours from two days ago? You were supposed to be bringing in bread. And you didn't bring any, we're sitting here with no bread! I can't leave Pavlik, and I'm due to go into hospital today! I lifted Pavlik up, like a stupid fool, and now I'm in terrible pain.

IRA. Mama, Mama, for God's sake, please . . . (*Lowers her voice.*) There's a long queue here, waiting to phone. I'll give you a buzz tomorrow. Anyway, love and kisses for now. Call up Auntie Nina, get her to come over and babysit. Tell her a fib, tell her I've gone off to the South with my lover. She'll come running. Well, anyway, I've got to go, before the roof floats away!

The YOUNG MAN *exits, still nodding to himself.* NIKOLAI IVANOVICH *enters, wearing yellow Bermuda shorts, Soviet made, and exactly the same sort of peaked cap as the* YOUNG MAN *had. He is also wearing sun-glasses..*

IRA. Oh dear, that's my money run out. (*Hangs up.*)

IRA *and* NIKOLAI IVANOVICH *sit down on a bench.* NIKOLAI IVANOVICH *has a look around him.*

IRA. So – tell me how you spent a whole twenty-four hours without me!

NIKOLAI IVANOVICH. Well, I didn't get any sleep, you know.

IRA. I'm glad to hear it!

NIKOLAI IVANOVICH. That's not very nice. As it happens, Alyona's a very light sleeper. I mean, there's three of us all in one room. You can imagine what it's like. And this is supposed to be a holiday! You can't so much as move a finger but Alyona

wakes up. 'Papa, you're snoring. You're snoring like a pig,
Papa!' Listen, I've only got a couple of minutes. They've gone
off for some ultra-violet treatment, for Alyona's tonsils, a
couple of minutes.

IRA. Well, anyway, I had a good sleep. First time in years. And I
went swimming yesterday, hardly came out of the water. Did
you see me on the beach? I swam up to where you were.

NIKOLAI IVANOVICH. Yes, I saw you.

IRA. So how about the bathing costume I bought?

NIKOLAI IVANOVICH. I had my back turned to you.

IRA. Yes, I noticed. I saw you turning away. You know there's
absolutely nothing to eat in this place. How are people with
kids supposed to manage?

NIKOLAI IVANOVICH. Yes, can you imagine Rimma's
situation? I mean, what the hell did I work my butt off for to
get a trip down here, eh?

IRA. Well, I've had a terrific time. I went swimming again last
night. I waited ages for you . . . the key was under the mat. You
didn't come?

NIKOLAI IVANOVICH. No, I stayed in bed.

IRA. God, if only Pavlik could come down here! I'm really stupid,
I could have taken him with me, picked him up still asleep . . .
just as he was . . . I could've got all his essentials together
quickly . . . his jacket and long johns . . . When I dropped in
to get my passport . . . But I didn't even give him a kiss on the
top of his head. I was frightened I'd wake him up. I didn't even
give him a kiss.

NIKOLAI IVANOVICH. So where are you off to now?

IRA. Pacific Bay, I think. Do you want to come?

NIKOLAI IVANOVICH. Listen, let me have your key for an hour
and a half or so.

IRA. My key?

NIKOLAI IVANOVICH. Yes, what did I arrange to come down
here for? Rimma's only human as well, you know what I
mean? I'll put the key back under the mat.

IRA (*hands over the key*). So where'll we meet up again?

NIKOLAI IVANOVICH. I've got a call booked at ten a.m. tomorrow. So come here. That's only if they don't decide to come with me. But if they're with me, don't approach, okay?

IRA. And then what?

NIKOLAI IVANOVICH. We'll play it by ear, don't worry. Right, that's their two-minute ultra-violet session about over now. God, Alyona's not well, she's been coughing. It's terrible. (*Exits.*)

Scene Five

Evening at the dacha. FYODOROVNA *is holding up the hem of the same ancient shabby dressing-gown with holes under the armpits, wrapped round a large, rusty key which she is turning in the door of* IRA's *room.*
SVETLANA, *supporting* LEOKADIYA, *is waiting to go in.* SVETLANA *has a chair in her other hand.*

FYODOROVNA. It's a good job this key's turned up. Otherwise you two'd catch your death, I can see that. (*Opens the door.*)

SVETLANA *helps* LEOKADIYA *into the room.*

SVETLANA (*re-enters*). She'll be a bit warmer in there. Anyway, when Ira gets back I'll tell her straight: while you were off having your little bit on the side, we had to make sure the kids didn't catch cold. So there.

FYODOROVNA. Well, she won't be back in a hurry. That Pavlik of hers is right poorly.

SVETLANA. I mean, I'll get a decent night's sleep now, for God's sakes! I can't get sleeping at all, you can't with the kids during the day, and then at night the patients keep you up . . .
Anyway, it's so quiet today. Maksim's been sloping around on his own since morning, with nothing to do. I wish to God it'd stay like that! He even sat down to read a book! Like a nice, well-behaved kid. And no fights.

FYODOROVNA. Well, if a person's on their own, who are they going to fight with? He should take a leaf out of my book. I can't help feeling sorry for your old granny, though. Just sits there saying nothing, off in another world, she is, her eyes wide open, never asks for nothing.

The women are meanwhile lugging various items into IRA's *room, folding beds, mattresses, bed-linen.*

SVETLANA. She gets everything brought to her, she doesn't need to ask.

FYODOROVNA. She'll be thinking about her son all the time.

SVETLANA. She'd be better worrying about her grandson, while I'm running myself ragged here.

FYODOROVNA. She's got one foot in the grave already. She's not going to run after your boy, her mind's somewheres else, the other world.

SVETLANA. Anyway, I can't be bothered with her. I've never heard so much as one word of encouragement out of her. She takes everything for granted. I mean, my husband was a lieutenant-colonel . . .

FYODOROVNA. A big wheel, eh?

SVETLANA. Yes, and she was a general's wife, quite the grand lady.

FYODOROVNA. I knew it. That's why she never asks for anything. She looks, but she won't ask. It's a real pleasure to serve people like that.

SVETLANA. Yes, well, it was after her son died, she went quiet like that.

FYODOROVNA. She must miss him a lot.

SVETLANA. So what? Loving your own kids is no big deal, you try loving other people's! (*Pounds her chest with her fist.*)

FYODOROVNA. Ah yes, but who can do that these days?

SVETLANA. Maksim won't be running after me in my old age, that's for sure.

FYODOROVNA. No, indeed he won't.

SVETLANA. It's a daughter I'd need! (*Hurrying past with bed-linen, etc.*)

FYODOROVNA. My Vadim certainly doesn't run after me. Nor his wife, that coalminer of his, she won't do it.

SVETLANA. We give them everything, and they give us nothing. Why's that?

FYODOROVNA. God only knows. I don't want nothing from nobody, I don't even ask God for anything. I live here on my own in the winter, wash my feet every night before going to bed, so's when they come to bury me I'll be able to show them a clean pair of heels. What do I need to believe in God for? I've got no sins on my conscience. I went to fix up a memorial service for my mother last year, and some old creature started shouting abuse at me in the church! I couldn't get rid of her, had to stuff money into her hand. I tell you, my legs were nearly giving way underneath me. So this year I've been turning it over in my mind, whether to go or not. I mean, I always do remember Mama, but where can you light a candle for her, outside of a church?

SVETLANA. What are you going on about her for? Church people are no better than you or me.

FYODOROVNA. I *do* like people with a bit of breeding, though.

SVETLANA. Well, I hate them, can't abide them.

FYODOROVNA. I've always liked them, my whole life. A really well-bred person never bothers anybody, they're the last ones to put themselves first, if you know what I mean. You'll never hear them swearing, either.

SVETLANA. Yes, well, you just try living with those people, the minute you step out of line you get a dirty look. I've been there, passed out with flying colours, I can tell you. My husband was one of that kind. Me, I shoot first and ask questions later. I'll think about it, and then my conscience starts to bother me. Then I'll give in, the whole way, but not before. Mama! You warm enough? Huh, not so much as a squeak out of her.

FYODOROVNA. No, she's nodding her head.

SVETLANA. Yes, she's so worn out that's the only thanks you'll get, and that's for your benefit. That's a fortnight's rain, two weeks I've been dragging her around everywhere, like a cat with a kitten, she's got all sticky with handling. Well, anyway, it's a good thing I don't like her, or I'd go nuts when I have to bury her. It's terrible even thinking about it. But this way, when she dies, I'll have good memories of her.

FYODOROVNA. A well-bred person always leaves a good memory behind them. I remember my own Mama like that, and I shall do till the end of my days. And my younger brother Pyotr as well. He died of a heart attack, and she went soon after, couldn't bear the shock.

SVETLANA. Yes, well, that one'll see us all out. It's in the blood.

FYODOROVNA (sighs). Oh well, no rest for the wicked. I'm going for a lie-down now. You stay here, and if Ira turns up I'll make up my mind about going to the church, and you can move in with me. I mean, how long are you going to suffer like this, Svetlana, eh?

SVETLANA (laughs). My whole life!

Scene Six

Koktebel, the phone-box as before. IRA is dialling a number.

LIFEGUARD's VOICE. Hey, you on the air-bed! Get back into the safety zone!

IRA. Hullo? Mama? Listen, I've very little change. Tell me quickly, how's Pavlik?

MARYA FILIPPOVNA (spot-lit). Hello.

IRA. Hello. How are you?

MARYA FILIPPOVNA's voice is dull and expressionless.

MARYA FILIPPOVNA. Pavlik's just the same. And so am I.

IRA. Mama, we've still got this roof . . .

A pause.

MARYA FILIPPOVNA. I don't want to hear about it now. Hold on, and don't interrupt. I've got to go into hospital today. I absolutely can't move. I didn't get a wink of sleep the whole night – the pain's just terrible. Can you hear me?

IRA. Yes.

MARYA FILIPPOVNA (expressionless). Oh, the pain, the pain!

IRA. How's Pavlik?

MARYA FILIPPOVNA. Pavlik's just the same, I said. He was coughing the whole night. You've got to come back right now. Pavlik'll be left on his own, you bear that in mind. Lyuba's gone to see her grandchildren, and Misha's not well. Nina Nikiforovna won't come to the phone . . . I've called everybody I can think of . . . There's nobody in . . . They're not answering. You'll just have to come home. I'm already packed to go, Pavlik'll be on his own, I've fed him for the last time. It's just as well you phoned, I can go away now to die with a clear conscience. Goodbye, Ira.

IRA (*in despair*). I'm coming! I'll just have to borrow some money! It's pouring here . . . Money for the fare! . . . The trains are all off, the track's been washed away! The timetable's suspended, do you understand? Suspended, there's a technical hitch!

MARYA FILIPPOVNA. What d'you mean, hitch? You'd better get out now, before it's too late.

IRA. Please don't leave Pavlik on his own! Wait for me, please!

The spotlight goes out.

Oh God, my money's run out! Look, I'm depending on you. Love and kisses!

IRA *comes out of the phone-box and sits down on the bench, stunned.*

Oh God, oh my God.

NIKOLAI IVANOVICH *enters, very rumpled-looking and furtive.*

NIKOLAI IVANOVICH. More trouble!

IRA. Oh, darling, I'm so glad! (*Clearly overjoyed to see him.*)

NIKOLAI IVANOVICH (*through gritted teeth*). Not now, not now!

IRA. Oh God, I've missed you so much! I love you more than my own life. (*Ecstatically.*) You're my only happiness!

NIKOLAI IVANOVICH. You don't love me at all.

IRA. You know it's so funny – I couldn't help gawping at you on the beach yesterday.

NIKOLAI IVANOVICH. Well, you damn well shouldn't have been!

IRA (*radiant*). I don't want anything from you! I'm just crazy about you!

NIKOLAI IVANOVICH. Yes, well, if you're crazy, they'll soon find a cure for that.

IRA. No they won't!

NIKOLAI IVANOVICH. Look, if you really loved me, you'd clear out of here sharpish! That's what I've come to tell you.

IRA. Clear off? Why?

NIKOLAI IVANOVICH. Because I say so.

IRA. You don't have to fling me out, I'll go of my own accord, when it suits me.

NIKOLAI IVANOVICH. No, you'll go now! Alyona and Rimma managed to pick you out in the crowd today. Alyona's been howling for a full hour! That was some carry-on, I tell you. You do your best for a person, go out of your way to keep them happy, and then they end up gawping at you!

IRA. So I'm not supposed to look at you?

NIKOLAI IVANOVICH. Damn right you're not!

IRA. All right then, I won't. Listen, I've got a favour to ask you . . .

NIKOLAI IVANOVICH (*dully*). How's your son? How's he keeping?

IRA. Much the same.

NIKOLAI IVANOVICH. And how's your mother?

IRA. Huh, the same old performance.

NIKOLAI IVANOVICH. Well, give me your key, in any case.

IRA. What, again?

NIKOLAI IVANOVICH. Look, you get on a plane out of here, right now!

IRA. First Mama shouting at me, now you!

NIKOLAI IVANOVICH. Alyona's highly-strung. She's started flying off the handle at people because of you!

IRA. She's fifteen, for God's sake.

NIKOLAI IVANOVICH. She's still a child!

IRA. Yes, well, I was a child once too, so what?

NIKOLAI IVANOVICH. You were a trollop!

IRA. Kolya, love, listen . . .

NIKOLAI IVANOVICH. Look, I'm not messing around, it's imperative you get the next plane out of here.

IRA. You just wait till she gets a bun in the oven, then you'll see!

NIKOLAI IVANOVICH. Yes, and I'll tear his fucking head off, whoever he is! Anyway, to get to the point, that's none of your concern. You know how much I care about my family, and you're just interfering! You've no right to be here.

IRA. I'm no different from them, I've the same right to be here as anybody else.

NIKOLAI IVANOVICH. You're nothing but a trollop! You've no self-esteem. Just take a look at yourself, the way you go about. I'm ashamed even to say it.

IRA. There's no shame, when a person's in love.

NIKOLAI IVANOVICH. It's disgraceful, absolutely shameful! I'm telling you to put a stop to this . . . this dogging my footsteps, d'you hear!

IRA. I can go where I like.

NIKOLAI IVANOVICH. You shouldn't have been sitting on that beach anyway. You haven't got a pass for it. Sitting there goggling!

IRA. What, there isn't room on the beach?

NIKOLAI IVANOVICH. Not for you, there's not!

IRA. So, do you own the place?

NIKOLAI IVANOVICH. No, but we'll just see who does!

IRA. Well, I like it here, and I'm staying.

NIKOLAI IVANOVICH. Right, in that case, *we'll* leave. I'll have to cancel everything, accommodation, treatment, the whole bloody lot! I'll have to drive them back up to Moscow, to the dacha! Is that what you want? Have you no decency?

IRA. What, aren't you frightened she'll spot me at the dacha as well? I mean, I'm going to be there all summer. And there's only the one river for everybody!

NIKOLAI IVANOVICH. Yes, you're right. Okay, bugger it, *you* go. Look, here's forty roubles . . . (*Takes out a roll of notes, slowly counts out forty roubles, and puts the remainder back.*) Here, take it . . .

IRA *won't accept, and* NIKOLAI IVANOVICH *lays the money on the bench.* IRA *gets up and walks to the phone-box, dials a number.* NIKOLAI IVANOVICH *rises, moves up, then returns and hesitantly retrieves his money.*

You know, people like you should be put down at birth. (*Exits, then re-enters.*) Have you any idea what Alyona might do to herself?

IRA. Yes, I do.

NIKOLAI IVANOVICH *slowly exits. Unexpectedly, he wipes away a tear, and his manner as he goes off is that of a deeply wounded man.* IRA *remains in the phone-box.*

Hullo? Pavlik, sweetheart, is that you? Listen, I need to speak to Granny, only you've got to call her quickly, I've absolutely no money for the phone . . . So how are you feeling, Pavlik? . . . Eh? . . . A little bit fine, I see. (*Smiles.*) Mama's baby boy. Anyway, be a good boy now and put Granny on . . . She's gone out? Well, that's great, that means she can still walk. You're all by yourself? Well done! Clever boy! What did she say? Oh, to the hospital . . . Well, of course! I'm coming home right now. I just thought I'd give you a quick call first, to see how you were getting on. Pavlik, have you got any water there? What d'you mean you don't know? I mean in the kettle? . . . Well, fair enough, then, you can't lift it up. Get it out of the tap then. You turn on the tap, and take a glass . . . Yes, of course you can, I'm letting you use tap-water now. Have you got a little bit of bread? (*Bites her lip, to stop herself crying.*) Right, that's fine, just open the fridge door, you know how to do that, don't you? . . . No, you're allowed to drink from the tap now. Open the fridge door, have a good look at what's in there, and I'll tell you what you can eat. You run and have a look, and I'll call back in a few minutes. Yes, love and kisses. Now run, there's a good boy.

IRA *exits from the phone-box, because the young man is already waiting. He is rather dishevelled in appearance, and carries a shopping bag.*

YOUNG MAN (*on the phone*). Mama? (*Laughs.*) Yes, it's me. Listen, we've a slight problem here. We let Sashka stay in the water too long. That's right. And we can't get a thermometer here . . . No, it's nothing serious. Listen, you wouldn't have sent off that parcel with the warm things yet? You haven't? That's great, you can put all the stuff out of the medicine chest in with it. We didn't think we'd need it, but . . . Yes, the whole lot. Including the mustard plasters . . . Yes, just in case. Anyway, go to the Moscow-Feodosiya train. Somebody'll maybe take it from you and bring it down. And I'll be there to meet it. (*Laughs.*) Well, I mean, how are we supposed to know, without a thermometer? . . . You're daft, that's what you are. Anyway, I'll call again this evening. And don't be using the phone, there's hellish long queues here at night. Right, love and kisses! (*Emerges from the phone-box.*)

IRA (*rushes up to him*). Listen, how would you like to buy a raincoat for your wife? It's very cheap, only forty roubles! It's worth ninety, honestly, it's practically new. Made in East Germany, see!

YOUNG MAN (*smiling*). No, no, Thanks, but no thanks . . . She doesn't need one. We've got a parcel of warm things coming from home. We don't need it.

IRA. But I haven't got any money! Take it for your wife, please! Take it! I need it for my plane fare right now, and I've still to get a bus to the airport!

YOUNG MAN (*smiling*). Listen, to tell you the truth, we've no money to spare. We're barely managing, you know? . . .

IRA. No, please, don't go away. *Please!* I've just got to make one call, and we can talk about it. (*She goes into the phone-box, dials the number.*)

YOUNG MAN (*still smiling*). There's nothing to talk about, I don't think you understand. We've no money.

IRA (*from inside the phone-box*). I'll send it back to you, the minute I get home. Oh shit, it's engaged!

YOUNG MAN. It's not up to me anyway. It's my wife that deals with the money side of things.

IRA. Engaged, that's all I bloody need! (*Keeps re-dialling.*) Engaged! Pavlik hasn't put the receiver back properly, that's what!

YOUNG MAN. Anyway, the thing is . . . (*Smiles.*) my wife never gives me any money. And the funny thing is, people are forever coming up to me in the street, and asking for money.

IRA (*still feverishly dialling*). That means you're a kind person.

Engaged! Oh God, Pavlik hasn't put the phone back. What am I going to do? (*Comes out of the telephone-box.*)

YOUNG MAN (*still smiling*). Anyway, you'll have to excuse me, I've got to get some milk, it's urgent . . .

IRA (*frantically smiling*). Let's go and see your wife, then!

YOUNG MAN. No, I'm sorry, I need to get milk, urgently . . . Someone's keeping my place in the queue . . . Our two kids are ill, you see.

IRA. All right, we'll join the queue. And then we'll go and see your wife.

YOUNG MAN. Well, you'll have to excuse us, but our house is in chaos right now. My wife hasn't slept the whole night, so don't be alarmed if she's a bit . . . you know. The kids are sick . . . so don't get upset if . . . it's the kids, you see.

IRA. Oh God, don't I know – I've got a boy of my own . . . (*She falters, trying desperately hard to keep cheerful.*) Listen, how long can a person go without food, if they've got water? About five days, isn't it?

They exit.

PAVLIK's VOICE. And while I was asleep the moon flew in to see me on her wings. She had tiny little black eyes, but I wasn't afraid. She had a blue body as well, with a big pink hook, it was pink at the tip and all shiny. She was so beautiful, just fluttering all over. She didn't say anything to me, but I told her about my troubles. And she said to me: 'I don't fly in Moscow.' That's what she said, she never flies in Moscow. She used to fly in Moscow, she said. She's a really great flier, and one day she flew in to see us. And I told her all about myself too, how I sometimes talk to myself at night. 'That's all right, my little friend, you can't help that,' the moon said to me, with her little hook. She said I take talkative people home with me and go for walks with them. She said she had some dinner left. She'd bought some meat . . .

This monologue may be subject to interference, in the manner of a radio signal. It should be intercut with the following dialogue scene, also heard only on loudspeakers.

ANNOUNCER's VOICE. Departure of the flight from Simferopol to Moscow has been postponed . . .

DUTY OFFICER's VOICE. Look, I've already told you, there are no more tickets . . .

IRA's VOICE. But he hasn't any bread!

DUTY OFFICER's VOICE. Well, you did leave him, for a start. That's not very nice, you know. I can't help you, no way. I can't print extra tickets. I can give you bread, though. Next!

WOMAN's VOICE (*with an accent*). We've got to go to a funeral – a funeral, d'you hear? Get away from the desk, miss, like you've been told. We've got a telegram to prove it, see, it's been stamped – we're going to a funeral.

IRA's VOICE. But I might not get there in time!

DUTY OFFICER's VOICE. And I can't dump other passengers off the plane, just to let you on. Next! Come on, move along!

WOMAN's VOICE (*with an accent*). For Heaven's sake, get up off the floor, it's dirty! Come on, miss, stand up!

MAN's VOICE (*with an accent*). They're forever jumping the queue, these people.

DUTY OFFICER's VOICE. Look, clear out of this office, and come in one at a time. For God's sake, miss, will you quit crawling after me! I've told you! What the hell do I want with a photograph? I don't know anything about any photographs. I've got a photo of my own son, d'you want me to show you it? Do you? Moscow's not accepting incoming flights, and that's it.

Scene Seven

The verandah of the dacha. TATYANA, SVETLANA, *and* FYODOROVNA *are drinking tea in the middle of the day. There is a pile of unwashed crockery on the table.*

SVETLANA. . . . . She kept saying: 'nobody wants me, nobody needs me.' But we need her, don't we? I keep thinking about her – thinking I hope to God she doesn't come back!

FYODOROVNA. She can come back when the warm weather's settled in. And you can move then into your old place.

SVETLANA. We can get along fine without her whatever the weather. I keep thinking about her the whole time.

TATYANA. Well, if she does come back, we'll have to clear out.

SVETLANA. Like hell we will! We've moved in, and that's it.

FYODOROVNA. Well, I'll let her stay with me. But from now on this dacha's not going for less than three hundred and twenty roubles for the season.

SVETLANA. That's all we need. We'll just use our own old toilet in that case.

FYODOROVNA. Well, that's your business. But don't say I didn't warn you.

TATYANA. Anyway, that's only from next year. (*Giggles.*)

FYODOROVNA. And she'll have to pay that from next year only. The toilet's hers, you see. I mean, it wasn't you got it put in.

TATYANA. Huh, that's bloody marvellous. She puts herself about and we have to pay extra.

FYODOROVNA. A hundred and sixty each . . . it's nothing if you say it quick.

TATYANA. Yes, and in fact there's three of you, and only the two of us.

SVETLANA. Make it a threesome, then, why don't you?

TATYANA. There's barely room to lie down here. Worse luck. (*Giggles.*)

SVETLANA. Well, that's your problem.

TATYANA. There's two of us, and three of you. Three plus two . . . Five into three hundred and twenty . . . (*Thinking it over.*) Six times five is thirty . . . Carry two . . . Four times five is twenty . . .

FYODOROVNA. That's a hundred and twenty-eight roubles from you, and a hundred and ninety-two from them. Plus the electric.

SVETLANA. But Maksim's hardly ever in!

TATYANA. And what about little me? I'm only here at nights.

SVETLANA. And I'm out at nights, so what?

TATYANA. I'd rather go to some holiday place right out of it –

otherwise it's nothing but these damn shops, back and forth on the train, greasy pans . . . You've got me absolutely pinned down.

SVETLANA. Me? Who is it has to sit with your Anton, then?

TATYANA. It's not you that sits with Anton, it's Maksim – he sits with him and bashes him!

SVETLANA. Well, Maksim's not going to turn out a wimp! I won't let him, he's not going to be like *some* kids I could name! (*Nods towards the room, in which old* LEOKADIYA *is sitting.*) I'm not going to let him die young either, like his father. That's why I'm doing gymnastics with him. And if your Anton doesn't like it, he can jolly well lump it.

IRA *enters, leading* PAVLIK *by the hand.* PAVLIK *is carrying a kitten.*

IRA. Oh, I see you're all here.

A silent tableau.

IRA. We've found your kitten, Fyodorovna. (*Takes the kitten from* PAVLIK.)

Enter MAKSIM *and* ANTON, *who stare as if mesmerised at the kitten, and stroke its fur.* PAVLIK *is also stroking it. He is wearing a headscarf, Granny-fashion, with a woollen hat on top, a checkered shirt, long johns with holes at the knees, and short trousers with braces: the standard dress of the kindergarten child.* MAKSIM *is in a fashionable tee-shirt with a logo, and shorts.* ANTON *is also wearing shorts and tee-shirt, though his is plain.*

IRA. Honest to God, we're just walking past, and there it is sitting at the corner, right there on the street, and a dog about to go for him! And he just arched his back, like this – (*Demonstrates.*) and didn't move. (*She is holding the kitten in one hand, and a holdall in the other.* PAVLIK *is hanging on tight to the holdall.*) Pavlik chased the dog away, and then we tried to catch the kitten, but it dived under a fence into some weeds. We started feeling around for it, but it turns out it's gone off behind a stack of wood! So I stood up, had a look around – there it was already outside some woman's house lapping up milk out of a saucer, and her stroking it! (*Laughs.*) She was really very nice.

TATYANA *nudges* SVETLANA *with her elbow, nods at* IRA.

IRA. Yes, it turns out he's been getting fed at her place all this time, he just went through the next two plots down to the third. God only knows how he survived. (*Presses the kitten to her cheek.*) I mean, there are dogs on these plots, Jack on this one, and Kuzya on that.

FYODOROVNA. Oh, there surely are. I'll go and get Her Majesty this minute! (*Goes off, calling in a high-pitched voice.*) Elka? Elka? Puss-puss? Here, kitty-kitty . . . What's she done with herself? Eh? Elka? (*Exits.*)

IRA (*still elated*). Oh yes, and my mother was taken into hospital, straight into the operating theatre. It turned out it was a strangulated hernia – a few more days and it would've been too late. I'd gone off for a couple of days, so I knew nothing about it, and Pavlik was left on his own for a whole day. And part of the night. I couldn't get a seat on the plane, no way, there were no tickets, and I'm having hysterics at the duty officer: 'You've got to help me out, my boy's left there all on his own, his granny's locked him in! His granny's gone into hospital, and he's sick!' And he says, 'Look, stick to one story or the other – either the boy's sick or the granny – maybe then it'd be worth getting down on your knees!' What a farce! (*Laughs delightedly.*)

TATYANA *nudges* SVETLANA, *as if to say, 'Look, she's laughing'.*

IRA. Then some business type says to him: 'Look, Captain, I have a container here, it's urgent freight, it's got to be flown out now!' And the duty officer's already writing out my ticket!

SVETLANA. I wouldn't get down on my knees before any captain, I tell you!

IRA. Oh, it gets better still! I had a ticket now, but Moscow wasn't taking incoming flights. (*Laughs.*) So I went to the pilots direct, and they took me on the first flight out. I told them, I said: 'It's just not possible my plane'll crash, because then my little boy would die!' And they fell about laughing! And then when I get home, and try to open the door, it won't budge! (*Roars with laughter.*) It turns out Pavlik's fallen asleep inside on the door-mat! And the rain in Moscow! And of course, I've no raincoat. (*Laughs.*) Sold it to a gypsy woman!

SVETLANA. Yes, the weather's just barely holding up here as well. Oh, look, it's started again! (*She stands up, moves in the doorway, looks out at the sky*) What the hell's the matter with it, are they all crazy up there?

TATYANA. There's mushrooms growing out the walls in that half of the house.

IRA. Oh, you've no idea how glad I am to be back! (*To the kitten.*) Are you glad too? His little heart's beating so fast! Look at him, he used to have such a dumb expression on his little face, like a baby. Now it shows traces of all the suffering he's been through. (*Hugs the kitten to her.*) And his little heart's pounding!

Enter FYODOROVNA *with her cat. The cat, as ever, is struggling to get away.*

FYODOROVNA. Where are you going? You lost him, now you just find him again! She's started hanging around them toms again. What, forgotten your own little offspring, have you? Eh? Clean forgot, yes. Milk probably dried up too. Well, we'll take them up to the loft. You can't leave a kitten outside in this place – that Jack'll be onto him in a flash.

The children, FYODOROVNA, *and* IRA *file out, running in the rain, carrying the cat and the kitten.*

SVETLANA. I told you, she was away having it off with that Nikolai creature. And Fyodorovna going on all the time about 'bad omens'. She dreamt somebody was spreading some black stuff on a bit of bread.

TATYANA. Maybe it was caviar. (*Laughs.*)

SVETLANA. So where do we go from here?

TATYANA. Where we agreed. We're not leaving this place.

Enter IRA *and* FYODOROVNA.

IRA (*elated*). I think they've recognised each other! Fyodorovna was holding Elka down, and I pushed the kitten up to her. The kitten started to suckle, and Elka jumped like a scalded cat!

FYODOROVNA. Yes, she'd got out of the way of it, you see.

IRA. But then the kitten started miaouwing, and Elka lay down again.

FYODOROVNA. Well, I'm sick to death of them tom-cats clattering above my head. They were rolling stuff all round the attic last night.

IRA (*happily*). Fyodorovna's letting Pavlik, Anton and Maksim stay up in the attic with the cats for a while. They're getting on really well.

FYODOROVNA. Aren't they brothers, more or less?

TATYANA. Third cousins, that's all, third cousins twice removed.

FYODOROVNA. Well, we're all brothers.

IRA (*laughs, excitedly*). No we're not – some of us are sisters!

SVETLANA (*after a deep breath*). Well, anyway, Ira. We're not leaving this place, I'm sorry. We've done enough traipsing back and forth.

TATYANA *titters.*

IRA. Then stay here, for God's sake! That suits me just fine, I've got to trail away into the hospital every day now, to see my mother. She's still in intensive care, so no one's allowed in, but they'll be transferring her from tomorrow afternoon. And that means I can leave Pavlik with you two.

SVETLANA. With *me*, that means.

IRA (*smiling*). Well, I can't rely on anybody else.

SVETLANA. You should learn to rely on yourself.

TATYANA (*giggles*). I mean, you've got that . . . the new bog.

IRA. So where are you planning to put Pavlik and me?

SVETLANA. We haven't touched your beds, you know. What d'you think we are, pigs? Right, Fyodorovna, look; Ira's back here now, so the old price can stay, two hundred and forty. That'll be eighty each from the three of us.

TATYANA. There's three of you . . .

SVETLANA (*firmly*). Eighty each! And if you don't like it, you can clear off.

TATYANA. But I'm only here at nights.

SVETLANA. Yes, and I'll only be here at nights as well, for the time being. Thank God I've already given Fyodorovna her hundred roubles!

TATYANA. And we've got to take turns doing the shopping and the cooking. And Maksim has to stop fighting! Okay? Bullies get put outside to cool off! You just bear that in mind, Svetlana, if any of the other boys gets beaten up. There's two of us now!

FYODOROVNA. Ira, you should bring your mother down here to convalesce, to my room. Two old folks like us, we'll get along fine. Old people get so bored, you've no idea.

IRA (*a wan smile*). I think I'd rather travel up to see her.

FYODOROVNA (*not listening*). I won't take much off her, say another seventy on top of your twenty . . . that should do it.

SVETLANA. That's some rain!

LEOKADIYA *appears in the doorway holding an umbrella.*

LEOKADIYA (*in an unexpectedly clear, ringing voice*). It's coming in through the ceiling.

The action freezes in a tableau.

Curtain

THE STAIRWELL

Characters

YURA (male)
SLAVA (male)
GALYA (female)
NEIGHBOUR (female)

The stage is set as a stair landing, with apartment doors. YURA, SLAVA *and* GALYA *emerge from the lift, wearing overcoats and fur hats.*

YURA. Which way?

GALYA. That's it to the right. (*She rings the doorbell a few times.*) My neighbour's not in.

YURA. Well, that's terrific.

GALYA *rings again, and listens at the door.*

YURA. An oil-cloth cover. Must've cost you a tenner.

GALYA. More like twenty. (*Rings the bell.*) Anyway, that's what my neighbour and I decided on, clubbed together. There's draughts on the stair, a lot of noise.

YURA. I'd have done it for free. For a kind look, you know?

GALYA. Yes, well, a kind look might cost me even more.

YURA. Not in money terms.

GALYA. Dearer, anyway.

YURA. What makes you think that? Why is it dearer for you, and not for me? Maybe it'd cost me more. The whole day buggering about with a door.

GALYA (*ringing the bell*). It's dearer for me.

The bell can be heard ringing above the stage very distinctly.

YURA. You're a strange person. I mean, you need it as much as I do. Why can't we just open up to each other, open our hearts, eh?

GALYA. Fair enough.

YURA. Right, then, you've got to admit that you need this no worse than me. It's not like we're playing blind man's buff here, are we?

GALYA. I suppose not. (*Rummaging in her handbag.*)

YURA. You want the same thing as me. I want the same thing as you. We're equals. I'm not offending you, and you're not offending me.

GALYA *rings the bell, and rummages in her handbag again.*

YURA. I mean, why did we tell you a lie, that there would be one person at the bus-stop, in a light-coloured coat, with a cake in his hand? Because me and my mate wanted to get a look at you, and if we didn't fancy you, we could quietly get on the bus and piss off. So there wouldn't be any offence. So as not to prolong the agony, you know? A clean break. But we didn't piss off, because we did fancy you.

GALYA. Honestly?

She pretends to be interested in the conversation, turns her back to the door, to face YURA, *and stops rummaging in her bag.*

YURA. Yeh. You've got the main thing, the kind of eyes I really go for. And I haven't seen your hair yet.

GALYA. It's black.

YURA. Brunettes are even sexier.

The conversation proceeds as though nothing has happened, but GALYA *is standing, in effect barring the door to her flat, and has no intention of letting anyone into her home.*

GALYA. You've got people pretty well sussed out.

YURA. Me? Yeh, I can do that. (*Animatedly.*) This is my mate Slavik, he works in one of the institutes. Get acquainted.

GALYA. I'm Galina Ivanovna. Pleased to meet you.

SLAVA (*holds out his hand*). I'm sure.

YURA. Slavik, his name is. Rostislav. A friend of mine.

GALYA. Your friend doesn't say much.

YURA. That's a sign of intelligence. Silence is golden.

GALYA. And talk's silver.

YURA. So you've noticed? That's true. I talk too much. I've put away a bottle of 'Surozh' since morning. That's a kind of port wine, 'Surozh'. I mean, it's Saturday for God's sake. That's when musicians play all their gigs. And people have been standing us drinks since morning already.

GALYA. You're musicians?

YURA. Yeh, that's right, musicians. But that'll keep.

GALYA. Why? I'm interested.

YURA. What d'you want me to tell you? A musician makes the human heart ache, while he feels nothing himself. Tears are just water to him, his grief's not forever, as they say.

GALYA. So what is it you play?

YURA. Basically Chopin. Marches.

GALYA. Really? And what instrument?

YURA. Well, there's an instrument called a French horn. I'm a French-horn player.

GALYA. And what's that?

YURA. Brass.

GALYA. Brass?

YURA. When I was a kid I split my lip on it. See? There. (*Turns down his lip under the lamplight.*)

GALYA. Ooh! Did you split your lip often?

YURA. Every month.

SLAVA. Come on, let's go.

YURA. Hold on. Slavik's saying nothing, but he definitely will say something, and it's always spot on.

GALYA. So how did they stitch it up for you?

YURA. Stitch it up? No. It healed over. You just don't play for a week, it heals over. Only I didn't let it heal, I used to pick at it.

GALYA. Was it painful?

YURA. Yeh, I hated putting up with the French horn because of that.

SLAVA. Look, come on, let's go.

YURA. Anyway, I studied at music school. An army school.

GALYA. Whether you wanted to or not, I can imagine.

YURA. Takes a lot of puff, you know.

SLAVA. Right, I'm off.

YURA. Slavik wants to go.

GALYA. Really?

SLAVA. Yeh, too true. Bugger this for a lark.

YURA. Actually, we're a bit offended.

GALYA. Really?

YURA. Yeh, we've come all the way out here, and now you won't let us in. That's not very nice. I mean, we agreed on the phone. And we met at the bus-stop. If you didn't fancy us, you should've said so, back then. Instead of which we get on the bus, and come out here. Chrissakes, what were you doing, giving us the once-over? That's not very nice. You ought to know your own worth, somebody like you. You're not in a position to mess around like that. Maybe dolly-birds can mess people around. But not you.

SLAVA. Let's go.

YURA. Hang on, let her answer that. How come you don't fancy us?

GALYA. Do you need to ask?

YURA. What d'you mean, ask?

SLAVA. Ask no questions, tell no lies. Here comes a poker to poke out your eyes.

YURA. I mean, we've got another three phone numbers noted down here, we could call them up. One's an English teacher. A cultured woman. She sat us down, a sort of tapestry table-cover, crystal chandelier, she lives on her own. 'Don't bother wiping your feet,' she says, 'the floor never gets washed, I'm in a state of depression, totally wrapped up in myself, nobody to live for.' She's lost her beloved Kolya.

SLAVA. It's not Kolya. It's her beloved *collie* she's lost. A dog. It's a breed of dog.

YURA. It's Kolya she's lost. So whose photograph's up on the wall?

SLAVA. That's a picture of Hemingway.

YURA. How do you know?

SLAVA. We've got one the same hanging up in the lab.

YURA. Our Slava knows everything. He works in one of the institutes. But you should see the junk she's got! All the old rubbish from the century before last. She won't chuck it out, it's all in memory of her ancestors. She doesn't come from around these parts. She told us her grandmother was one of the Smolensk women, whoever they were. And she's obviously carted all this garbage out of Smolensk with her. Anyway this Smolensk granny of hers used to go about in sack-cloth, never wore scent, a woman ought to smell of fresh water, she says. Back straight as a ramrod to this very day. Even sits upright in her wheel-chair, does this granny.

SLAVA. Yeh, I'd marry her granny.

GALYA. I've never been to Smolensk.

YURA. I've never been to Smolensk neither.

GALYA. So where have you been?

SLAVA. That's his bloody business.

YURA. Or to put it more simply, it's none of yours.

GALYA. I used to go to Sochi.

YURA. And you didn't hunt out a man for yourself down there?

GALYA. What gives you that idea?

YURA. Nobody was dazzled by your beauty?

GALYA. I'm asking you again, what gives you that idea?

YURA. Well, it's a fact of life, isn't it. There's some people nobody needs, nobody's interested in them, they're just stuck on their own, like rejects. I mean, everybody's interested in me and Slavik, people need us. But with you, well, it's a one-night stand, and there's others . . . Like there's this English teacher, she's thirty-eight, teaches in an institute. She's got a chandelier – crystal and bronze, it is.

GALYA. You've already told me about her.

YURA. No, no, there's more. Another woman. Actually several.

SLAVA. Come on, let's get the hell out of here. Best of luck, sweetheart.

GALYA. And best of luck to you.

YURA. It's been nice meeting you. Not especially, of course. Still, that's life, isn't it. To tell you the truth, we didn't fancy you much either, we just had a debate between us – like, it was worth going, maybe she'd have some grub out, a bottle to seal the introductions.

GALYA. Yes, I'd set the table.

YURA. So in fact if we hadn't come up to you at the bus-stop, you'd have had to manage all your grub on your own. You'd have sat down to it all on your lonesome, Well, here's to your good health, Galina! And yours too, Galka, let's party! And you'd have kept yourself company with the bottle. But we came, so you're not on your own, I mean, people aren't animals, right? And it's not as if we didn't like you, there was something about you, you've got nice eyes, and I like your coat.

GALYA. Anybody can put on a coat.

YURA. Don't you believe it, Galina. A coat just hangs on some people like a sack. But everything's nice and neat on you, very smart. That's how a Galka ought to be, sort of like a jackdaw – a perky little black bird.

SLAVA. Christ, you don't even know her, and it's Galka straight off already.

YURA. I'm calling her Galka because I like her. I call all the Galinas I know Galka. The serving-lady in our canteen's a Galka. There's even two Galkas – an old one and a middle-aged one. Galchonok, I call her.

GALYA. Do you stay in the barracks?

YURA. No, I've got a room. Eat barracks food, that's all.

GALYA. So what about your mother?

YURA. I don't have a mother, never have.

GALYA. Is that the truth?

YURA. Just put it out of your mind, Galka.

GALYA. All right, I will.

YURA. Anyway, let's go in and get settled down, see what develops, eh?

GALYA. Yes, that's easily said.

SLAVA. Yura, let's piss off, come on!

YURA. Well, okay – best of luck to you, Galka, keep your chin up!

GALYA. Oh, hang on . . .

SLAVA *is pressing the lift button.*

GALYA. It's a No. 10 bus you take, to the terminus, where it turns round.

YURA. Well, that's us then, Galka. You're really something else. I wasn't expecting this. You'll think about me, eh? You'll remember? You'll wake up tomorrow morning and it'll all come back to you. You'll cast your mind back, you'll think about me, only I won't be around any longer.

GALYA. What do you mean, you won't be around?

YURA. The usual thing. (*Improvising.*) Down off the fourth floor without using the stairs. (*Pause.*) And we don't have a lift in our block. So that'll be it.

GALYA. A likely story.

YURA. Seriously. Tell her, Slavik.

SLAVA. Look, come on, let's go.

YURA. Because you never know what might happen.

SLAVA. Yeh, he'll slide down the drain-pipe.

YURA. And I'll play Chopin's Death March for myself. And that'll be it then – the old zinc coffin!

SLAVA. No, the zinc coffin's for out-of-towners, when they're sending the corpse off some place. It's not for locals. Where would they send you?

YURA. Well, I'm not from around these parts. Actually I'm from Brest.

SLAVA. You haven't got anybody in Brest. Who needs your coffin?

YURA. They've taken their time with that lift. Anyway, I'm off. I'll send Galya my galvanised coffin. And you can play the sousaphone, Slava. Okay, Galka, the funeral service'll be the day after tomorrow. (*Makes to kiss her gently on the hand, but she won't give him it, so he kisses her coat flap.*) I swear to God, I've always loved stubborn women. Through gritted teeth, eh? An unapproachable woman means some man gets a good kind wife. That's a sort of inner beauty. Isn't that right, Galochka?

GALYA (*smiles*). How should I know?

YURA. Teeth clamped shut, eh, Slavik? Anyway, here's to the next time. You know, I really loved your braids, sort of like ringlets, I had you in my mind as a Zina, Zinochka. I actually wrote a poem, when I was ten years of age. *I called you Zinochka for love . . .*

GALYA. Was that somebody you knew?

YURA. No, it was just somebody. A nurse in the medical room. But you can change it, you can substitute Marinochka or Irinochka. For all occasions. *I love your braided ringlets, let me call you . . .* (*Thinks.*)

SLAVA. Piglet.

YURA. I'll call you Galinochka, out of affection. Take off your hat, then, let's see what your hair's like.

GALYA *removes her hat.*

YURA. Mm, not bad.

SLAVA. Terrific. The lift's arrived. *Au revoir, mam'selle.*

GALYA. What?

YURA. *Arrivederci, signora.*

GALYA. So, how is it?

YURA. The hairdo could be better.

GALYA. It's a perm.

SLAVA *drags* YURA *to the lift, they exit.* GALYA *goes up to the lift door and listens to them descending. The sound fades away.* GALYA *leans against the wall, takes out her comb. She rings the bell several times, listens at the door, knocks. She presses her face to the door, stands like that a while.* YURA *and* SLAVA *creep quietly up the stairs.* YURA *covers her eyes.*

GALYA. Oh! Who's that! (*Tries to break free, but* YURA *won't release her.*)

YURA (*in a squeaky voice*). Guess! Who is it?

> GALYA *immediately calms down, stands motionless, as if listening to her own feelings.*

GALYA. It's Yura, isn't it?

> YURA *releases her. In that moment something has happened between* YURA *and* GALYA, *and their whole tone changes.*

YURA. So why aren't you inside, sitting down at table?

SLAVA. Don't you see, she's forgotten her keys.

YURA. Why didn't you say, you gormless creature?

SLAVA. Where's your neighbour, then?

GALYA. I don't know. She ought to be back soon, if she's not stayed over at her daughter's.

YURA. Well, anyway, we'll break the door down for you. Always ready to oblige.

GALYA. No way. No, no. I'll be late for work tomorrow because of the door. Getting a new lock on, running around looking for a locksmith. And my neighbour won't be able to get in, if it's a different key.

SLAVA. What, never been late for work?

GALYA. No, of course I haven't. It's not worth it.

YURA. Oh, well . . . are you spending the night out here?

GALYA. Look, please go.

YURA. Go to your relatives.

GALYA. I don't have any.

YURA. None at all?

SLAVA. Same as Yura, whereabouts unknown.

GALYA. My father got married again . . . to my girlfriend.

SLAVA. He's no fool.

YURA. And you're suffering? Has your mother been gone a long time?

GALYA. My mother's in hospital at this minute.

YURA. She's taking it bad, then? Won't she give him a divorce?

SLAVA. You've got a friend, surely? Somebody you can go to.

GALYA. That *was* my friend.

YURA. Well, what the hell, it'll pass. It'll pass.

GALYA. My mother tried to kill herself.

YURA. It'll pass, I tell you, Galina Ivanovna, these things happen all the time. Don't be too hard on your father, you know, a man's got to live three lives, minimum: a first youth, a second youth, and a third youth, from sixty onwards. You can't run his life for him. You've just got to accept him for what he is, and don't nag him too much. I mean, he's already done everything for you in life, set you up. He's given up two of his youths for you. Now he's got to live for himself, for his own benefit. And as for your mother, well, she'll forget, and she'll be forgotten.

GALYA. I'm taking her in here after the hospital, she can't go back there.

A silence.

YURA. You're her daughter.

GALYA. She wants a grandchild, then she'll be able to forget herself, she says.

YURA. So, a grandchild, just like that. (*Pause.*) It's only cats that drop them that quick. It'll take you at least nine months. Plus whatever time it takes to find a man. And it's not everybody that'll agree. There's not many would want to get mixed up in that sort of business. I mean, who needs an illegitimate kid, for Chrissakes?

GALYA. No, Mama doesn't want it that way. I did suggest it to her, but she's terrified just hearing about it. If I get myself . . . I don't care how bad it is, she says, as long as it's a registered marriage.

YURA. I mean, then you've got a mother-in-law, and a family, and a baby, all in one room. That's some mess.

GALYA. Well, anyway, I told the whole story to Anna Dmitrievna. And I gave her my phone number for the purpose.

YURA. Which Anna Dmitrievna?

GALYA. The one that's acting as go-between.

YURA. The hairdresser?

GALYA. Well, yes.

YURA. And you think you'll get a husband that way? Oh, I'm telling you, never trust a man. D'you really think we want to be lumbered with all that? A man just wants a bit of fun with a woman, a good time, that's all. What's he need with all these other complications, rushing to get married? Don't trust us, just don't. Nobody but an idiot would get married like that. Who needs it? No, don't you believe it. Anyway, it's not as if you yourself even want to start a family like that, it's for the sake of peace, just to console your mother, right? I mean, you're not coming clean here; a man'll think you fancy him, but it's not him you need, except as a means of shutting up your mother. And husbands don't like mothers. A husband doesn't like it when everything revolves round the mother-in-law, he wants it to revolve round him. To be for his benefit, and that's it. And you'll be operating on two fronts. You'll do what your mother tells you, and the husband'll piss off, but if you obey your husband the whole time, your neurotic mother'll wind up hanging herself off the light-bulb. No, that's no use at all.

GALYA. And what's your opinion, Rostislav?

SLAVA. I don't think you wanting a husband's got anything to do with your mother.

GALYA. Really?

SLAVA. Yeh, why do you keep going on about it? It's for your own sake, and that's that.

GALYA. Living alone's nothing to me. I come home from work, everything's clean and tidy, I've got the television, a wardrobe, everything I need. I was really happy when I got this room. My mother and father hadn't been getting along recently, they were fighting the whole time. It was no picnic, I can tell you. And now Mama's blaming us all, that we've all betrayed her. You started it, she says, it was you that brought your girlfriend home. You can't talk her round, she just keeps crying.

YURA. That's where you got it from, that stubbornness of yours.

GALYA. Me? I'm not stubborn.

SLAVA. Just let your father go.

GALYA. She won't give him a divorce.

YURA. That's families for you.

GALYA. She just cries, turns her face round to the wall.

YURA. Yeh, that's family life. The hell with it! Well, we just wanted to spend a nice evening, and there you are. But I'm okay, I've no mother or father, nobody, just call me Brestsky. Nobody's suffering on my account, and I'm not suffering on theirs. I mean, take our Slava here, he lives with his mother-in-law, that's why he's out on the tiles every night.

SLAVA. What do you mean out on the tiles?

YURA. Along with me, of course.

SLAVA. That doesn't count. I didn't undertake to sit staring at four walls.

YURA. Well, you could pick up your wife, and go out with her.

SLAVA. That's *our* business.

YURA. So there you are – you see, Galya?

GALYA. See what?

YURA. How families can't exist these days.

GALYA. How do you mean?

YURA (*philosophising*). Because on the one hand there's a race of wives with their young, and on the other, there's solitary males.

GALYA. Is that a fact?

YURA. And of course there's some females, like you, that can transfer to the race of wives.

GALYA. Is that so?

YURA. But what's absolutely the worst thing, is females without young. I mean, like your mama.

GALYA. And what will you be?

SLAVA. Put a sock in it, Yura. Brestsky here's the biggest bullshit artist in the whole funeral band. Once he gets started, you'd have to gag him to shut him up.

YURA. That's why Anna Dmitrievna warned us. 'Galina's a nice girl,' she says, 'but she's forgetful. That's one of her shortcomings.' Did you forget to take the money to her?

GALYA. I didn't forget. I'll hand it in the first payday.

YURA. You're likely to forget everthing: boiling kettles, the gas, switching off the light. I mean, you've forgotten your keys, for Chrissakes!

GALYA. Me?

YURA. No, me.

GALYA. I didn't forget.

YURA. I did.

GALYA. I just didn't want to let you in. I didn't like you, either of you.

YURA. Well, you wanted to plenty, you were delighted, I mean you waited at the bus-stop. Ten minutes in the freezing cold.

GALYA. Never! It wasn't ten minutes!

YURA. Ten minutes by my watch. Slava checked it.

SLAVA. That's no lie.

GALYA. Because I could see it was you.

YURA. How come? A man in a light-coloured coat with a cake?

GALYA. I could see it was you. You were whispering and looking over at me.

YURA. Yeh, that's because nobody'll look at you for nothing.

GALYA. I wouldn't have said that.

SLAVA. It's weird. I mean, it's not as if you're that bad-looking.

YURA. Standing in the dark, at a bus-stop.

GALYA. That's the lift!

GALINA's NEIGHBOUR *emerges from the lift.*

NEIGHBOUR. What are you doing here?

GALYA. I've forgotten my keys.

NEIGHBOUR. Huh, crazy girl. Good evening.

YURA. And a very good evening to you.

SLAVA. Hello.

They bow from the waist.

YURA. She's quite an attractive bird.

The NEIGHBOUR *goes into the flat,* GALYA *behind her.*

YURA. Yeh, a nice-looking bird, and now she's pissed off.

The door slams shut.

SLAVA. Ring the bell!

YURA. You ring.

SLAVA *rings the bell. The door isn't opened immediately.* GALYA *appears wearing her indoor dress and slippers.*

YURA. I mean, she's really not bad. Hey, Galya, we're standing waiting out here for an invitation, like spare parts.

GALYA. An invitation to what?

YURA. To spend a nice evening. We can sit for while, have a chat, it'll be great. We'll sing to you.

SLAVA. You've got the table already set, I mean really. It's a shame to let all that work go to waste.

YURA. Just two mates and a girlfriend, that's all.

GALYA. So? Then what'll happen?

SLAVA. Well, anything can happen.

GALYA. I don't need that.

YURA. You did need it, though, for whatever reason.

SLAVA. We're still the same guys, we haven't got any shorter.

GALYA. That's got nothing to do with it.

SLAVA. Galina, you need to take a modern view. You've got a day in front of you, and you've got to live through it so it's not a terrific pain in the arse. But so it's terrific, right? And you do that day by day. So nothing's permanent, so what? Take each day as it comes, and be happy by the day. Why look ahead to the future? You know what's waiting for us all up there? I mean, the bottom line's Chopin's Death March, if you're lucky. Unless they don't even order that for you. And there's not many people more full of the joys of life than us. We earn plenty, we spend plenty, there's nobody sitting at home waiting up for us . . . My wife's got used to it, and she's filed for a divorce . . .

GALYA. Your wife's thrown you out?

SLAVA. She would have thrown me out. If I'd married her.

YURA. We're bachelors for today, Galochka. Our wives can wait.

GALYA. That makes no odds to me.

NEIGHBOUR (*looking out*). What's this door doing open?

GALYA. It's all right, I've got a key.

NEIGHBOUR. Shall I close it? There's a draught coming in.

GALYA. Yes, go on, close it.

NEIGHBOUR. And don't be standing there with them, with those drunks. Damn wine-moppers, I'm fed up with them.

YURA. Well, what a sweet old lady, thanks a bunch.

NEIGHBOUR. Huh, for two pins . . . (*Slams the door.*)

SLAVA. Hey, Yura, you can't make a fool of a fool.

GALYA. What does she mean, wine-moppers?

YURA. You shouldn't repeat bloody silly remarks.

SLAVA. She doesn't even know us, attacking strangers like that. Does she attack everybody? She needs treatment.

YURA. Yeh, acupuncture.

SLAVA. Anyway, we've still got to decide the question of the supper table. What'll we do?

NEIGHBOUR (*emerging*). You do what you like, Galya, but I'm not letting them in. After eleven o'clock I've got the right. (*Slams the door.*)

YURA. It's not eleven yet.

SLAVA. Ten to.

YURA. So, we can polish it off in ten minutes. We'll manage that.

GALYA. There's too much.

SLAVA. You don't know us.

YURA. We can do wonders.

SLAVA. Well, at least we can conclude our debate here.

GALYA. What, out here, do you mean?

SLAVA. I've even got sort of used to it.

YURA. It's quiet, it's warm, it's light.

SLAVA. For the love of Christ, as the beggar said.

GALYA. I'll bring it out to you.

YURA. You could put it on a newspaper.

GALYA. Hold on. (*Exits.*)

SLAVA. It's time to get the first drink in, eh?

YURA (*nonsensically*). Yeh, it's time we were doing what we were doing at this same time tomorrow!

SLAVA. Come on, she's a decent bird.

YURA. What sort of bottle's she got in there? Possibly vodka, somebody like her.

SLAVA. It certainly won't be dry wine.

YURA. Remember how that one brought us it in little tiny glasses.

SLAVA. And this is good, without all these tablecloths and mats.

YURA. I'm not used to all that.

SLAVA. Out in the entry, that's where we belong.

YURA. I'm sleeping outside, said the groom to the bride.

GALYA *emerges*.

GALYA. Here you are . . . a bit of bread. I've cut up some sausage . . . some cheese. And there . . .

YURA & SLAVA. Hey, you shouldn't have, thanks a lot.

GALYA. Only you've got to go down a floor. Otherwise my neighbour'll chase you again.

YURA. Okay, Galina Ivanovna. We'll do just that. I'm sorry, Galina Ivanovna, if we've annoyed you in any way.

SLAVA. Yeh, for God's sake, forgive us.

YURA. Just two mates and a girlfriend.

SLAVA. Okay, mam'selle? I'll maybe even marry you.

YURA. Yeh, me too! What do you reckon?

SLAVA. Listen, I'll tell you what – keep this in mind – if your mama should . . . I mean, God forbid, but we'll all play for her. Chopin's Death March.

YURA. No kidding, if you need that kind of thing, get in touch with me right away. Give me a call. Slava and me'll organise the lads. They'll do anything for a mate, for a reasonable fee, i.e. gratis.

SLAVA. We can't do much, but this we can manage any time. Tomorrow if need be.

YURA. Everything's ace, Galchonok. You'll have terrific kids, really beautiful.

SLAVA. And anything that's in our line – you've only got to call! We're ready and willing with our music.

YURA. It's not often we can, but once in a while – no problem. Once in a while.

They descend the stairs.

The End.

LOVE

A One-Act Play

Characters

SVETA (female)
TOLYA (male)
YEVGENIYA IVANOVNA, SVETA's mother

The scene is a room densely cluttered with cheap furniture, to the extent that there is almost literally nowhere to turn round, and all the action takes place around a large table. There is a new shoe-box on the table, tied with string. Enter SVETA and TOLYA. SVETA is wearing a simple white dress, and carrying a little bouquet of flowers. TOLYA is in a black suit. They are silent a few moments. SVETA takes off her shoes and stands in her stockinged feet, then sits down. The point at which she puts on her slippers is at the discretion of the director, but the process of SVETA putting on her slippers is significant.

TOLYA. So where's your mother?

SVETA. She's gone visiting.

TOLYA. Really?

SVETA. Actually she's taking a trip out to Podolsk, to her family.

TOLYA. Has she been gone long?

SVETA. She went straight after the Registry Office.

TOLYA. So, as far as I can estimate, it'll take her an hour and a half to get there, one way.

SVETA. Less. An hour and a quarter, including the metro.

TOLYA. She'll be worn out. And it'll be too late for her, travelling back. Podolsk's no joke, a lot of riff-raff out there.

SVETA. She doesn't like staying the night anywhere.

TOLYA. Well, what the hell . . .

A pause, during which TOLYA moves a little closer to SVETA.

SVETA. Er . . . do you want something to eat?

TOLYA. I was poisoned good and proper in that restaurant.

SVETA. I liked it.

TOLYA. Well, I'm poisoned.

SVETA. Yes, well, I liked it.

TOLYA. Because you're not used to it.

SVETA. Not at all, I just liked the way they did the food.

TOLYA. The chicken tabaka?

SVETA. What do you mean the chicken? I had the beef stroganoff.

TOLYA. Yes, well, you'll pay for it tomorrow, you'll find out what beef stroganoff means. D'you know what kind of fat they cook it in?

TOLYA *moves closer to* SVETA, *at which point she gets up and goes to the other side of the table, to look for a pair of slippers.*

SVETA. I enjoyed it.

TOLYA. The chicken tabaka was fine if you were a dentist.

SVETA. I had beef stroganoff.

TOLYA. Yes, well, the chicken was ideal for dentists, that's all.

SVETA. Meaning what?

TOLYA. You'd need your teeth fixed, urgently, after that.

SVETA. You haven't got bad teeth, have you?

TOLYA. I've got excellent teeth, never any trouble with them.

SVETA. So what's bothering you then?

TOLYA. The fact there was nothing on it but bones.

SVETA. You could've got it changed, you could've asked the waitress.

TOLYA. I don't like making a fuss in restaurants.

SVETA. Yes, well, you had a row with the waitress right at the start.

TOLYA. That wasn't just for the hell of it. They were sitting us at a table covered in crumbs, and leftovers.

SVETA. Who was? You sat down there yourself.

TOLYA. The place was full of empty tables, and they're telling us to wait.

SVETA. We could've waited.

TOLYA. I mean, your feet are blistered.

TOLYA's *statement produces a reaction which might be described as the sound of a breaking string!*

SVETA. I've been cursing everything in sight because of these shoes. I've been chasing after them nearly the whole of this month, and I ended up having to take a half-size smaller, just the day before yesterday.

TOLYA. Was that when I phoned you?

SVETA. The same day.

TOLYA. Were they difficult to get hold of?

SVETA. Yes, I couldn't get white anywhere. Because it's summer, of course.

TOLYA. You should've got them earlier.

SVETA. So? I forgot.

TOLYA. I mean, in the final analysis you could've written to me. I did leave you my address.

SVETA. I left you my address as well.

TOLYA. Well, I was running around all the time, what with selling the house.

SVETA. And I was working.

TOLYA. You know, you can pick up some good stuff there, that place I was staying in. At the market on Saturdays, they sell deficit items, you know?

SVETA. I don't like buying from people. It might've come off a dead person.

A pause. TOLYA *is still standing.*

TOLYA. Well, anyway, I need a wash after that trip to the restaurant. My suitcase is around here somewhere, there's a towel in it.

SVETA. Take one of ours in the bathroom, there's red ones hanging up.

TOLYA. You know, for a start, when you get right down to it, it's unhygienic, a shared towel.

SVETA. I'll give you another one of ours, it's red as well.

TOLYA. So how will we distinguish them?

SVETA. I'll sew on a bunny-rabbit for you.

TOLYA. No, don't bother. Actually I've got a whole bottom
drawer with me. I've got sheets and underblankets even.

SVETA. What, are you planning to sleep on your own sheets?

TOLYA (shrugs). We'll see how it goes.

SVETA. Well, I'll sleep with Mama, you can make up your own
bed. Then your sheets won't go to waste.

TOLYA. And all that hard labour won't be in vain, as Pushkin
says. I've been washing and ironing every spare minute. I
bought them, then had to wash and iron them.

SVETA. Yourself?

TOLYA. Well, I'm on my own, as you know. I was on my own in
my home town as well, although actually Mama wouldn't agree
to me marrying this local girl, a while ago. She said she knew
her parents right back to three generations and they were all
thieves. So that's how I do all my own washing and ironing to
this day.

SVETA. So they taught you to wash *and* waltz, then, at the Naval
College?

TOLYA. Well, you missed your chance for the waltz with me
anyway.

SVETA. My feet were killing me, you could have got Kuznetsova
up.

TOLYA. She had her own husband there for that, and he was
sitting it out.

SVETA. He wouldn't have been offended if you'd asked her up.

TOLYA. No, *he* wouldn't have been offended.

SVETA. Anyway, at least they taught you two things at that
College of yours: how to waltz, and how to wash sheets. The
one goes with the other – the ideal modern man.

TOLYA. What d'you mean? We got everything done for us at the
Nakhimov, we didn't have to wash sheets. It wasn't like that at
all. Nobody taught me. Even when I was working on the oil-
rigs in Kazakhstan, in the steppe, we had a cook that did the

washing. And actually when I was in lodgings in Sverdlovsk, there again I had an arrangement with my landlady about the sheets.

SVETA. You've told me all that.

TOLYA. This is the first time I've mentioned the sheets. The first time in my life I washed sheets, was when I was coming here. I bought them, washed them through with soap-powder, and ironed them. You can't just sleep in bought sheets straight away, they've been through so many hands; the machinists, not to mention the weavers, then Quality Control, then the warehouse, then after that the salespeople, and other shoppers.

SVETA. Terrific. You're really hygiene-conscious.

TOLYA. Yes, I'm a very fastidious sort of chap, very fussy.

SVETA. What, are you fussy about our towels as well?

TOLYA. Me? No, why should I be?

SVETA. So why did you bring your own?

TOLYA. Well, because . . . Actually, I'll tell you. As a matter of fact it's because you haven't got that much to spare.

SVETA. No, maybe not, but I always give myself a present for the New Year: I buy two new sets, and we sleep on clean sheets.

TOLYA. Right, that's the first priority. We'll do the same, and I'll make you a present of them. In our own family.

SVETA. Where d'you get this idea from – our own family? There's none yet, and there maybe won't be.

TOLYA. We'll see what we'll see.

He approaches SVETA, *and surprises himself by placing his hand on her breast.*

SVETA (*recoils*). Get off!

TOLYA. What's the matter? What's up? What are you scared of? Nothing's going to happen.

SVETA. What, d'you think you're home and dry now? The deep-sea sailor?

SVETA is seized with laughter.

TOLYA. What are you doing that for? You're my wife.

SVETA. No, indeed I'm not, and don't even think it.

TOLYA. Look, it's no big deal.

SVETA. And if you're going to try it on, you can just go back home.

TOLYA. Go where? Where can I go?

SVETA. That's up to you. (*She is still trying not to laugh.*) Go to your mother's.

TOLYA. She's living with my sister. There's no room there.

SVETA. Then go back to your place in Sverdlovsk. To your landlady.

TOLYA. I've already been signed out of there. That's finished. I've been de-registered out of everywhere, and I've sold my mother's house back home. I'm nowhere! So here I am standing at your table, for the moment I'm at your mother's.

SVETA (*laughing*). Well, if you're going to stand, you might as well sit.

TOLYA. That's all right. We'll stand and wait a bit.

A pause. TOLYA *takes everything seriously.*

SVETA (*laughing*). And he's making a pass at me!

TOLYA. So how come a husband can make a pass at his wife? In actual fact, that's not possible. As long as a husband respects his wife, that's all that's needed.

SVETA. Look, let's give it a rest.

TOLYA. I mean, your mother's gone away deliberately, she's put herself out, hasn't she, to go and spend the night in somebody else's house?

SVETA. I'm telling you again, she doesn't like staying overnight. And she said nothing about any overnight stay, so that means she won't be. She does what she says she'll do, and I'm the same.

TOLYA. That's terrific. (*Muses, silently.*)

SVETA. I just say what I think, I'm not dependent on anybody – why should I make up some lie or other, and then have to tell more lies? I say what I think.

TOLYA. But she won't be back that soon, if that's what you're scared of.

SVETA. Well, for a start, how long did we sit on in that restaurant? And secondly, where d'you get the idea I'm scared? I'm not scared. And I'm not in the habit of telling lies. I mean, what do you know about me? I always tell the truth, and I'm not scared. You just don't know me. I've got nothing to be scared of. You really know nothing about me.

TOLYA. I had a good look at you, in five years as a student.

SVETA. A good look maybe, but you don't know me.

TOLYA. I know plenty, more than I want to know. There were two guys chasing after you, but they wouldn't commit themselves.

SVETA. Look, we're not going to discuss me, right? But if you ask me, I'll tell you the honest truth.

TOLYA. I don't need to ask you anything – I got to know you in five years at university.

SVETA. Yes, well, I just don't know you at all. You were in a different crowd, we graduated, and not once in those five years did you come near me. Not even at parties, nowhere.

TOLYA. That just means I was observing, and making notes.

SVETA. And then you got your posting to Sverdlovsk, and went away. And that's just not on. '*If you love somebody, let them know; don't hide your feelings, and simply go.*' That's from Griboyedov. D'you remember Mamonov gave us a whole lecture on that quotation, on the difference between the sexes?

TOLYA. It took me all those years to make my choice, and the various candidates all dropped out, one after the other.

SVETA. That is, what is the role of women in this world, and what is the domain of the masculine principle?

TOLYA. I even went away to Sverdlovsk, with nothing decided.

SVETA. They all dropped out?

TOLYA. Well, I went off to Sverdlovsk, without having made up my mind.

SVETA. Yes, but if you'd fallen in love with one of them, she wouldn't have dropped out.

TOLYA. I can't love anybody. There's nothing I can do about it, I just don't know how. In that respect I'm a moral freak. I just can't do it. I told you. I told you all that quite openly: I don't love anybody, but I want to marry you. Or wanted to, rather.

SVETA. And now you don't want to?

TOLYA. Now I *am* married, from today onwards.

SVETA. People say that's a good test: to ask a man if he would marry the wife he's got now again – so what would you answer to that?

TOLYA. You suit me, you're just what I need, as far as I can see. I mean, I took my time, didn't I, looking around? I was twenty-five when I entered university.

SVETA. You've told me that today already.

TOLYA. And I can only repeat what I said: there was plenty of competition, but they all dropped out, one after the other. Apart from you. All except you.

SVETA. But you don't love me. So tell me . . .

TOLYA. And what are you going to do now? I'm giving it to you straight, I'm not hiding anything. You were the only one that appealed to me, out of the whole lot. But what could I do then, when we were waiting to be posted? You didn't know me at all, was I to just walk up and propose? I mean, would you really have married me then, immediately before the postings? Of course not.

SVETA. No, of course not.

TOLYA. But now you *have* married me. And that's the long and the short of it.

SVETA. So it took you two years to prepare yourself for this? Biding your time, were you?

TOLYA. What do you mean, biding my time? It's not like I was sitting waiting, making up my mind, thinking back, it wasn't like that. I didn't love you. But I'd already spotted you at university. So then two years went by, my mother wrote to me in Sverdlovsk that she was selling the house in our home town, our family home, my inheritance, which I wasn't counting on anyway, since there's nothing to keep me there any longer. In our home town, that is.

SVETA. Why not? You could settle down there.

TOLYA. Well, actually there wasn't any work for me. Anyway, my mother wrote to say she was selling the house and going to live with Tamara. And so that I'd go and sell it, a third of everything would come to me. It's a good house, practically two storeys. So, I was travelling home via Moscow, there was a bit of money coming my way, and I decided to look you up.

SVETA. Yes, you've told me all that perfectly well already, so that's enough of that.

TOLYA. But that *is* actually the case, so what are you going to do now?

SVETA. You know, it's as if you're not like other people. Everybody else says one thing, while they mean something different, and they're trying to guess at something else again, and because of that they never suspect how wrong they are.

TOLYA. Well, I'm telling you it like it is.

SVETA. You come out with the whole story right away, so you've got nothing left to tell, and all you can do is repeat yourself.

TOLYA. Well, that's how it is, in fact, so what the hell.

SVETA. It's like you have one leading idea, and nothing else in your head, just your own version of the truth.

TOLYA. Well, that's right.

SVETA. But I'll tell you what I think – I think you're just the same as me, and everybody else. And when you're hanging on like grim death to your own version, I get suspicious, that maybe there's something totally different behind it all.

TOLYA. There's nothing different, honestly. I hardly ever lie. I mean, I can tell a lie, if it's something I don't know about. But what I do know, I tell the truth about.

SVETA. Yes, well, you know this whole story doesn't quite match the picture you've just painted. You know it, actually, and so do I.

TOLYA (*monotonously*). It's actually nothing of the kind. Look, this is how it was: I went to university when I was twenty-five, so I wasn't particularly young for my age, you know, and I'd made up my mind to get married, only I was having a good look round, just because I wasn't young. And one by one the various contenders dropped out, so by the time of the diploma exam there was only you left. I mean, I already knew I wasn't capable of love, and actually, after observing somebody for a while, I used to get this distinct feeling of hostility. But in my relationship with you, that didn't happen. My relationship with you, and you only. At first, I felt absolutely nothing towards you, a sort of level, flat calm, you know? But afterwards, turning things over in my mind, it began to dawn on me, albeit dimly, that that level, calm aspect of the relationship meant something. In fact, that *nothing* was actually a very precious *something*, and I needed that more than anything, more than any other kind of relationship. But we got our postings, you stayed on in Moscow because of your mother's illness, I couldn't propose to you, and so I went off to Sverdlovsk. And the fact is that in any case I was only just starting to work all this out myself, and that continued in Sverdlovsk. I worked there for two years, and it was the same end product, I just didn't fancy anybody. Out of the lot, there was always only you left; after I'd subtracted all the rest, you were the remainder. And then Mama wrote to tell me she was selling the house, and if I managed to get the right price for it, a third of it would be mine. So I immediately quit work, got de-registered from Sverdlovsk, I mean, my mind was really buzzing, and I set off to sell the house, passing through Moscow. I still didn't know how much a good two-storey house in our town would fetch, but I had some sort of money to look forward to, besides which I'd saved a bit in Sverdlovsk. So I came to you in the library and proposed. I asked you for an answer the next day, so I could put in an application to the Registry Office. And you agreed. And that was that.

SVETA. And what if I'd said no?

TOLYA. You wouldn't. I was sure of that.

SVETA. You were that sure of yourself?

TOLYA. Well, that's me.

SVETA. Not one shred of doubt.

TOLYA. That's the whole point, I knew right from the start. I knew what you were like.

SVETA. Like what?

TOLYA. Like what you are.

SVETA. And yet you don't love me. True?

TOLYA. I've already explained that to you, and if you want, I'll repeat it again. I'm not in the habit of deceiving myself, and during those five years, I analysed all the various candidates and they all fell by the wayside, one after the other.

SVETA. Oh, give over, I've heard that already. That's not the whole story, and it's out of order besides.

TOLYA. It is the whole story.

SVETA. In point of fact you *did* love somebody at university.

TOLYA. I did? Who?

SVETA. You know perfectly well who.

TOLYA. I do?

SVETA. You were in love with Kuznetsova.

TOLYA. No, I wasn't.

SVETA. And then she went and married Kolya Dobachev.

TOLYA. That's rubbish!

SVETA. She married him.

TOLYA. I'm telling you – I *wasn't* in love. I can't love anybody. I absolutely can't, it's not in my power.

SVETA. No matter what you say, Kuznetsova told me you proposed to her. On the stairs. So there.

TOLYA. I did not!

SVETA. That's what she said, she said it, so calm down!

TOLYA. I'll tell you what I said to her, I said, 'You should get married'. And that's all. I just told her, 'You ought to get married'.

SVETA. So, that's what I'm saying.

TOLYA. That was advice.

SVETA. That's what you said to me as well.

TOLYA. Not quite. There's a difference.

SVETA. Yes, I just knew your standard proposal formula.

TOLYA. Not quite, it's a matter of the intonation and the circumstances. I mean, I said to you, 'You ought to get

married', and you said 'To you?', and I said, 'Yes', but I was
giving advice to Kuznetsova, and she said, 'Yes, but who'll have
me?', and I didn't say anything else. That's the formula – it's
ambiguous, made out of two statements. 'You ought to get
married', and 'Yes', in the case of me proposing. But in the
case of straightforward advice, I don't make the second
statement, and I've advised a lot of people to get married that
way.

SVETA. You've been in love with a lot of people, then.

TOLYA. How many times do I have to tell you – no! I wasn't
even in love with Kuznetsova, I can't love, it's just too bad. I'm
not able to fall in love with anybody, and I never could. I
mean, everybody at Naval College kept falling in love, but I
couldn't.

SVETA. You were even in love with that Azerbaijani woman
Farida.

TOLYA. Since when!

SVETA. You went up to her room, didn't you?

TOLYA. Well, I'm a man, for God's sakes, you surely understand.

SVETA. No, you were just in love with her, and she gave you the
elbow.

TOLYA. I dropped her of my own accord, as soon as I realised
she didn't suit me, not in every particular. I mean, the closer I
looked into her, the more she repelled me. I told you about the
various candidates I had. Well, one after the other, those
candidates just dropped out of the reckoning.

SVETA. So what other candidates did you have?

TOLYA. God almighty, what do you think! I'm a grown man, I'd
started out in the submarine service, only thank God I got
discharged on account of my blood pressure. I mean, what am
I supposed to do? I went on the rigs, out on the Kazakhstan
steppes, and the only woman in the whole place was the cook,
yes, and she already had a husband *and* a fancy man, besides
which she was fifty-three, no less! I mean, what do you think,
after what I'd been through I was going to come up to Moscow
University, and I *wasn't* going to be playing the field?

SVETA. So tell me about these candidates of yours, what were
they like? Who were they?

TOLYA. Everybody, the whole year group! Literally the whole faculty, and the girls in the hostel, you can count them as contenders.

SVETA. You're telling lies.

TOLYA. I never lie, except white lies.

SVETA. You're telling a lie. In actual fact you were in love with everybody.

TOLYA. I can't love, I'm absolutely incapable. I don't have the capacity. Oh! My blood pressure's going up! It's as if the back of my head's been thumped. It's going to rain, for sure. Now I'm starting to go red.

SVETA. Mama'll get caught in the rain.

TOLYA. I can predict the weather, with my blood pressure. I can tell it's going to rain five minutes before it happens. Have I gone all red?

SVETA. Mama'll get soaked because of me.

TOLYA. Have I gone red?

SVETA. Not really.

TOLYA. Maybe it's not going to rain. You've got to take a close look. Have a look.

SVETA. I don't know.

TOLYA. Have a really good look.

SVETA. I'm telling you I don't know.

TOLYA. You've gone all red.

SVETA. That'll mean sleet, then, will it?

TOLYA. I don't know what it'll do.

SVETA. I just want to tell you straight: you were in love with everybody, barring one person.

TOLYA. And who was that?

SVETA. Who do you think?

TOLYA. Look, I'm telling you again, the fact is I wasn't in love with anybody.

SVETA. But you fancied them.

TOLYA. Who?

SVETA. Your candidates.

TOLYA. Well, I'm not going to argue about this. Of course I fancied the candidates, same as any other raw kid just out of Naval College.

SVETA. So, it doesn't make any difference, then, how you describe it? You fancied them, or you loved them?

TOLYA. Look, loving somebody and fancying them are different concepts – totally different.

SVETA. How would you know? I mean, you've never been in love, you can't compare them.

TOLYA. That's right, I've never loved anybody, not ever, I'm just not in a position to love anybody. As far as that goes I'm a freak.

SVETA. Okay, let's call it love, then, your fancying everybody. We'll just call it that. What you call it doesn't matter. You were in love with everybody, so did you love me as well then?

TOLYA. I can't love anybody.

SVETA. But you fancied your candidates?

TOLYA. Yes, at first I did, then it was as if they all just turned me off.

SVETA. They didn't turn you off, more like brushed you off.

TOLYA. No, it actually was as if they turned me off. That's how I often used to think of it, in my own mind: like, they've turned me off again. So what could I do? I just marked down one candidate after another.

SVETA. Yet you picked me out from among all of them?

TOLYA. Well, up to a point, yes.

SVETA. But you fancied them all.

TOLYA. Look, I picked you out, yes, but that was later, actually.

SVETA. Before the graduation party?

TOLYA. Before? No, afterwards. It was much later, in fact, when I was in Sverdlovsk, it was then I started to think seriously about you. You settled me down, somehow, you used to keep me calm. And I often remembered you as if you were the only one.

SVETA. Yes, but at the graduation party you were dancing with that Farida again.

TOLYA. Well, she was going away for good, it was the farewell waltz.

SVETA. And Kuznetsova was already in the club.

TOLYA. Well, believe me, I don't remember. You remember everything.

SVETA. So let's cut all this stuff down to size, to the one thing. You fancied them all, that is, you loved them all.

TOLYA. I'm telling you again, I didn't.

SVETA. And you picked me out of the whole lot. I was the exception that proves the rule.

TOLYA. That's right, you were. You're a different kettle of fish, I've told you.

SVETA *goes very silent.*

Sveta! Hey, Sveta, love! What's up?

SVETA. So you looked on me as a kind of last resort, whatever was left, after all the rest had dropped out. A standby last resort, that wouldn't turn you down no matter what. Isn't that so?

TOLYA (*moves towards her*). Come here.

SVETA *moves away from him, round the table.*

SVETA. Leave the easiest to the last, of course. I mean, where you're not going to be refused, why bang your head off a brick wall? It's only me you were never in love with.

TOLYA. I was never in love with . . . (*Sits down.*) Look, what's all this love stuff? What good is it? What does it get you? Look at your Kuznetsova, she was passionately in love with Kolya, and him with her, so she married him, and now they're completely nuts, the pair of them, she's calling him a sex maniac, while their kid sits on his pot in the middle of the room howling.

SVETA. How do you know this?

TOLYA. I spent the night at their place. Two nights.

SVETA. So, you were hiding out at their place.

TOLYA. What do you mean, hiding out?

SVETA. Well, what would *you* call it? You phoned up just two days before the wedding, and then disappeared again. Of course you were hiding. We could've gone out together, done something.

TOLYA. I bought the rings, what else had I to do? I bought them a month ago, and gave them to you for safekeeping.

SVETA. Yes, there's no point talking about it now, but that was some month.

TOLYA. It was a good month, I had a good time, got a lot of things done while I was waiting, looking forward to seeing you.

SVETA. So why did you come to Moscow then, and not want to see me? All you did was phone: let's meet at eleven, and I'll bring the witnesses.

TOLYA. I ordered supper at the restaurant.

SVETA. We could've had a good time, gone out places.

TOLYA. Well, anyway, that's all in the past, and the important thing now is that we got married without any hitches, and we didn't change our minds. If we'd met up before the wedding, we'd have got talking, silly bickering about who loves who, and how much, and all that.

SVETA. Yes, and we're having these discussions now, just the same.

TOLYA. But now that's all behind us.

SVETA. And that was a really good month. The leaves smelt so nice.

TOLYA. Eh?

SVETA. I didn't sleep much.

TOLYA. Well, that's all past.

SVETA. So you arrived, and went straight to Kuznetsova's place to spend the night. You went to visit your old flame.

TOLYA. I had to get a bed for the night.

SVETA. Not necessarily.

TOLYA. What do you mean, not necessarily? A person's got to spend the night somewhere, get a sleep.

SVETA. You could've spent the night here.

TOLYA. That would've been awkward.

SVETA. But you've decided to stay here tonight?

TOLYA. Yes. But we got married today. We've been registered.

SVETA. So, it won't be awkward for you tonight.

TOLYA. It's legal now.

SVETA. Oh well, if it's legal, there's no shame, is there. It's down on paper. But it's just a scrap of paper that's appeared, all the rest's the same.

TOLYA. No, that changes a lot of things.

SVETA. What, you've now got rights over me?

TOLYA. Of course.

SVETA. But how can you? I mean, you don't even love me. How can you actually bring yourself to touch me?

TOLYA. The same as any man touches his wife. (*He doesn't budge from the spot.*) You're my wife now.

SVETA. Don't you come near me, you don't love me.

TOLYA. It's only now I'm getting to know you.

SVETA. And of course you thought, well, so what if they have all dumped me, I wouldn't dump you.

TOLYA. Yes, I'm only getting to know you now, and I can *see* why those other two wouldn't commit themselves.

SVETA. They all bloody well dumped you, all hundred and fifty of them.

TOLYA. They had damn good reasons, those two, the first one sussed you out, then the second. One after the other. I understand now.

SVETA. Yes, well, Kuznetsova really enjoyed telling me how you'd stood on the stairs, shaking, and how you'd said again, 'You ought to get married', and she'd answered, 'Yes, but who'll have me, I haven't got anybody, and nobody wants me.' And you were afraid to say, 'I want you', because you knew what the answer would be.

TOLYA. Is my face red?

SVETA. Yes, it's red.

TOLYA. It's going to rain.

SVETA. Mama'll get soaked, she didn't take an umbrella. Anyway, now I understand why you spent two days in Moscow without me. You were afraid I'd dump you as well beforehand.

TOLYA. No, I wasn't. I was a bit uneasy about your mother.

SVETA. Well, I mean, you knew that, you were well aware, I told you Mama would live with us always, that I'm going to live with my mother always, even when we get our co-operative flat.

TOLYA. So go ahead, who's stopping her?

SVETA. Anyway, I'm sleeping with my mother tonight, you can stay overnight here in your washed and ironed stuff, but tomorrow we'll go and apply to have the marriage annulled.

TOLYA. I'll stay the night at Kolya's.

SVETA. What for? You'll only have to go and tell him the news, what's happened, and it's none of his business. Stay the night here. You can have my bed, it'll be comfortable, like on the train. You've just got no luck, have you, not a single one of your proposals.

TOLYA. Yes, well, you never know who's the lucky one.

SVETA. Right, you know what you can do? Actually, you can just pack your suitcase and go now, you can tell them you've been given the heave again.

TOLYA. I don't need to pack it, I haven't even unpacked it.

SVETA. Right, go, then.

TOLYA. So how will we get an annulment?

SVETA. I don't know, it doesn't matter. You go and make out an application, and I'll do the same. What would we go together for, like a devoted couple?

TOLYA. Right then, if you'll excuse me.

Enter YEVGENIYA IVANOVNA, SVETA's *mother*.

YEVGENIYA IVANOVNA. Good evening.

SVETA. Is that you, Mama? What are you doing home so early?

YEVGENIYA IVANOVNA. Good evening.

SVETA. It's still only evening.

YEVGENIYA IVANOVNA. Good evening.

TOLYA. A very good evening to you.

YEVGENIYA IVANOVNA. And a good evening to you, son-in-law.

SVETA. Mama, what's the matter?

YEVGENIYA IVANOVNA. You mean, why have I come home early? Yes, I did set out for Podolsk, but then I thought better of it, me going there uninvited, without letting them know. I mean it's just not done, everything in a mad rush like that – new shoes, new dress, a bed for the night. And there's me going off to spend the night with people, right out of the blue. I mean, what are they to me? I've got a bed of my own, besides, it's not as if I'm keeping anybody out of it, I can stuff my ears up. I live here, and I'm going nowhere, do what the hell you like.

TOLYA. I'm clearing off, you don't need to worry.

YEVGENIYA IVANOVNA. Well, I'm not holding you back, do what you like.

TOLYA. I'm leaving, just the same, right now.

YEVGENIYA IVANOVNA. Well, if you're going, go. I didn't take to you in the first place, I just wondered why's my Sveta got mixed up with him. All he wants is a Moscow resident's permit, that's all, it's just a marriage of convenience.

TOLYA. What do you mean convenience?

YEVGENIYA IVANOVNA. Don't try and con me, just don't bother. Sveta's too good for somebody like you.

TOLYA. Why are we talking like this?

YEVGENIYA IVANOVNA. We need you like a hole in the head. We'll get along fine here, just the two of us, even if we are both old, and both ill, we'll do just fine. I've got no husband, I've slept in a cold bed for thirty years, and she'll do the same.

Rather that than with you. Living with you'll bring nothing but heartache. So on your way, and don't look back.

SVETA. Why does he have to leave? He's got no place to go. And he has a perfect right to stay here.

YEVGENIYA IVANOVNA. He wants to leave himself, don't you see?

SVETA. Who asked you to get involved?

YEVGENIYA IVANOVNA. This is my room, outsiders have no business here. I can see what's going on, I'm not blind. The bed's not been disturbed. You've gone through a phoney wedding with him, what d'you want to get mixed up in that nonsense for? Did you just fancy having the stamp in your passport?

TOLYA. She didn't do that, it wasn't a phoney wedding.

SVETA. Maybe it'd be better if we just left. Tolya, let's get out of here.

YEVGENIYA IVANOVNA. And where do you think you're going! I'm not letting him in here, he just does what the hell he likes, and you'll see, he'll get his resident's permit, he'll get a flat, and throw us out. You see if he doesn't. I'm not letting him in. And he's only too pleased to leave. Well, go on then, go. Huh! He turns up in Moscow one day – proposes, and she accepts. Then he disappears, spends the time God knows where, and you're kept waiting, running to the phone every time it rings. Well, go on, get out, don't stand on the doorstep.

She advances on TOLYA.

SVETA. Tolya, wait a minute, I'll get dressed, wait for me. (*She puts on her shoes, wincing.*)

TOLYA. Put on the other ones, those are cutting into you.

YEVGENIYA IVANOVNA. What did you run after him for?

SVETA. These burst ones?

TOLYA. We don't know how far we might have to walk.

YEVGENIYA IVANOVNA. Go on, get out. There's your suitcase, bugger off. (*Trying to screen* SVETA *behind her back.*)

SVETA. Hold on, there's something I've got to pick up.

TOLYA. We've got everything here. We can buy anything else we need in the morning.

SVETA. We can't afford to waste money like that now.

TOLYA. Take your raincoat, it's going to rain.

SVETA. You've gone bright red.

TOLYA. And the back of my head's aching.

YEVGENIYA IVANOVNA. Will you get out!

She forces him out through the door, while he manages to hold it half-open.

YEVGENIYA IVANOVNA. I'll squash you!

SVETA (*grabs his outstretched arm through the gap*). Tolya!

YEVGENIYA IVANOVNA. Huh! That's some start in life.

SVETA *and* TOLYA *exit*.

The End

NETS AND SNARES

A monologue

WOMAN. This is what happened to me when I was twenty years of age. Actually, my being twenty doesn't come into it – I could've been seventeen, or thirty: the main thing is, it was the first time I'd found myself in a situation like that. And I never found myself in that sort of situation ever again: you could say that the minute I got a whiff of the possibility of winding up like that again, well, I promptly escaped, slipped through the nets that had been spread for me. Actually, there never were any nets spread, nobody ever – not even that first and only time – had the slightest intention of driving me into any kind of net; to tell you the truth, there were no wicked designs on me, or snares set for me on anybody's part, neither that first time, nor on any subsequent occasion, there wasn't even a basic, minimal interest in me as a person; I was of interest, and necessary in that situation, not in my own right, but as my husband's wife, and nothing else.

Anyway, there were absolutely no nets of any sort spread for me at that point when my husband, the future post-graduate student, found himself still involved in his work, while I, his wife, being in what they call an interesting condition, set off for his mother's house in another town. My husband was supposed to follow on soon after me, to see me settled into the new place, get us both registered, and eventually celebrate our wedding, sit his post-graduate entrance exam, and begin our new life.

So, while the immediate future was clear and unclouded, the remainder could only be worked out in the longer term, which is in fact how it turned out.

The situation I found myself in was absolutely straightforward and clear, or rather it would have been quite straightforward, and simple, if I'd possessed a document confirming that I was Georgy's wife. In all other respects, everything was fine: I'm Georgy's wife, I'm travelling meantime on my own to his

mother to have my baby, since he can't possibly tear himself
away just yet; he wants me to have the baby in his home,
because you need to give birth to a baby in peaceful
surroundings, and not in the atmosphere of that hole where
Georgy and I were living. True, I could have gone to have the
baby at my own parents', who lived some distance away;
however, I liked the idea of linking my fate with that of Georgy
as closely as possible, with his family, and his mother, whom
I'd still never seen, and who knew of my existence only through
her son's letters.

Well, anyway, everything seemed perfectly okay, if you discount
the fact that I still wasn't Georgy's wife. And I wasn't Georgy's
wife for the simple reason that he'd been married before me,
and had a five-year-old child, and his first wife lived in that
very same town where Georgy's mother lived, and where he
himself had spent the greater part of his life. Georgy had
divorced from his wife a long time ago, and it wasn't simply a
consequence of the prolonged separations you get when a
husband is working in one town, and his wife and child are
living in another, so that gradually communications break
down, they get out of the habit, and stop going to see each
other, although there aren't any obvious reasons, either for a
formal divorce, or for a full-scale showdown. In the case of
Georgy it was all much more cut and dried: they got divorced
while they were still living in the same town, Georgy's wife took
her child and went away to her parents', and Georgy got posted
to another town a short while after, where I also arrived from
the Far East, and he's now paying maintenance for his son.

So, that's the story of my acquaintance with Georgy, and at the
same time, the story of how, one hot summer three years after
the start of my studies, I came to be travelling to my husband's
mother in a strange town, with a suitcase, a raincoat, and a
handbag, in which was a letter from Georgy to his mother.

To tell you the truth, Georgy wasn't too pleased that I was
going to have the baby at his mother's. However, I was able to
get my own way, or more accurately, simply took matters into
my own hands, insofar as I was prey to the fears typical of
someone in my situation: if I were to go away to the Far East to
my parents, while Georgy went off to study for his post-
graduate exam, we'd be a long time getting together to start our
own family life. I'd be well looked after in the Far East, my
child would receive excellent care, I'd soon be going out to

work or study, and the whole tenor of my life would already be settling into a groove without Georgy. In point of fact I'm more afraid of that than anything: peace and a quiet life without Georgy. I preferred all the turmoil and instability of an existence *without* Georgy, because I knew how conscientious and noble he was, his nature just wouldn't allow him to abandon me and the baby in an unstable state. I knew that in a situation like that, if things got difficult, he would come to my assistance, meaning he would simply appear and organise whatever was needed.

That disorganised life automatically entailed a kind of striving towards order and stability, while any form of organised life – in the Far East with Mama, or in the town where Georgy and I lived, and where I could have asked for a place in the student hostel, if need be – any settled life of that kind would mean postponing a *truly* settled life, since Georgy's mind would have been at peace for me and the baby right from the outset, and he could begin his new life at the institute with a clear conscience, so that making him do anything – apply for a divorce, take me and the baby in with him – would be virtually impossible.

However, all of that in no way explains the state of mindless ecstasy I felt then, rushing into the arms of a strange family, Georgy's mother, that is, Nina Nikolaevna. She lived in a big, solidly built old house, and what a real delight it was for me, after the dusty summer road, to go into the bathroom, where there was an ancient porcelain sink, with a blue pattern and a crack, and the enamel at the bottom of the bath was worn right through to the cast-iron!

Our first meeting passed, nonetheless, without a surfeit of joy. Nina Nikolaevna, I have to admit, didn't conceal her doubts. She read the letter very carefully, while I stood in the hallway, poised to turn on my heel and leave right there and then. I'd put my case in the left luggage and had even spent half the day (I arrived in the morning), trying to find some place near the station where I could get a bed for the night.

At this point I must confess that I'd been relying on the fact that no one would take too much account of me in Georgy's house. In that respect I'd anticipated it all, since Georgy, who was ten years older than me and had seen much more of life, had given me a very clear picture of the set-up in his house, and of his mother. He told me it was all up to me, and me alone, to what extent I turned out to be intelligent and free-standing – that's right, free-standing. He repeated that word in various contexts, explaining its significance to me: a free-standing person is one who stands by him or herself, doesn't lean on anybody, doesn't make any demands on anybody. Only a person like that, Georgy informed me, could count on success with his mother, only that sort of individual, and not one in any way weak, looking for sympathy, ready to give in, to help, so as to show how good and decent they were. And Georgy furthermore told me he didn't like my eagerness to accommodate people, to please everybody, to put my trust in anybody instantly and unreservedly, he didn't like the way I was prepared to open my heart to all and sundry, in order to reach an understanding. Georgy wanted more firmness from me, and he turned to absolute stone, so to speak, whenever I tried to have guests in the little room he and I lived in after I left the hostel. Georgy didn't like my servility, my willingness to laugh at any sort of joke, and to take any show of interest for current gold, as a friendly overture, and nothing else. Whenever Georgy's friends left, Georgy wouldn't speak to me for days afterwards, annoyed that all his teachings had gone for nothing, that I wouldn't ever make that kind of stoical, free-standing person, who could treat coarse jokes and small talk with disdain. And even the way I reacted to those silences of Georgy's, the way I wept and tried to get back into his good graces – even that he felt to be some sort of marked deviation from the norm, from the normal behaviour of a proud, free-standing person. 'If you would just *once* show a bit of pride!' – Georgy would end up saying to me, and then fall silent again.

That last month we were living together it was quite impossible to get any kind of sense out of Georgy: he would turn up whenever, say nothing about his plans, and say nothing either about how his studies for the exams were going, as if I was trying to worm something out of him, even in that trivial enquiry about his work for the exams, as if I needed those details. He defended them, nonetheless, against my incursions, as if that information was somehow essential to me, and frankly I just couldn't live without it, without assailing him with questions, about how he'd spent the day, and how it had gone. He zealously guarded his notebooks from me, his books, his files, odds and ends he bought.

Anyway, he sat down with the greatest of ease and wrote a letter to his mother, when I told him I was going to her place to have the baby, because I hadn't enough money to get to the Far East. He wrote that letter, not just because I got down on my knees to him, but I think also because he himself wanted me to go, and quickly, no matter where or how, but go regardless. And actually my going down on my knees, all that grovelling, was a bit over the top, needless to say, and nobody ever persuaded anybody to do anything by that method, so Georgy informed me, getting on his high horse yet again. He started going on at me, saying I had no sense of occasion, and that in general I couldn't see beyond my own nose, that I was a person with no independence and that I'd get nothing out of my trip to his mother for that very reason – that I wasn't a free-standing individual. At that point he read his familiar lecture on the theme of how he would like to see me, which was a distinctly rare event, manifestation number one in the past month, insofar as he'd practically stopped paying me any attention whatever, just kept defending his private world, limiting my incursions into it, as best he could, gradually extending the no-go area, so that I spent almost all my time in the kitchen. It was summer, but I sat up the whole night in the kitchen, since I didn't want to miss the moment when Georgy would be leaving to sit his exams. Besides which he might quite easily have left me without a key, and I'd have had to travel out of town to our landlady, and the landlady wasn't all that receptive to me, because she'd very soon spotted the peculiar nature of my condition, and quite often used to say how she'd let out the room to a single engineer, and now a whole brood's living in it.

So anyway, Georgy sat and wrote his letter, and I said nothing to him in response, just took the sheet of paper and went back into the kitchen. That's when I began to put into action what I'd decided about a radical reworking of our relationship, about cultivating some pride in myself. And accordingly, without saying a word, I picked up the letter, waited until Georgy had gone out, then quietly packed my things and left, without so much as a note.

I pondered long and hard as to why Georgy had so coolly shipped me off to his mother, without demur, but I couldn't come to any sort of conclusion. I knew relations between him and his mother were strained, that his first wife hadn't got along with his mother, initially, and only later, with Georgy.

Still, for some reason or other, that didn't frighten me, I just kept turning it over in my mind – then I gave up, the train was on its way, and it eventually brought me, after a day and a night's journey, to the station in Georgy's home town, where his legal wife lived, along with his son, where the house stood, in which he had spent his childhood, and so on – all these thoughts troubled me a great deal, and it was some time after my arrival before I started doing what I'd made up my mind to do, that is, find a place to spend the night.

Thus, if the reception I got from Georgy's mother wasn't too polite, well then, I wasn't counting on it in the first place. Nina Nikolaevna read through the letter in the hall, without letting me into the flat. To tell you the truth, I looked perfectly decent – I'd had a wash at the landlady's, where I'd taken a bed for the night. And I'd also sewn a little white collar onto my dress there, since the attraction of pregnant women lies first and foremost in cleanliness and tidiness, in the particular charms of hygiene, and certainly not in keeping up with the fashion.

When she'd finished reading the letter, Nina Nikolaevna didn't greet me any more warmly, but she did invite me inside.

Her room was vast, and rather dark, with beautiful old furniture, and an almost black parquet floor. I fell instantly and totally in love with that room, my heart was filled with unbounded joy, and a desire to remain there forever.

However, in response to her question, as to where I was staying, I said I was staying with friends and that everything had been fixed up. To the question, had I any money? I said that I had, and that I'd actually just walked over to make her acquaintance, since I'd arrived in town anyway. To the question, why had I come? I said I was going to wait for Georgy there, along with the baby. 'And will the baby be soon?' asked Nina Nikolaevna, and I said I didn't know for sure, since the doctors were saying one thing, but I knew differently. Nina Nikolaevna asked what I meant by that, and I said I had to count from the November holiday. Then Nina Nikolaevna asked if this baby was Georgy's, and I said yes, and burst out crying.

I couldn't hold back that terrible weeping, in which I was obviously pouring out all my sufferings of the past months, when I hadn't cried, but laughed, rather, in response to Georgy's remarks about my lack of independence. It was that idiotic, irrational laughter, I might add, that infuriated Georgy particularly, but there was nothing I could do about it, it just burst out of me involuntarily, the same way as I began to cry quite involuntarily after Nina Nikolaevna's question about whether this baby was Georgy's.

My weeping made an impression on Nina Nikolaevna. It was as if she now understood whom she was dealing with, since she thereafter began to treat me in such a way that her every action produced in me a feeling of immense, indescribable gratitude, and of such bliss, as if I had found myself at last in a much-loved family home – the only difference being that I wouldn't have wanted to find myself in my own family home. In point of fact, the worst thing was that nowhere, no home whatsoever on this earth, not even subsequently Georgy's and my new flat, ever exerted such a pull on me as this house of Nina's Nikolaevna's, this beautiful, dear house, in which nothing had been meant for me, where everything existed as it were on a superior level to me, was more noble and splendid than me – and which at the same time was my only hope of happiness. With what awe I inspected the paintings in their heavy frames, the beautiful cushions on the sofa, the carpet on the floor, the grandfather clock in the corner!

I even found myself admiring all sorts of tasteless knicknacks, various little boxes and shoes from forty years ago, stuck with mussel shells, little empty scent bottles. I would have lovingly wiped all these things with a duster and displayed them beneath the mirror. In fact I eventually tried to do that, but Nina Nikolaevna foiled every such attempt, and wouldn't allow me to touch anything in her room, no matter what. To tell you the truth, the room wasn't all that beautiful, and she didn't tidy it all that carefully. Nonetheless, the very special magic of a long life lived within it, the charm of its solid old objects instantly communicated itself to me, struck me between the eyes, so to speak, like the sight of food to a starving man, or a safe haven to a wanderer.

Let me say again, there were never any nets spread for me, in the hope of trapping and destroying me. And moreover, I myself marched blindly forward, without any inkling that at some time, somewhere, there might be nets spread for me. I mean, I could scarcely regard that sensitivity and motherly – no, not motherly, something rarer – and finer – protectiveness, which I felt in Nina Nikolaevna, as a trap! I'm putting it badly:

not motherly – rarer and finer, because a mother doesn't act like a generous patron. Anyway, with all that, I was so enchanted, that I shouted one day from the room to Nina Nikolaevna in the bathroom that I would like to call her 'Mama'. She couldn't make me out, asked me to repeat it, but the noise of the water drowned my words, and I never again attempted to make such a far-reaching proposal.

It was like being in Paradise. If initially I was still tempted to slip away to the old woman's by the station, and make some sort of arrangement, just in case, about a bed for the future, then subsequently I never so much as mentioned it to Nina Nikolaevna (I did very quickly reveal my secret to her, about having booked a bed in advance).

Nina Nikolaevna wouldn't let me out of her sight that first day, and with each day that passed she grew more and more attached to me. She literally wouldn't let a speck of dust fall on me, and before going to work she would somehow get down to the bazaar for vegetables, and grate me a carrot for the morning.

Nina Nikolaevna, as I've already said, wouldn't allow me to touch a thing – she herself cooked the food for the whole day, and left me just to heat up my dinner. In the evenings, I didn't eat supper, but waited for her, sitting by the window. She would arrive, we would eat then, and go for a walk before bedtime. I slept on the vast wide sofa, on linen sheets.

Now and again Nina Nikolaevna would give me presents: she and I went to the shop and bought two floral print dresses, with box pleats, so they could be let out; she bought me nightdresses also, and open sandals for my feet, which were beginning to swell a little more each day, and so on.

Assuredly I have never – neither before nor since – felt so happy. The seal was set on our union as soul-mates, in that she loved jokes, and I also loved a good laugh, and we used to chuckle long and heartily, delighting in any occasion to do so. Nina Nikolaevna confessed she would have been bored without me, that the sound of my voice ringing through the house enlivened her quiet, solitary existence.

Meanwhile there was no news whatsoever from Georgy, we had no idea how his preparations for the exams were going, or even where he was. I wrote him several letters in the presence of

Nina Nikolaevna, but received neither an answer, nor my own letters returned with 'Gone Away' marked on them.

Having no new facts, Nina Nikolaevna and I spent long hours rehearsing old information about Georgy – we used to tell each other anecdotes from his childhood, about which I knew at least as much as she, if not more, indeed. I told Nina Nikolaevna things she didn't know – for example, about Georgy's fall from the roof at the age of ten (he concealed it from her at the time), about his first love, and then about his later life, Georgy's work, his friends, his habits, his relationships with his boss. Conversations like that were meat and drink to Nina Nikolaevna, and she quickly got excited, demanding ever more fresh details of our life together, how we divided up the responsibilities within our family, how Georgy received the news of his future child, and so on. I told Nina Nikolaevna about how Georgy and I got to know each other at a party in our institute, when two boys walked me home – he and a friend of mine ('What friend?') – right to the door of my hostel ('And where's this friend now?'). I knew well what was going on, I realised she was comparing dates – she wanted to know dates – and names, and places, in order to make quite certain it was Georgy's son I was carrying under my heart, her grandson, and not the child of one of my other hangers-on, who had also walked me home some dark night, then disappeared, leaving Georgy to feed his brat. To tell you the truth, I even found such guileless interrogations endearing, her thinly veiled suspicions – indeed, at the time, they proved all the more clearly how frightened she was of being betrayed in her hopes, how fiercely she cherished and protected her dreams of her future grandson!

Nina Nikolaevna used to visit her first grandson once a week with little gifts, she travelled to see him at the dacha, and I liked that habit of hers, the fact that she remembered, and kept up her duties towards the child, who was in no way to blame. On several occasions I even asked if I could go along with her, but she became unusually stern, and in an instant put me firmly in my place with a few simple, merciless words: it was clear that she too had her own particular world, quite distinct from the world of her relationships with me – a private world, again, like Georgy's; that world of hers, to which I had no access, formed gradually, imperceptibly, but also inexorably, and she began jealously to guard it against my incursions; I, totally drained once more, was left with nothing. She used to have long-distance telephone conversations with somebody, and wouldn't say with whom. She started going out for the whole evening, without leaving me a key. Our evening conversations became very one-sided – now it was me that kept asking, I did all the talking, praising Nina Nikolaevna's fine figure, pouring out the sour cream for her, while she said: 'It's my house, I've done the cooking, I'll take my own, and you just help yourself.'

Just how this metamorphosis came about, I have no idea. I suddenly got the impression that she had been transported high above me, that she was hanging poised over my head, like a mountain, weighing down my every movement. I now found it difficult to move in her room, difficult to speak with her. Everything irritated her, sometimes she wouldn't even bother to answer my questions.

Of course that situation, which I had experienced once before, was a familiar snare to me, a well-known net – although, I must repeat, it was neither a snare nor a net – but there was no getting round it, it was a disastrous situation for me, and under those circumstances, even more of a disaster than previously, since in the business with Georgy, at least if I found myself in an impossible position, I still had my hopes in his mother, in her nobility.

I continued to drag out my ambiguous existence in Nina Nikolaevna's house, since I had nowhere else to go. The old woman beside the station, in whom I confided, advised me to stay where I was, since nobody would give me a room with a baby.

I began going to the so-called 'exchange' – where the people who owned and rented flats used to gather. Summer declined into autumn, and Georgy had long since arrived. I felt sure of it, felt it physically, that he was in town, although he hadn't shown himself at his mother's, and she grew ever more harsh. Suddenly, as if she was shedding some kind of obligation, whatever it might be, she began talking about some friend of hers with her daughters, who were going to be staying with her, and then she would be going to them, and the flat would have to be locked up – her neighbours were out of town, they had entrusted the flat to her, and no one would allow a stranger to live in the flat, someone not a member of the family.

I suggested we have a talk, to clear the air. She said she'd had enough, it was disgusting, quite frankly, trying to get a stranger's child registered in somebody else's name, somebody who had absolutely nothing to do with it, when there had been all kinds of outings to dances and people walking me back to the gate.

I started to laugh, and the conversation came to an abrupt halt. My clothes were dumped out in the corridor, Nina Nikolaevna locked herself into her room, and I spent the night in the kitchen. In the morning Nina Nikolaevna carried my things out onto the stairs.

Thus ended my adventure. There's nothing more of interest – after that I stayed with the old woman beside the station and kept going to the exchange, trying to conceal my bulging tummy under my raincoat, and the upshot was that some crazy guy, who had signed up for work in the North, gave me his room literally for a song. I can't help mentioning that there was an absolutely bare iron bedstead in the room, with a kind of steel-mesh base, and I slept that first night in the new place, on a bed made up from my raincoat spread out on the bare metal, happy and serene, until the time arrived for my morning trip to the maternity home.

On that note, this period of my life is concluded – a period which won't ever be repeated, thanks to the fact that I've now learned a few simple tricks. It'll never be repeated, that time when I so strongly believed in happiness, loved so deeply, and surrendered my whole being into everybody's hands so unreservedly, to the very depths of my soul, like something which has no value whatsoever. That time won't ever be repeated – quite different times have come and gone, and different people, the life of my daughter is already under way, of our daughter, whom Georgy and I are somehow or other managing to bring up, and whom Georgy loves with such devotion, as he has never loved me. But that doesn't bother me that much – I mean, this is another period of my life, quite different, entirely different.

THE DARK ROOM

The Execution

Characters

Two actors in each scene

Scene One

FIRST MAN. There wasn't any courses on it, no training, nothing. No way am I doing this.

SECOND MAN. So what would they train us on?

FIRST MAN. They could have trained us on monkeys.

SECOND MAN. Okay, so the monkey's walking on its hind legs, with its hands tied, and it doesn't look back.

FIRST MAN. It would be a moving target, at least.

SECOND MAN. What do you need that for? You're one step behind, you'll hit the target, don't worry.

FIRST MAN. Supposing he makes a sudden move?

SECOND MAN. Well, there's no kind of training'll save you there. You can't foresee which way he'll jump.

FIRST MAN. What, he's free to walk?

SECOND MAN. Yes, his hands behind his back, if you call that free.

FIRST MAN. You mean his legs'll be free?

SECOND MAN. Yes, so what?

FIRST MAN. They should tie his legs as well.

SECOND MAN. What do you mean tie his legs? We'd have to drag him, then. If his legs are tied. He'll move one way or another anyway. Just watch you don't shoot at me. Possibly he'll fall on his knees. He'll turn round.

FIRST MAN. He's not permitted to turn round.

SECOND MAN. You can't give orders at a time like that.

FIRST MAN. So he should have his head fixed too. In one direction.

SECOND MAN. You'd want to make the man a dummy.

FIRST MAN. It's a problem. Yes, it's tough.

SECOND MAN. What's tough is that you've been dumped on me at a time like this. That's what's tough. Me and Kolmakov have been taking him out every morning. Just round and about, walking. And he's going without any panic already. And then at a time like this, suddenly they change the guard and he'll start to flap. I mean, the first morning we took him out he fell down on his knees.

FIRST MAN. In front of you and Kolmakov? What, is he stupid or what?

SECOND MAN. No, he just fell down. Didn't turn round. Just like that: three steps, then plop, down on his knees. So, we pick him up. Then it's another step, and the same performance.

FIRST MAN. What, was he praying?

SECOND MAN. Praying? No, far from it. Obviously he just couldn't stand it.

FIRST MAN. Ah, shit, it's going to be difficult. I'm new to this, though, he'll understand.

SECOND MAN. Understanding's as maybe. He'll feel it. It'll get to him.

FIRST MAN. Shit. Well, maybe he'll look at it this way: all right, so it's not Kolmakov, but I've got the same rank. Maybe he'll think it's completely *different* people that come to do the business on him.

SECOND MAN. He thinks all kinds of things, this and that, never stops. Falls on his knees the whole time. You'd be the same.

FIRST MAN. Yes, well, I haven't murdered anybody. They've got nothing on me.

SECOND MAN. Well, you're going to murder somebody today, what the hell.

FIRST MAN. I'm not murdering him, I'm implementing an order.

SECOND MAN. You're implementing a murder.

FIRST MAN. Well, thanks a lot. I'm not coming with you, that's really nasty. Shit!

SECOND MAN. I mean, what the hell? He killed one way, you're killing another. However you cut it, it's killing just the same.

FIRST MAN. You'll be killing as well.

SECOND MAN. I'm shooting. Firing squad.

FIRST MAN. And I'm shooting too. Shooting for a reason. I mean, this has got to be a real bastard – an animal. Nothing but a beast. Killing somebody, and then cutting up the body.

SECOND MAN. That's what I told you, you see? You've made up your mind to kill. You want to kill him for something, right? Well, he killed for some reason, and you'll kill him for that.

FIRST MAN. And you won't?

SECOND MAN. I don't know who he killed, or if he killed anybody at all. They could've made a mistake in the investigation.

FIRST MAN. He killed them and cut up the body, it was proved. Dismembered them.

SECOND MAN. How proved?

FIRST MAN. By investigation, that's how.

SECOND MAN. Yes, a mistake in the investigation.

FIRST MAN. A fat lot you know.

SECOND MAN. Well, I don't know, and you can't know either, that they didn't make a mistake. Have you seen *Twelve Angry Men*?

FIRST MAN. No. Anyway, I should've had a dry run.

SECOND MAN. How'd you make that out? It's been proved to you that you can't train on monkeys. What d'you want, mice?

FIRST MAN. Well, I won't hit him!

SECOND MAN. That's okay, I'll hit him.

FIRST MAN. No, I mean, shit, the hell with this. The point is, I can't cope with it. This isn't my business. I'm not doing it.

SECOND MAN. Oh, so now we're getting picky, are we? Look, it's your job to shoot him.

FIRST MAN. He'll make a move.

SECOND MAN. That's not your problem. You just fire down the corridor then. I'll handle it.

FIRST MAN. I don't know why I've been landed with this gig.

SECOND MAN. So complain to the major.

FIRST MAN. I will complain.

SECOND MAN. You're chickenshit already.

FIRST MAN. That's right, I'm chicken.

SECOND MAN. Kolmakov picked the wrong time to sprain his arm.

FIRST MAN. Picked the right time, you mean. Absolutely the right time. I know what the score is now.

SECOND MAN. I'd be better doing this job with a cripple, than having to smell your chickenshit.

FIRST MAN. Yes, well, Kolmakov certainly put his trigger-finger out of action. Self-inflicted, if you ask me.

SECOND MAN. I mean, what am I to you? Your guide and mentor, for Chrissakes? Your instructor? Vigilance at all times, combat readiness, all that crap.

FIRST MAN. Yes, well, you should be committed to your work. If a job's worth doing, it's worth doing well.

SECOND MAN. I tell you, you wouldn't just fall down on your knees, you'd be crawling around the whole time.

FIRST MAN. So? I'm not a murderer. I'm telling you again. It's not me that's in jail.

SECOND MAN. My God, I can just imagine you being sent to the Front. You'd make some mess there.

FIRST MAN. Yes, well, the world's at peace now, thanks to us. I mean, what have we established world peace *for*?

SECOND MAN. Well, it's no skin off my nose. I couldn't give a shit whether you go or not, frankly. You're nothing to me.

FIRST MAN. Yes, and I'm a babe in arms, joined with Frankenstein's monster.

SECOND MAN. That's tough, but there's nobody else. No substitutes.

FIRST MAN. Nobody to stand in, right? Well, I'm turning the job down. I'm withdrawing my services. So that means everything'll get postponed. He can live a bit longer, until Kolmakov comes off the sick list.

SECOND MAN. Well, that's just terrific. You know, I just thought straight away, I wondered when you'd show up in your true colours? So, when are you going to shit yourself?

FIRST MAN. Look, it's *this* shit I can't take.

SECOND MAN (*looks at his watch, a call sign, then the national anthem*). Fine. Oh-six-hundred hours. Stand . . . up!

FIRST MAN *stands up.*

SECOND MAN. Right . . . face!

FIRST MAN *right turns,* SECOND MAN *right turns.*

SECOND MAN. One pace forward . . . march! Halt, one-two! Port . . . arms! Left shoulder forward, prepare to advance . . . by the right, quick . . . march! One-two, one-two!

FIRST MAN (*on the march*). I'm not doing it.

SECOND MAN. Leaving the guard-room, forward . . . march! Come on, come on, get outside, it won't kill you, what's the point of sitting here?

FIRST MAN. Well, all right, we'll go, but I've had it for the rest.

SECOND MAN. Look, that's his cell door. Keep your voice down, don't start a panic. Don't spoil the man's death.

They walk out towards the door.

Scene Two

DOCTOR. Comrade Major, may I come in?

MAJOR. What do you want?

DOCTOR. Medical report?

MAJOR. Yes, right.

DOCTOR (*hands the* MAJOR *a sheet of paper*). As you'll see, typically, the heart continued to beat an additional eighteen minutes.

MAJOR. What were you waiting for?

DOCTOR. To despatch him.

MAJOR. You could've been waiting for him to survive. He might've survived.

DOCTOR. No, he was being despatched.

MAJOR. Despatched, despatched – what the hell do you mean? What sort of word is that?

DOCTOR. It's the term we use at the clinic. So as not to alarm the patients.

MAJOR. So who managed the no-hit?

DOCTOR. Well, there were two wounds – one trifling, in the region of the clavicle. The other had a lethal outcome.

MAJOR. Huh, experts. Who was responsible, the new chap?

DOCTOR. I can't say at present.

MAJOR. I could set up an investigation, you know. Honest to God, I mean, what would you do with these people! A top-flight criminal, five people he's murdered, and they couldn't even finish him off!

DOCTOR. So everything's fine, what's the problem?

MAJOR. You've got to chase after them the whole time, in person. Did he remain conscious for eighteen minutes or what?

DOCTOR. That's difficult to say.

MAJOR. You see? We're running a torture chamber next. They can't even kill the man cleanly. He lived on for eighteen minutes! I can't believe it. No doubt he was aware of everything that was going on.

DOCTOR. It's hard to say, we don't know that much about death's secrets actually.

MAJOR. But he did definitely die?

DOCTOR. Look, why are you taking this tone? I mean, I'm certifying that he was despatched. And I'm responsible for my report.

MAJOR. You're new here, I don't know you, *or* how responsible you are. Supposing he's still alive.

DOCTOR. I can say categorically, no, he isn't.

MAJOR. Hm – you never know. You just never know.

DOCTOR. Actually, I've dismembered the body.

MAJOR. You sure you haven't cut him up alive?

DOCTOR. What do you mean?

MAJOR. You'll find nothing out now, except maybe by forensic examination. These bloody civilian experts have no intelligence, you can't do a thing with them. Doesn't matter whether you trust them, or keep checking up on them, they make a balls of everything. They'll take the skin off a living man out of sheer ignorance. Out of bone bloody idleness. And instead of a clean execution, they've spun out his death Christ knows how. You too, I mean, what did you do, sit up with him?

DOCTOR. I felt his pulse.

MAJOR. Eh? What is he, wounded in the line of battle, for Chrissakes? Stupid buggers. You could have finished him off a bit more humanely. Instead of all crowding round him, waiting. My God, like a bloody peep-show. You haven't done exactly a first-class job here, not first class at all. Right, you can explain to the guard where they've to take it. There's a car, thank God, at least they've given us a car.

DOCTOR. The head's to go to the crematorium, the rest of the body to the Medical Institute. I know. I've been instructed.

MAJOR. The driver's not one of ours either, as if it wasn't bad enough.

DOCTOR. What can you do? It's summer. Everybody's on leave. But that's some organism, I tell you!

MAJOR. What? Where?

DOCTOR. Quite literally worn out. The liver's four fingers deep under the ribs. I've had a look at it.

MAJOR. Huh, you bloody experts. Okay. I'll have a look at your report, now go.

Scene Three

DRIVER. It's not my job to hump this stuff around.

FIRST MAN. Look, mate, what's the problem?

DRIVER. Yes, I know, I know.

FIRST MAN. You want me to hump it out on my own, is that it?

DRIVER. It's not my job. That's your business.

FIRST MAN. You think it's mine? Well, there's a certain smart comrade here who's just fallen on the stairs, and managed to sprain his arm. He can walk, but he can't carry anything. Allegedly on the stairs, but more than likely he just did it in the door.

DRIVER. Yes, like I said, that's your problem.

FIRST MAN. Occupational injury, hundred per cent compensation. You slam the door on it, one-two, bingo. Then you walk down and lie at the foot of the stairs. It's no big deal.

DRIVER. That's your business, anyway. So tell me, who is it? It's him, isn't it? The murderer, right?

FIRST MAN. You don't need to know.

DRIVER. Hey, come on, soldier, tell me. I thought they sent them to the uranium, uranium miners? Why didn't they send this one?

FIRST MAN. They've left him for you.

DRIVER. What was he like, did he cry out?

FIRST MAN. What's it got to do with you? Let's go and load up.

DRIVER. I've told you, that's not my job. Anyway, what was it like? This is my first and last time with you people. I want to pass it on to the grandchildren.

FIRST MAN. Oh yes, smart guy. I tell you, and you tell your grandchildren. Come on, there's two boxes.

DRIVER. Hump out two of them, what's this?

FIRST MAN. Don't worry, relax, it's only one.

DRIVER. One man in two boxes?

FIRST MAN. One man what, what's it to you? It's just two parcels.

DRIVER. Identical?

FIRST MAN. Come on, you'll see.

DRIVER. Hey, look, I'm not touching any horrors.

FIRST MAN. It's just a polythene cover.

DRIVER. And what's under it?

FIRST MAN. Some sacking.

DRIVER. And then what?

FIRST MAN. Boxes.

DRIVER. Identical?

FIRST MAN. No.

DRIVER. I see. Listen, is it him, the murderer?

FIRST MAN. Come on, let's go and you'll see, maybe it is him.

DRIVER. Listen, what I'm going to see, what I'll see . . . I mean, will it be visible? God, I won't be able to sleep at nights. No, you drag it out yourself, I'd rather sit in the cabin. Why the hell did I get involved in this bloody caper?

FIRST MAN. Look, it's two boxes, boxes, that's all. Just two boxes.

DRIVER. Why two?

FIRST MAN. You're really paranoid, you know? Look, you can take whichever's the lighter.

DRIVER. Yes, well, I wasn't hired to weigh stuff.

FIRST MAN. Listen, I'll probably give it to you myself, I won't cheat you. You've got to take these no matter what. And you can't take them if they've not been loaded.

DRIVER. I don't do loading jobs.

FIRST MAN. What, and do you think *I* do?

DRIVER. I don't know what you're making a fuss about.

FIRST MAN. Yes, you're right, why should I bother if other people don't? My job's escorting. But I'll report you to the major right now.

DRIVER. Makes no difference to me. I've done my time in the army.

FIRST MAN. Have you no conscience?

DRIVER. Yes, I've got one, I'm not complaining.

FIRST MAN. Are you looking for a tip, a bottle maybe?

DRIVER. Listen, I've got a grade six ulcer.

FIRST MAN. Right, I'll sit down here, and I'll stay sitting. You go back to the garage. I'm not going to sign your sheet.

DRIVER. And I'm not going to load those sort of horrors.

FIRST MAN. Well, you can just drive away empty.

DRIVER. A real bullshitter, eh?

FIRST MAN. No, I'm not, but the job's got to be done. You do what you like now, but you can't leave him lying around.

DRIVER. What was that?

FIRST MAN. You can't leave him lying. The dead murderer.

DRIVER. That's true. That's the first true thing you've said.

FIRST MAN. He took a bite out of his hand. My mate's hand. Out of sheer spite. If you want to know the truth.

DRIVER. He did the right thing.

FIRST MAN. Yes, well, that's why I'm left on my own to load this. You see what I mean?

DRIVER. Yes, yes, I can see all right.

FIRST MAN. So let's go, we can't leave him lying.

DRIVER. Yes, but I'm scared of these things.

FIRST MAN. I used to be scared as well. But it's got to be done, you understand? I mean, they'll be carrying you out as well some day. But if you're alive now, you've got your duty to the dead meanwhile. Somebody'll do the same for you eventually, don't worry.

DRIVER. D'you know how many friends I've got? You wouldn't dream how many.

FIRST MAN. And he's got no friends.

DRIVER. When they carry me out – boy, that'll be some day. The whole garage. They'll be sounding the horns full blast.

FIRST MAN. So you can sound your horn for him.

DRIVER. Oh, let's go, what the hell. We'll bury him.

FIRST MAN. We're not burying him. He's going to the Medical Institute.

DRIVER. So, it's the Institute – shit, what the hell.

FIRST MAN. You see? And you said you were scared!

They exit.

The End

The Meeting

Characters

A MOTHER
HER SON
A LOG

The SON *finishes chewing some food, wipes his mouth.*

MOTHER. Aleksandr Aleksandrovich sends his regards.

SON. What did he actually say?

MOTHER. He said, give my regards to your son, and be brave.

SON. Did you meet him?

MOTHER. Well . . . not really. I rang him up.

SON. So what did he say?

MOTHER. He advised us to go higher up.

SON (*shakes his head*). As if we didn't know that, without him.

MOTHER. He said he's always thought something would happen,
he's an unusual man, he said, I knew there was something in
store for him.

SON. Why the hell are you phoning everybody, eh? What for?

MOTHER. Will you have some stewed fruit?

SON. I couldn't get it down.

MOTHER. I'm trying to get advice, and what can I do? What else
can I do?

SON (*irritated*). What the hell are you asking me for? I don't know.

MOTHER. I can't sleep at nights. Why did you do it?

SON. Shut up! Bitch . . . !

MOTHER (*recoils, nods at the log*). Look, take some stewed fruit,
won't you? I boiled it up last night. My God, I've got to keep
myself busy somehow. I had to call the emergency doctor last
night, they gave me some sort of injection. They suggested I
should go into hospital.

SON. You should have gone.

MOTHER. And what about you, then?

SON. For God's sake, what are you going on about me all the time for! Think about yourself. Did anybody phone?

MOTHER. That Borya of yours phoned. Passed on his regards.

SON. And who else?

MOTHER. They're not phoning any more, they're just waiting now. It's awkward for them, I can understand that.

SON. What do you mean awkward?

MOTHER. Well, you know, you know how it is . . . They don't want to bother me. But I'm saying the same thing, all the time, it doesn't matter. We're still waiting.

SON (*smiles*). Still waiting! It's all over. Just stop waiting.

MOTHER. They've allowed us a meeting.

SON. There you are, you see. That's it.

MOTHER. No, no, quite the reverse. I've been taking advice, and they said that means it's not going to happen.

SON. Oh yes? It's pointless. Who said that?

MOTHER. A lawyer.

SON. Which bloody lawyer? Matveika?

MOTHER. Somebody else.

SON. Have you been borrowing money again?

MOTHER. This isn't an advocate, it's just a lawyer at the citizens' advice bureau. A woman, Zbarskaya, her name is.

SON. So what did she say?

MOTHER. She says, according to all the indications, if you've been allowed a meeting, you can expect a favourable outcome. That's what she said. She had a case once, and they allowed a meeting in it, and then there was a reprieve. Now they're waiting for him to be released, already. That's fifteen years gone by.

SON. What article were they charged under?

MOTHER. Oh . . . it was a particularly serious offence. Article 58b.

SON. There's no such article.

MOTHER. There was, and this Zbarskaya's an experienced woman, she's retired now, acts as a consultant in the citizens' advice bureau. Maybe I've got it mixed up.

SON. So what was it in any case?

MOTHER. It was housebreaking, he killed an old woman, and murdered her niece, who was pregnant. And now he's being released.

SON. Ah, you see. Two people.

MOTHER. Three. The baby in her womb.

SON. Well . . . Did anybody else phone?

MOTHER. Lerka hasn't phoned anyway. That's right, Lerka. She's landed up on her own in a nice apartment now, the same one you worked on. That's always the way of it. She's doing nicely, and you're in here. You've dropped yourself in it, as they say.

SON. Mama!

MOTHER. Yes, it's Mama, isn't it, but I warned you you were biting off more than you could chew. I told you you were destroying yourself. Didn't I tell you? I did, I warned you. And how has it turned out? That I was right all along. That Lerka's a bitch!

The SON *silently nods towards the log.*

Listen, drink up a little drop of fruit juice. Borisovna brought me some Yugoslavian prunes. I'm on the sick list, you know. I can be on the sick list for at least a year, my heart can't stand the strain. Maslennikova's extending my sick leave without even looking at me. It's just a pity I've got to drag you down to the clinic, to the surgery, she says, I'd sign you off right now, to the end – you've got pain enough here as it is.

SON. To the end of what?

MOTHER. To the end of my life. I won't see it out. And all on account of that Lerka. If I could only just get my hands on her . . .

SON. Mama, why did you come here?

MOTHER. Drink up your prune-juice. Your stomach'll digest it. It'll do you good.

SON. What do you know about her?

MOTHER. Well, she's alive, no matter what.

SON. Is she on her own?

MOTHER. Yes. You should be delighted. Nobody wants her.

SON. Is she working?

MOTHER. No, how could she?

SON. What do you mean?

MOTHER. What are you looking at me like that for, son? Eh? If I got my hands on that Lerka . . . Now drink up your juice, it'll save me carrying it back.

SON. Tell me, or I'll kill you!

The MOTHER *looks towards the log.*

Please tell me. What's up with her?

MOTHER. I didn't want to upset you. That Lerka of yours . . . she's a bitch, a bloody bitch. (*Begins to cry.*)

SON. It's all right, it doesn't matter, tell me.

MOTHER. She's had a baby, that's what.

The SON *stares into space.*

You're so pure Lerka!

SON. What did she have?

MOTHER. A son, that's what she had. In memory of its father.

The SON *slumps to his knees.*

MOTHER. What are you doing! Don't do that! (*Points to the log.*)

The SON *gets up and sits down again.*

MOTHER. Drink some juice. Fish out the prunes, they're nice. Yes, she was living with him even before the wedding. It's not been nine months, seven and a half. The proof's there, staring you in the face.

SON. What are they calling it?

MOTHER. I wasn't interested.

SON. Who told you?

MOTHER. I phoned the maternity hospital. It's a boy. Three and a half kilos. Fifty-one centimetres.

SON. What the hell . . .

MOTHER. Well, what do you want?

SON. So who's meeting her now? Coming out of the maternity hospital?

MOTHER. Her girlfriends, I suppose.

SON. No, she hasn't any now.

MOTHER. Oh, that's right.

SON. Her mother won't be meeting her, nor her father. Nor her husband. Her whole family and friends, they've all been killed.

MOTHER. Yes.

SON. What about her neighbours?

MOTHER. What neighbours? They didn't even live there. They got some flat at the back of beyond, at Chertanovka.

SON. Yes . . . she didn't reply to a single one of my letters.

MOTHER. Yes, well, she wasn't even at home, she was in hospitals all the time . . . From the wedding, and straight into the ambulance.

SON. Yes, I remember.

MOTHER. She actually locked herself in the lavatory, in the toilet.

SON. What did she lock herself in for, as if I couldn't have broken the door down? . . . If I'd needed to. She locked herself in and that was that, she didn't want to come out, fine. I was crying, but what the hell. So who called the police?

MOTHER. The people downstairs.

SON. I wouldn't have laid a finger on her. I just wanted to have a talk with her, just a talk. I just wanted to kill those . . . nobody else. It was them that wanted her to have an abortion, they took her away from me, yes, to a new flat. No bloody forwarding address! Bastards!

The MOTHER *nods in the direction of the log.*

SON. Her girlfriends as well. When I came in they started laughing at me. Her dear mother and father making faces. And her fiancé just shrugging his shoulders.

MOTHER. You'd taken on more than you could handle, I told you.

SON. We're all equal! That's the law. She's my wife.

MOTHER. What are you saying?

SON. She's my wife, you bitch! Yes! And that's my son!

MOTHER (*signifies with a look, that the log is at hand*). What are you saying, God help you!

SON. You go and meet her from the hospital.

MOTHER. What would I do that for?

SON. Buy her . . . whatever she needs. You can send me a note through Matveika, tell me who he looks like.

MOTHER. What for?

SON. I won't be here much longer, you've got to help her.

MOTHER. We'll have to tell Matveika that this is your son, that it's your son! Oh my God!

SON. What's the matter with you, do you think it'll change anything?

MOTHER. She'll say it's not. She'll deny it's yours.

SON. No, no, she won't. It was them that turned her against me, they set her on me like a dog. They kept on at her, beating her eardrums, it was them that dug up that boyfriend, that soldier boy from wherever it was. They did it. She was just feeling low, and they were forcing her to have an abortion.

MOTHER. You don't kill people for that.

SON. Yes, you do! Bitch! They wanted to kill my son. Didn't they want to kill? What else is abortion?

MOTHER. Yes, I know, I know.

SON. And I killed them for that.

MOTHER. I know, I know.

SON. It was her girlfriends got her into hospital. That Milka and Tomka. Bloody stupid.

MOTHER. I know.

SON. Milka and Tomka, the stupid bastards.

MOTHER. You're right.

SON. The nurses, they do these abortions . . . They're whores. Murderers, Milka and Tomka. They're murderers, they've done abortions for everybody.

MOTHER. That's true . . . that's right . . .

SON. They do thirty abortions a day each. I mean, I killed five people! There's no comparison! There isn't!

MOTHER. All right, all right. Calm down. If that's true, you'll be released soon. I'll just go and see Matveika, have a little chat with her.

SON (*agitated*). Thirty abortions in each department! And how many hospitals! I mean, these are living beings! They can hear what's going on, take food! They can turn somersaults! I read it. And every one has a mother and father, grandmothers and grandfathers! And they have to be killed? What for? Live children! Just imagine it!

MOTHER. I know, I know, it's all right.

She starts to pick up the jars, leftovers, packages.

SON. That Milka and Tomka, they were doing the killing. Lerka's mother and father, that husband of hers, they were forcing her. As sure as God! (*Begins to cry.*) Christ almighty, they torture, they murder people every day . . . Every day, non-stop. What can you do, take them all to court? They won't charge them . . . My God, have mercy on the little murdered children . . .

MOTHER. He needs to see a doctor, we need to call a doctor urgently. Isn't your poor head hurting, eh? (*Hugs her* SON *to her breast.*) Thank God, thank God, I've waited this long! I knew it! (*To the log.*) He's got to see a specialist, urgently, he's gone out of his mind, a sick man needs expert medical attention, not execution. You don't execute sick people, you isolate them. He's ill, thank God, he's not responsible. He's being tortured by his own thoughts. What are you doing, shooting sick people? If he's killed somebody, all right, kill him, but he didn't kill anybody. He didn't! He only dreamed he did. Let's go home. Let's go home and I'll put you to bed, I'll make up your bed for you again. Your cot-bed's just waiting for you . . .

Everything's nice and clean, I've scrubbed the whole place, just as if I knew. I hadn't been cleaning, but I cleaned the whole place just yesterday, as if I knew this would happen. Borisovna brought some Yugoslavian prunes. You have a rest. Your poor little head hurts. We'll go, I'll take you away . . . just quietly . . . (*Looks at the log.*) Can't we? He's a sick man. He's insane. (*Looks at the log.*) What d'you mean, I can't? Is he thinking straight, eh? (*Looks at the log.*) No, I'll hurry and see Matveika. Don't cry, don't cry, you're not normal, you're not right. They'll give you a certificate. (*Looks at the log.*) Is that it? Is the meeting over? Thank you.

They exit in different directions.

The End

A Glass of Water

A dialogue

Characters

A. (female)
M. (female)

M. He's a wolf. A genuine, honest-to-God wolf! You'll see now, you just have a good look, and you'll see what kind of a wolf he is. I've always called him that, and now you'll call him the same. A lot of people think I hung onto him after my first husband dumped me, after my twins died. A lot of people think I've clung onto him at any price. That he took pity on me, and picked me up, after I came out of the Grauerman maternity, empty-handed, with two coffins. But I'm telling you for a fact, they gave me nothing, they burned them in the boiler-room furnace, the boiler-woman burned them. Did you know they did that kind of thing? On the quiet, of course, all hush-hush. Later on, I turn up at the office and the boiler-woman's there drunk, kicking up a fuss because they weren't paying her enough for disposing of the premature births, you know? She kicked up all holy hell in that office, because she wasn't getting overtime. And I'd just arrived that minute to collect the death certificate. My God almighty! I mean, just imagine my situation, I'd have given her money, dress lengths, whatever – I'd have given her a thirty-rouble note even, the old money was really big then, huge notes. She'd have handed over the whole lot for peanuts, and I could've buried them. Sly old bugger! They'd have been forty now, oddly enough. There's been a lot of water passed under the bridge since then. Probably it was for the best. Yes, they'd be forty now, both of them, and I don't even know who they are. Just two little boys, I suppose. That's how it seems. One time I had a dream, it was before the birth, and for some reason or other it was just the one, I'm holding him in my arms, hugging him, and I can't figure it out, I don't know whether it's a boy or a girl. He's wearing little short trousers, so it's impossible to tell. Anyway, if you can't tell, I'm thinking in my dream, that means it's probably a girl. But you always dream things the wrong way round. I dream the wrong way round all the time, for instance, that that Wolf of mine loves me. Yes, she was some crafty old bugger, her! Well, anyway, it doesn't matter, I've come to terms with all that stuff, I've planted a big wooden cross on my life. A wolf's a wolf, and that's that. You know what distinguishes wolves from other animals? It's that they'll devour another wolf out of their own pack, on the spot, if it gets wounded. Or else if it's sick, or old, as in my case. But this is a wolf we're talking about, the scavenger of the woods and fields, they even protect them. Anyway, he'll be here any minute, and you'll see him at last, just hang on another while and don't go away, for God's sake, because if he finds out a young woman like you came to see him, and went away again, he'll swear blind I showed you the door, and bad-mouthed him. I mean, you're a smart girl, eh?

A. Sure, I've got plenty of time.

M. Thanks. Last time he had a thing going with some auxiliary out of that hospital of his. I mean, you know nowadays it's mostly shoplifters they send to be auxiliaries in hospitals, people that've been caught stealing, they serve out their term there. They carry the stretchers, take round the bedpans, hump out the dead bodies. Drag out the garbage. Anyway, it was one of these little auxiliaries he pulled. We do our housekeeping separately here, he does his own cleaning, does his own washing and shopping. I'm at work anyway, I mean, not to work in my situation would be equivalent to starving to death. You take my meaning? Well, anyway, that's how it is. He does his own washing in the sink, travels to the special diets canteen at Mayakovka, and he suddenly decides to improve his life, and he says that from now on he'll have a non-resident wife here, a cook and laundress all rolled into one, because he just hasn't the strength to put up with me any longer. Do you understand? Eh? Do you understand me? (A. *nods*.) Of course, I gave that little auxiliary the bum's rush, as soon as she appeared on the doorstep, before she could even open her mouth she was standing the other side of the door again. I don't understand what he saw in her, I mean, she's only five years younger than me, not like you – true, she's well kept, she's been well looked after on prison bread. She'd had her hair permed, sprayed herself with perfume, made up her silly face, thinking, I'll just go and turn up. Wolf himself didn't appear, of course, he sent her on ahead, like a scout, thinking, she'll cope. That's how he's sent you. But *I* can deal with it, pretty damn quick too. I'm not decrepit yet, you know. I'm not on my last legs yet, no way. Just case-hardened. Take a look, see, not a wrinkle. And that's not from having an easy life. I reckon I can put up with

anything, after what happened to me in that office at the age of
twenty. When that boiler-woman was shouting, that she wasn't
going to burn them, she wasn't accepting any gift parcels, they
could just damn well take them back, there were three items
lying down on the bricks in her shed, under the rafters, and if
they dumped any more on her, they'd bloody lie there as well,
till they got somebody else for that job. Well, right there and
then I flung myself at her, they had to hold me back, and she
was punching me while they held onto me, all I wanted was to
have a look, to see who was in her shed. I mean, they could
have let me have a look, but they dragged me into the hospital,
to the violent ward. Can you imagine it? They had to tie me up
with strips of cloth, torn-up towels and nappies. And of course,
after that, who am I now my whole life – a psycho case,
certified, as they say, I can get away with anything, albeit what
have I really done in my life? Practically nothing. I'm not afraid
to say anything to anybody at work, no way. The minute I start
to speak, they all shut up, including my boss, but I'm his
deputy, and he exploits the fact that I'm such a terror, so he
can come on as Mister Nice Guy. At any rate they won't let me
retire, though I'm dying to go. Oh no, he says, we'll sack
whoever we feel like, but we'd better not sack you. I've never
come across work like you do. But if anything happens, it's me
that gets it in the neck, it's time you retired, it's time you had a
break. So they keep offering me a voucher, a free pass,
Saturday–Sunday, at a holiday home. That's because Wolf's free
at weekends, bear in mind. So he'll go there instead of me,
living it up, the people at my work like him, he goes out
drinking with them. I mean, you just phone up, I'll tell you
where Wolf is. Either that or I'll just bloody hang up, when
he's driven me to it, or I'll say: 'I'm sorry, miss, you've got the
wrong number. There's nobody here by that name.' Well, he's
got his own life, he goes where he likes with whoever he likes,
that's up to him, there's hellish few women would put up with
it, right under their noses, when you come home and there's
somebody else's dirt in the bath, hairpins and hair. And I've
got to get rid of all that shit, before I can lie down and have a
decent rest. Very few people would put up with that, no way.
But I wash it out, give it a good scrub out, then lie down on
the bed, everything's spotless on me and under me, all the
cleaning up's always left to me. I can't abide other people
interfering. I love cleanliness, and I'm a clean person myself,
they used to call me Snow-White when I was young. Two
husbands I had, married twice. During the war, in the

evacuation, you had to live however you could, from hand to
mouth, and I was left to bring up two kids, but I had starched
net curtains, I made the starch myself, you grate up potatoes
and make it that way, on my own with two kids, can you
imagine? But I had a full military ration. Wolf sent on his form,
he'd got right through to the colonel, but my children, that I
had in 1940, the twins, tiny little mites they were, they had
diarrhoea and vomiting, they'd travelled in a goods van, and I
was in charge of arranging medical services, and children's
homes, but my kids were left on their own, with a wet-nurse,
can you imagine it? That's how they've come to haunt me,
they've been dead and gone a long time already, they both died
in hospital. I had to hand them over, they had colic, and I'm
travelling around all over the place, they gave me a cart with
old Masha as the driver, you know? Anyway, somehow or other
Masha got me home, but I suddenly see the house is empty,
there's nobody there, no wet-nurse, and I start screaming the
place down at the children's hospital and they come out to
meet me with corpses, they carry them out all blue, like
plucked chickens. Well, I kicked up hell, and they all got sent
for trial, yes and worse, in the children's hospital there was
pilfering going on from top to bottom, without exception, all
the children had colic, they won't take the bottle, they won't
eat, that suits them just fine, they're delighted, they drag all the
food home for themselves. I'm looking for my own kids, they
keep asking me – is it a boy, is it a girl, what's your name? –
but I've forgotten everything. I can't say a word, I can't answer,
just howl, like a stuck pig. When I came to I was already in a
ward, there were nine of us, and I lay there the whole time,
while the trial went on, the whole court case with these
wreckers, these doctors and technicians. One of the auxiliaries
told me later how you can stop somebody getting colic: just
force a few drops of fresh cream between the baby's teeth, if it's
got any teeth. Some babies die, you know, if they've no teeth.
What are you looking at me like that for, do you think I'm
crazy? I've had children, dear, I really have. I've given birth.
But I got pregnant and the foetus stopped developing, my
weight stopped increasing and everything, and my belly started
to go down. I ran around all over the place, seeing people, and
they put me in hospital, that's it, they say, your foetuses aren't
moving, it's twins you've got, in fact, it's been confirmed, we've
done an X-ray. So what am I supposed to do? You'll just have
to wait for the birth now, they say, they'll come out
mummified, they're like mummies in there, right inside your

womb. So what can I do? Now I just have to wait, just keep waiting. They keep sounding me, there's no heartbeat, and I'm shrivelling up day by day. I complain to my husband, but that's the last thing I should have done. You can open your legs to them, but you don't open your heart – the women quoted that old saying to me afterwards, I didn't know it, and I kept on complaining. I told him everything, and the upshot was I never saw him again, he stopped visiting me, and he was missing presumed dead in the war. And divorces were easy then, so he got a divorce on his side. Well, anyway. A week went by, he didn't come, two weeks, and I'm lying there, the other women are getting flowers, trays of fruit, but I'm getting nothing, my late mother brought in some food, but I couldn't eat, I'm just lying there listening, maybe that's even just one heartbeat starting up? It seemed like that the whole time, right up to the end I kept hoping. I didn't want to believe I had two mummies inside me. Then I had to give birth, the contractions started, and there was nobody near me, not a soul, and I'm lying there, waiting. I didn't shout, I just waited for them to start howling, you know? And one of the midwives said to me: 'What's the matter with you, you should give birth without any bother, all you've got are dead sticks'. They all just gave me the brush-off, crowded round the live births, of course. The midwife says: 'Well, anyway, you just lie there on your own a while,' and she went away, and I started to shout, I started to scream the place down! I had no idea what was going on, I didn't know a thing about it, the midwife came running up, and she says: 'That's it all over with you now, can you open your eyes?' I didn't open them. Well, they cleared everything up, took it all away, and I lay in hospital two days and then went home. Home to mother, like a single woman. I didn't even take a look at them, and I blame myself for that, I had the chance, but I didn't look at them. What there was to see then. You can judge for yourself. The children were still quite small. Well, no matter, that's what happened, and that's why there's nobody now to chuck a glass of water into my gob, in my old age, as my Wolf says. But I'll be the first to go, that'll be the end of my torture. He'll carry on living still. I won't outlive him. And he'll get married right away, like an idiot. He says, your sons would have been drunks, your daughters would be old crones already, fighting with each other, but what the hell, now it's you and me doing the fighting. Of course, we've taken the place of the whole world to each other now, we fight for everybody. And you know, Wolf's either got, or had a son. A young woman turned up here once, younger than you again, by about fifteen years, though not exactly a girl. She drank a glass of tea, dumped the kid on the floor, and says to me: 'Well, you're a woman, you should tell him just the same, you just ask him whether his child can survive without a father, it makes no odds to you, you won't have any kids now, that's for sure, but my little baby's a year old, exactly, and I've got to make my own luck. You just tell him what's the main thing in life – children.' So I say to her: 'You can just sort it out between you, leave me out of it, it's your business, but I can tell you Wolf's none too pleased when they come at him like that, you know, like a bull at a gate.' Well, anyway, that was that. She kicked up hell and pissed off eventually, and that son'll be eighteen by now. Wolf's never once set eyes on him, he's managed perfectly well without him. And he never gives money to nobody, no way, he's a miserable sod, you ought to bear that in mind. Anyway, why would he dump me, you might ask, when we'd starved together at the start of the Blockade, that really terrible winter, and later on, after that unattached female, I heard him saying on the phone to somebody, I don't know who: 'My wife saved me from dying, she fed me with her own hands, she boiled up seven cats for me, and for the sake of some nameless kid or other, I'm supposed to do the dirty on her, yes, and I didn't even want to have this kid,' he says, 'she just did it to wind me up, an appeal to my pride, my manhood, you know?' She made him tea, would you believe, and then she comes away with it, so brazenly: 'Well,' she says, 'are you staying or going?' And he did stay, so now he's got a kid. But that was what actually happened in the Blockade, I exchanged all my clothes for fresh cats, stewed them up, bit by bit, kept him alive. I mean, he was a huge man, a real glutton. And my two children had died not long before. That was during the Blockade as well. I couldn't save my children, but I managed to save him. So anyway, what the hell have you plonked yourself down here for?

A. I'm waiting for Leonid Vitalyevich.

M. Like hell you are. You're not waiting here for him. Didn't you get the message? Do I have to call the police?

A. Go ahead.

M. There was another one like you, another of his young women turned up here and stayed on. 'I'm not leaving,' she says, 'and that's that.' So we started living together as a threesome. Like the Beryozka Trio. He'd drop a book, and she'd shout at me:

'What's the matter with you, you crazy woman, can't you see a person's dropped something?' A two-roomed flat, and there's the three of us. I tidied up, did the washing and the dishes just for myself, and they looked after their own stuff. They did their own cooking, he stood at the cooker himself, they had a honeymoon, and he cooked for days on end. Besotted with it. But what'll he have left, once they've retired him? Anyway, he cooked, washed his own socks in the wash-hand basin, like he used to, and she just lounged about. But he's delighted: he's got somebody to fuss over. It sort of roused feelings in him he'd forgotten, I mean, I was the one that did all the caring, and that's why he'd got out of the habit of caring for other people, you know? I've worked that out for myself, he's a human being too, he wants to live like a human being, and think about somebody else. That's what he bragged to me in the kitchen. And she's beside herself with joy, sheer ecstasy, she's found a whole new feeling, every day she'd make up her eyelashes, she'd found somebody to warm her ribs against. 'I've suffered so much in my life,' she says – she's telling him that, and I've got to listen to it all as well. 'I've had thirty years of utter loneliness,' she said, 'there's been husbands, three men, proper marriages, I've never just lived with anybody.' That was a hint, for his benefit. 'The last one,' she says, 'spent a month with me as my husband, that happened all of seventeen years ago, and since then, no way have I been able to get rid of him, he conned half the room out of me, that's all I had that he could manage to take off me. And now his relatives are living in his half, they just breeze in from Sverdlovsk, they sit up eating and drinking the whole night, to the point my eardrums are bursting, although we've got a plasterboard partition, but what use is plasterboard!' That's how she kept complaining to my Wolf. They'd already had a nearly grown-up son from that month-long marriage, the son kept pining for his dad all the time behind the partition, and she put her whole life into that son. She hadn't had an easy time, we could all of us see that. Anyway, she stayed on, and stayed on, and Wolf stopped making himself out to be the Good Samaritan, and went into hospital to have his large intestine examined, same as usual. That's sort of like a sign of impatience with him. Anyway, that's when I asked her to clear out. I says: 'You've got fish of your own to fry, on you go home.' She says: 'I've only got my son.' 'Well,' says I, 'go and give him my regards. Otherwise your son'll forget who you are, and there'll be nobody to give you a glass of water in your old age. And what did you raise him for,

you might ask. On you go, before you let this chance slip as
well.' So she started bawling and shouting, struggling, bashing
herself against the wall. But there was damn all she could do,
she was nobody here, not a wife, not even half a wife. So she
runs off to the hospital, to take some fruit or something in to
Wolf, and explains what's going on between us: 'She's saying
I'm nothing to you,' she says, 'that's what that one's doing to
me.' But Wolf doesn't say anything specific to her. She dropped
a clanger there as well: 'Which is it to be,' she says, 'am I
staying or going?' Those were her very words. And he didn't
say anything definite – go if you want, do what you like. She
actually told me that later, she said that signifies a refusal, and
she asked: 'What do you reckon?' What did I reckon anyway,
what business was it of mine? But I got used to her. She was a
decent enough woman, not malicious, no backbone, though,
she's like strawberry soap, as Wolf puts it, he's that damn
clever, is my Wolf. He'd get home, and she'd have tidied up
already, I mean it's easier with two women, I wash the floors,
she shakes out the rugs, carries out the slops, wherever there's a
nail needing knocking in, she'll do it, any repairs. She'd
become a dab hand, living on her own all that time. Thirty
years on her own, one minute it's a beating up, next minute it's
burst blood vessels. But what can you do? She sits crying,
smoking. I'd already started holding onto her, deliberately, so's
she wouldn't think we were driving her out, I'm saying, you can
carry on living here, nobody's throwing you out, Wolf's just
Wolf, he's not committed to anybody, he's always got one eye
on the forest. And she says: 'You go, go and see him at the
hospital, he didn't leave me a visitor's pass, the auxiliary said
he's not allowed visitors, he's in isolation, you know.' Well,
anyway, I went, I mean I am his legal wife, so I sneaked my
way in, you have to wear a white gown and all that. And I tell
him, I say to him, 'Let her stay with us, I've got used to her,
you'll get used to her as well, she's a good woman, I've
forgiven her everything, it's easier for me with her there,
although you've got her practically destroyed with grief,' I says.
But the minute he heard that, that was it, he turned away – no,
no, no. So I says to him: 'What d'you want me to tell her? And
he says – Who cares, what's she giving herself a hard time in
somebody else's house for? We don't want anything from her.'
So then I said to him myself, 'Well, I'm not going to be your
accomplice in that sort of business, no way, I'm not passing any
message onto her, she can stay where she is, it's just not
human, flinging her out. You shouldn't have got yourself into

this mess anyway,' I say, 'you're wasting your energy on that kind of damn nonsense, it'd suit you better to start thinking about a job, where you're going to get one, supposing it's just a lift attendant, that would be something at least.' Anyway, he turned chalk-white, his blood pressure had gone up, and there's more to come. She stays on here, my unofficial step-sister, still dug in. He didn't stick to his original 'no', he couldn't get rid of her decently – not everybody has that sort of false pride, you know? Some people only have tears. He shouted at her, called her up from the hospital phone-box, to get her to bugger off, saying people round about would be thinking all kinds of things, what the hell's going on here, he'd maybe be forced to call out the police. She holds the phone away from her ear, starts crying, then listens again. Then she slumps onto the couch, and tells me the whole story. 'He probably suspects something,' she says, 'he's jealous, but I've had nothing to do with anybody, it's a mistake, I've never gone behind his back and I never will, and you can tell him that.' I'm to tell *him*! But as it turns out, he got the idea she was still involved with her husband, behind his partition, when she dropped in there to see her son. Anyway, that's the version he's clinging onto, the husband story. And she's shouting: 'He's no husband of mine,' she's even going to the extent of hunting him out from behind his stall, he sells haberdashery at a market stall, this husband of hers, and she's going to take him to the hospital in a taxi, to prove he's got a new marriage, and he doesn't live there any longer. She actually wanted to get somebody in to break down the partition, to prove her husband's been signed off the register there, but I talked her out of that. 'It's only a temporary measure,' I said, 'Wolf's already walking out of your life, and when he goes, you'll be living with no partition, and a grown-up son, that kind of thing can lead to murder, if he can't have his privacy behind his wall, and that's the only way you'll keep your pride, and have somebody to chuck a glass of water in your gob.' Then she started trying to strangle herself with her bare hands, that's all a performance for my benefit, so's I'll relay it to Wolf, she's spewing up into his pillow, all the same she managed to choke on her own tongue, I don't know how. Of course Wolf had a fit, when I told him about the pillow – pounded his knee with his fist. Anyway, he's to be discharged, and she's lying on the couch, it's still unmade, and she hasn't combed her hair, or washed, and she's smoking. But they've made up their minds to discharge him, they've no intention of doing any more to him, that's it. So I brought him home from the hospital in a pretty weak state, and put him to bed in my room. She stood by the door, and started to shake her head. He says, somebody call the police. As if we don't have enough carry-on in our entry, all the women in our block know what's going on, and they'll cross the street just to say hello to me, you know? Anyway, she kept on and on, shaking her head, then next thing she's whipped a bottle out of her pocket, and bingo! she's swallowed a whole bottle of sleeping pills, crunched them up. She took the pills, fell back, and started muttering: stomach pump, stomach pump. She closed her eyes, and kept muttering. I phoned for an ambulance, they started to pump out her stomach, and managed to tear open her gullet to a depth of twenty centimetres. Everything in our hall was drenched in blood, you understand? You see?

A. I see.

M. Anyway, they dragged her out, and I went to visit her later, fed her out of a drinking cup through the rubber tube in her nose, I went there for a month. Wolf turned up twice as well, could hardly look at her, she's lying there, tubes sticking out everywhere, like a hedgehog. He could hardly stand up. She didn't say anything to the detective. She was just visiting, she said, and she got upset. Her son came to see her as well. I trained him, showed him how to feed her, I mean, I had work to go to. He learned how to cook porridge for her as well. He turned out to be a real good lad. Later on he came to us to collect her clothes. He was lucky we opened the door to him, we were trying not to open the door to anybody at that time. I got everything ready for him, he hadn't even brought a case, and she'd arrived without a case as well, just a shopping bag. It was only later on she bought all her bits and pieces. Anyway, I tied up all this junk into a decent bundle, he picked it up and lugged it away. He's got his own room now, her son, but his mother practically lives off him. A wolf is a wolf, it seizes its prey, and devours it. The scavenger, d'you understand that? It'll eat and kill. That's what you're headed for. So you just pick up your suitcase and beat it, on your way.

A. I've nowhere to go.

M. Here we go again! What d'you mean nowhere?

A. I've no place to go. I've come to you, to Leonid Vitalyevich.

M. And there's no place for you here! D'you get it?

A. But you don't understand – I'm looking for advice. I just want a little bit of advice.

M. Huh – so what kind of advice is it, with a suitcase?

A. My father and Leonid Vitalyevich used to work together, a long time ago, at the ESI.

M. At ESI? Really? Who is he?

A. Zhukov. Yuri Nikolaevich Zhukov.

M. I don't know him.

A. The director of the Planning Section.

M. I don't know anybody by that name.

A. While my mother was still living, and I was out of work, she said to me: 'Go and see Leonic Vitalyevich.'

M. He wouldn't concern himself.

A. It was my father that got him the job.

M. So where is your father?

A. Father walked out on us, to another family, then he died. Mama was left with the two of us. We grew up, and I quit work. I'd had a row with one of my colleagues, and I handed in my resignation . . . I was left to live off my mother. A year ago my mother died . . . I haven't any money, only a very small pension.

M. How come you've got a pension? You're just young.

A. It's a pension for schizophrenia.

M. You're joking.

A. It was my brother advised me, after my mother's death, to go into hospital, it makes no odds, you're bedridden anyway, if you go in there, you'll be able to stay in bed, and at least they'll feed you. That's true, they found out I had a depressive condition, after Mama's death.

M. You don't say.

A. In point of fact I was just upset at Mama's death, ordinary human feelings, that was all. Well, anyway, I came out, and it was tough after the hospital, I had to live somehow or other . . . But my brother calls out the doctor again, 'We can't get her out of her bed,' he says, 'she's impossible to lift, she can't take care of herself, and I haven't got the resources to feed her. I'm not spoonfeeding her, no way. For twenty-seven roubles?' 'Well, it's not your business,' he says, 'so don't feed her. Leave her in peace.' But obviously my brother fancied living on his own, so he stuck me in hospital again, and that's a second diagnosis, you know? They brought me in, and I was screaming blue murder, so they put me in the violent ward.

M. Is that a fact?

A. Damn right. Anyway, three days ago now I got out of hospital again. He wasn't at home, so I picked up my things and went to the station. I left my stuff there, and collected my pension. Then it's back to the station. I turn up this afternoon, and my brother's already home. Why's he at home? I mean, he has his work to go to. 'Where are you wandering off to,' he says, 'this vagrancy's in your blood, you can't take care of yourself.' I just snapped.

M. Well, what the hell, you'll need to get yourself a job. But where? I don't know any place they're taking on schizophrenics these days. Leonid won't help you.

A. I used to work in a publisher's.

M. Well, you can forget publisher's. Sewing on buttons, glueing boxes. Going out early morning, getting home late at night. Then cooking yourself something, having a bite to eat, then into bed to sleep.

A. I can't sew on buttons. I'd go nuts.

M. What are you now? It's not like you're normal. Maybe you've just imagined it all, that your brother's after you. Maybe he couldn't care less about you.

A. No, he's sitting there now, he's writing out the committal papers again.

M. So tell me, how did you find our address?

A. My mother kept it, to be on the safe side.

M. But where did she get it from, who gave her it?

A. Papa gave her it, when she went to see him in hospital. Papa said: 'This man owes me a favour, I once got him out of a very bad business.'

M. What business, there was no business.

A. Mama noted it all down, all the facts.

M. There was nothing, there wasn't anything of the kind. So where's the note, then?

A. The note? Here it is.

M. You certainly are off your head, going around waving notes at people like that. Give it here. (*Reads.*) When was this? What are you hoping for? This is ten years ago. It's long past its expiry date. He's been a pensioner for ages, what has this business got to do with him? D'you think you'll force him with this?

A. All right, then, give me back the note.

M. No way, I'm giving you nothing. It'll be better if I just keep this out of sight from now on, and if you poke your nose in here again, I'll let people see it. I'll have you put in the clinic, for pestering people with crazy nonsense. I mean, you're a diagnosed mental case.

A. So what am I going to do?

M. You'd be better to get the hell away from here right now. You'll get no help here. Don't bother crying. This is the wrong house.

A. What would I cry for? I've shed all my tears, I've cried them all out, forty years' worth.

M. Are you forty? You're well preserved. That means you never married. Well, on you go. Wolf doesn't like strangers. Go on.

A. I was married, and I left him. He blamed me because we had no children. But I'd had an operation, and that was me finished.

M. Yes, well, and you've come for help to people like us. Go on, get away from here. Pick up your case. Blame your own brother for it all. Blame your husband. But not us. We're nobody to you, just the same kind of people as everybody else. Why should we help?

A. When Mama was dying, she kept saying: 'You've got to support each other, children, you're all alone in the world, there's nobody closer to you.'

M. Yes, a husband loves a fit wife, a brother loves a rich sister.

A. You were born on the same day, in the same hour, that's what she kept saying, begging us.

M. You're twins?

A. My brother and I are twins.

M. I had twins as well . . . Well, in memory of them, what I can do is . . . I told you about my twins, they would have been forty . . . Your dear mother was lucky . . . Look, wait just now on the stairs, otherwise Leonid'll fly into a rage, if there's somebody in his apartment. I keep out of all that. You can just turn up, here's your note back. (*Gives her the note.*) That'll be more convincing. You'll just say: I'm out of work. And that's all. Because he gets mad hearing other people's misfortunes. Only don't tell him about your twin brother. Or he'll start shouting at me – you've dreamed all this up, he'll say, you're having hallucinations again, you're dragging in twins again. You're sure you're not an hallucination?

A. Yes, yes, of course.

The End

Isolation Box

Characters

A, aged forty-two (female)
B, aged sixty (female)

A. Well, as soon as they told me, I went to the morning show at the cinema. I turn up there, there's only a couple of people, all old women, only one other young person, and me.

B. Well, I don't ever go to the pictures now.

A. I'm thinking, all these poor people, here they are at the morning show, they've obviously nothing better to do. Fair enough for me at least, I've just been sentenced, I've gone there to relax.

B. Yes, well, I can't relax. Marusya tries, she goes to see people, runs round her friends, here, there and everywhere, she's brought home a boyfriend next. He was smoking, too.

A. Anyway, this young chap was standing at the buffet, drinking beer. The film starts, and he's bought another two bottles. And it turns out that's what he's there for, to drink beer. Good for him, he didn't even go into the hall. There was about a dozen old women sitting in there, and me. A ticket for the morning show costs a kopeck, so he'd bought a ticket to drink beer at the pictures! But he didn't show his face in the hall.

B. This young man of Marusya's, right? Well, he came in and sat for a while with us, yes, but he couldn't stand it for too long. Irochka's little card's hanging on the wall, with its black ribbon round it. Of course, that's all he's needing. So he got up and went. Marusya's in tears. We're no use to anybody. What did you have to mention Irochka for, Mama? I'm to blame, of course. Irochka's to blame.

A. Anyway I remember now, they were showing some crap film or other, about the Young Pioneers. I mean, who were they showing it to? All the Pioneers would be in school long since, unless they were playing hookey, that's the only way they'd be at the cinema. And the rest of it was an adult audience. Still, there was nothing we could do about it. I mean, that's the absolute end, that we've turned up there to watch the bloody

Pioneers. And I'm thinking, well, that's terrific, here am I just sentenced to death. It's okay for me, I'll go to anything, just for a bit of quiet, and so people won't stare at me. But my Vanya doesn't know, I haven't told him a thing. If I could just support Vanya, raise him for another couple of years, that's all. Right? Just a couple of years. Till he's past sixteen. Till he starts work, at least.

B. They've given me two years.

A. They're giving me ten years, all going well. That's if there's a lot of remissions. I'll try anyway. Ten plus fourteen, that'll make him twenty-four.

B. So what do I want two years like this for?

A. They're saying now that some quack's been curing people with shark liver oil. He's a complete crank, he doesn't take money, all he cares about is his method. He almost cured some old man of seventy-five! I mean, that's some patient he's found himself. There's young people dropping like flies, but he goes and picks him, so there's less of a risk. I would take the risk, but who's going to speak up for me? Vanya would have made the effort, but they won't give him the address. Anyway, he hasn't got the time. He's got a full schedule at that boarding school, it's like drawing teeth, getting them to let him out, so he can visit me during the week.

B. I mean, what's another day, or another two days to me? Marusya doesn't need me, I'll clear off, and she'll be free to bring in whoever she likes. She'll start a new life for herself, have another baby. Then she'll forget all about me, totally, she'll abandon me and Irochka, and we'll just lie side by side, we don't need much. We'll lie there for thirty-five years, waiting until Marusya comes, an ancient old crone.

A. He'll be twenty-four by then, Vanya, he'll get married, that's what I dream about. And once he's got himself hitched, he won't need me any longer.

B. They only let you lie for thirty-five years in the cemetery, then they get rid of you. Just as long as they lay Marusya beside us, then they can reshuffle us. They'll level us out off the face of the earth with a bulldozer. They'll put up a new building, it'll be a new Church of the Holy Bones. But that'll make no odds to Irochka and me. I haven't tended my own husband's grave since the year nineteen thirty-eight – why should I go there, it just makes me cry. And it upsets the dead, people visiting. Like now, Irochka's getting upset these days, what are you doing, Granny, why should you be crying for me? Live as long as you can, you'll come to me soon enough, and we'll rest in peace. Live on, Granny, live on, dearest darling Granny, she's ordered me to have a long life. I won't manage, but I'll take whatever time I can. Maybe even ten years, but what for?

A. They've given me ten years, Lagutin gave me ten years. They're wheeling me in here yesterday on a trolley, and they laid my case history on my chest. I had a look at it, and there it says it: another ten years.

B. Lagutin?

A. The porters were waiting for the lift, and they went to ask about something or other. So I took a look at it, I couldn't believe my eyes, there it's written: 'Ten more yrs'. I mean why, what for? Doctors generally don't put the life expectancy down. But they'd written it for me. That's pretty rare. Ten, it said.

B. Isn't it ten litres?

A. No, years. What d'you mean litres? D'you think they're all drunk in there?

B. If I've got ten years, I'm just thinking how much mischief that Marusya can get up to in ten years, she can give birth to twins, work her way through three husbands. But I'll be left with Irochka, who's going to think about her? Well, anyway, I won't, I won't, I'll stop. Dear Granny, don't cry. Granny love, don't come and see me so often, don't cry. Dear child, how can you say often, when I've been laid up in this place a month already? Your grave's all overgrown with weeds now. Well, Marusya's got to work, of course, she finishes at seven, she comes to see me on Saturday, on Sunday she's got to do all the washing, have a breather. She can't come and see you, Mama's poor heart aches, her poor head's splitting. But I'll come and see you, I'll come, my darling little flower. Granny dearest, don't come, not until you're feeling better.

A. Why would it be litres here? It's ten years. It'll take us the first three years to finish school, that's one bit. My little Vanya's a first-class scholar, gold medal. And even without the gold medal, they can still get into an institute. He can go in the evenings. They won't take him into the army, I'm an invalid, he'll be the only breadwinner, right? He can study in the evenings as well. And as soon as he graduates at twenty-four, he'll be finished and I'll be finished. I'll open all the doors for him, he'll have his own room, my boy'll be big then, grown up. Actually it's a good thing that I'm an invalid. I can go up to people at anytime, and fall on my knees and say: you've got to take in my little Vanya, I've got cancer, cancer, I haven't got long to live, and he'll be left on his own. And a certificate with the diagnosis, Nina Ivanovna promised she'd give me a personal copy.

B. Was it Nina Ivanovna that told you?

A. No, it was Dr Gogoberidze, at the out-patients clinic. It was after that I went to the pictures. What about you?

B. I guessed it myself, that that's why they brought me here. Nina Ivanovna only told Marusya, Marusya started to shake, burst out crying, that's all we need, she says, what am I going to do now? Does that mean another funeral? I've just buried one, now it's the same again. I've had enough of it, she shouts, I've had to bury my daughter. Have they all gone crazy there? she's shouting, isn't that just too much for one person? And I was lying in intensive care right there, I could hear every word.

A. Well, Dr Gogoberidze told me right away, she says, you've got to keep your head up, take hold of yourself, there's nothing else you can do. If you want to bring up your son, you'll have to be brave. Well, anyway, it was after that I went to the pictures to watch the Pioneers. I can't even look at children, I feel so sorry for them, they take them into children's homes when they're still tiny, send them away out of the city. They dish out the bread in penny numbers there, two slices each, I went there with our company's aid project, and I just dissolved in tears. But they won't take Vanya in now, he's too big. Two of them got into our bus, started unwrapping the sausage. The driver chased them out: these orphans have been sniffing at all the sausage. But I mean, for God's sake, they didn't eat any. Anyway, they won't take Vanya there, he's too big, he's fourteen. And at twenty-four, well, he can hardly go then! Meanwhile he's still fourteen. For me it's the same as if he were twenty-four already, the years just fly past, you don't even notice. It's not as if he needs much from me. I've got my pension, but I'll try to spend time in hospitals. So by the time I go, he'll be used to it. I'll have been away, missing, and suddenly I'm gone for good. It's the same thing, really, only he'll get all my money. To teach him how to live

independently. He's looking after himself even now, on a
Saturday evening and a Sunday he comes home by himself,
cooks for himself, brings me a snack, all on his own. What are
you wasting your money on, son, I say. I don't need anything, I
get fed here. You do need it, Mama, you do. He's got money
now. My pension for a month, plus he gets his meals free at the
boarding school.

B. Marusya's got my pension as well as her own salary and she
just throws it away. She's got nothing left. The minute I'm not
here, she's chucking it around again. One minute she's off to
Tallinn, next she's scooting off to the Baltic somewhere. She
can't sit still. She goes where she's not known, you see. Where
she is known, they run a mile. She's obviously trying to catch
herself a husband some place. But it doesn't matter how you
try to hide it, the minute a man turns up, he'll see the whole
show, he'll soon know the score. You can't hide Irochka, I tell
her, you'll blurt out the whole story yourself. Every second
word with her, out pops Irochka. And people get scared!
People don't want to hear it, naturally. They soon get sick of it.
Marusya, I tell her, don't give people your worries. But who's
she going to tell it all to? Beating my ears with it's the same as
beating her own. She's got to tell other people. It's the same
everywhere, it's shameful.

A. Well, I'm not ashamed of cancer. Let other people be
ashamed. But I'm not ashamed of it. I know my own situation,
other people damn well don't. They don't know, they know
bugger all about me. I'm not flapping my arms about for
nothing. I'm doing it on account of Vanya. I've got to live a
long time for Vanya's sake. I'll make it my business to give
everybody a good shake-up, yes. But they've got children of
their own, naturally, they're looking out for their own. But I
don't give a damn about their kids, I've got my own. So we'll
put up a fight, see who comes out on top. Survival of the fittest,
it's called.

B. Well, I don't need anything. I'm not standing in any queues.
And Marusya even less. We don't need anything. She'll only
queue for plane tickets. She scrimps and scrapes, saves up, and
then bingo! she's on the plane. Fly Aeroflot, that's her motto.

A knock on the wall.

A & B. Who is it? Is it for me? It's for you. Is it me?

B. It's for me. Oh dear, I wonder what it is? Oh – where's my

dressing-gown? Oh, I shouldn't even be up. Marusya's come,
my little girl. Don't cry, Granny. I won't cry, my angel, no, I
won't. (*Exits*.)

A. *is sitting, covering her face with her hands.* B. *re-enters carrying some
parcels and plastic bags.* A. *remains sitting, her face covered.* B. *spreads
out the things she has brought in.*

B. You see, she doesn't visit, she doesn't come, suddenly she
splashes out on all this. Why should she buy all this, eh? Now
she's flown off to the Baltic, and bought all this stuff there. I
can feel it in my bones, she'll soon give me a little grandson
from the Baltic. They don't know her there, they're not scared
of her there. But it's all one to us, isn't it, where he's from?
Granny, don't wring my heart, don't come to see me so often.
What d'you mean often, dear child, when I'm stuck here in the
hospital? Your dear mother'll soon come, I feel it in my bones,
she'll soon settle down and come to you, she'll pull out all the
weeds and she'll water the flowers. Granny, I'm fine, it's not so
bad under the grass.

A. She's gone mad. She's off her head. Our old dear's gone right
off her trolley.

B. Look at all this stuff she's brought me, she wants to make me
happy, and she has done. Mama, she says, they paid out our
bonus recently. These are warm Hungarian stockings for you.
Here's a nice clean brassiere. Here's some nice apples. And this
is jam.

A. Vanya's a boy, I can't get him to bring things like that: a bra.
He gets embarrassed. He's a first-rate scholar. (*Covers her face
with her hands*.)

B. But they'll come to you, they'll still come to you, don't worry,
dear Mama. You're all your son's got in this world, he'll come
running, the shops are so busy, it's Saturday after all.

A. But he's only just got out of school. I'm not worried, actually,
I mean, you don't know, but he drops in all the time. I mean
really, you don't know anything, this is the first time I've ever
clapped eyes on you. They brought me into your ward and I
sat down and that was that. Vanya still doesn't know where I
am. This is a convalescent ward. I'm not telling Vanya anything
at all about my illness, he's not to know this.

B. Huh, that'll be right. Convalescent ward. After the one that was here before you, they had to spend the whole morning washing it down.

A. How do you know?

B. I live here.

A. Have you been here long?

B. A month.

A. Well anyway, it's a convalescent ward.

B. Don't you believe it. It's a terminal ward.

A. Yes, a terminal treatment ward. They stopped giving me pills yesterday, I've to have injections now.

B. Well.

A. Nina Ivanovna said convalescent.

B. Yes, well, the one in here before you was convalescing as well. Up till this morning. Now they've wheeled her out with a towel over her face.

A. They gave me ten years.

B. Ten years? Ten litres, L T R S, not Y R S.

A. Are you drunk, or what? You're seeing litres in your sleep.

B. They drew off ten litres of fluid from your body.

A. What, yesterday?

B. That's right, yesterday.

A. But what about Vanya?

B. He's coming today?

A. Yes, he is. He is coming.

B. Tell him everything, when he comes. Get everything organised. Everything. Write it down, call up some woman. A neighbour, a friend, your husband, even if he's a pig. Call them all.

A. So how many days have I got?

B. You just write it all down now, right away. I mean I'm just waiting too, any day now, and I'm still here.

A. No, it's a convalescent ward. Nina Ivanovna said.

B. This is a box!

A. What?

B. It's a box, I tell you. It's an isolation box for us. So as not to frighten people. We're in a good hospital. They don't want people frightened.

A. But what about Vanya?

B. And what about Marusya? I mean, what about you, haven't you buried your mother?

A. No.

B. Then call her. You're lucky.

A. But I've got no mother or father, that's the thing. My father dumped them, and my mother just walked out. Died, for all I know.

B. Well anyway, they'll outlive us. They won't die along with us. Write to whoever you like. They're left behind to live on. Really, you're a fool. I mean, you just suppose you were to outlive Vanya. You would have to bury Vanya. Well? Which is better? Marusya buried Irochka, and now it's me. Well, I tell you, I don't envy her. No. Like, in our block a mother and son died in the same little room, the two Satanovskys in a one-room flat. I suppose they should be thankful she died a day earlier, it's only right and proper for the mother to go before the child. He was twenty-seven, she was fifty, so there you are.

A. What has this to do with me? I've got my life, they've got theirs.

B. No. I've had to listen to you, now my patience has snapped. Your boy's independent, praise God for that. Apply to your own firm, get them to take him on as a trainee. All kinds of people had to start off as trainees. What's the matter with you? I mean, how did we grow up, eh? What are you scared about?

A. Just let him get an education, that's all I want.

B. There you go again! Have you no relatives?

A. I've got a sister in the country.

B. Well, send for your sister then.

A. You just try sending for her. She's got a house, a bungalow, a cow. She's got kids. You try sending for her . . .

B. Then let them take him.

A. But we'll lose our room.

B. Well, you're just being downright awkward. Nothing suits you. You won't lose your room in any case. There's a lawyer here, call the lawyer to your bed. (*A knock.*)

A. Who's that for? Is it me? I'm coming! I'm coming. Oh, thank God, thank God. It's him, he's here. He's alive, you're right, you're absolutely right, he's alive. (*Exits.*)

B. *covers her face with her hands.*

B. Don't, Granny, please don't, dearest Granny. I promise I won't, child, truly. We've still got our dear Mama. Mama'll have a baby for us . . . a little brother . . . or maybe even a little sister . . .

The End